Apple

and the

Thorn

The
APPLE
and the
THORN

Emma Restall Orr
Walter William Melnyk

Thoth Publications
Loughborough Liecestershire

A CIP catalogue record for this book is available from the
British Library.

Cover design by Avanson Design

Printed and bound in Great Britain

Published by Thoth Publications
64, Leopold Street, Loughborough, LE11 5DN

ISBN 978-1-870450-66-9
Web address www.thothpublications.com
email: enquires@thoth.co.uk

Nota Bene

This story is not true in the sense that most
people use the word. It emerges out of the mists
of time, rooted deep in the heritage of Britain.
It is a weave of mythologies, theologies
and histories. It is the story of two
people, and a story of our peoples. It has
no beginning and it has no ending.

Dedication

In honour of my goddess, I offer this tale
of the powers of love and change.
And in doing so do I bow to all who have honoured her, each
priestess and seer of the land and the waters, of the dark womb
and the setting sun, all who have heard her songs and the songs of
the dead, since first my ancestors settled upon these sacred lands
of Britain.
Hail grandmothers.
May your songs be ever sung.
So mote it be,

Emma Restall Orr

I offer this tale to Glyn, my life partner, who has walked
with me through the mists of countless adventures, and to the
walkers between the worlds in every age who have had a desire to
understand and the courage to be changed.

Walter William Melnyk

Ynys Y Niwl
c.45ce

Marsh

Forest

Marsh

Vivian's Community

Orchards

Orchards

Bryn y Afalau

Glyn y Ffynhonnau

Eos' Camp

Bae Fyrtwydd

Bol Forla

Dolgwyl Waun

Bryn Ddraig

Bryn Fyrtwyddon

Forest

Impassable Bog

Summer Grazing

Walkway to Crib Pwlborfa

Marsh

Bryw Waterway

Affalon
c.45ce

Brynfau'r Mendydd

N

Bryn
Llyffaint

Pruddy

Llyn
Cimwch

Llw Ffynnon

Pentreflyn

Llyn
Hydd

Llynwen

Ynys
Y Niwl

Crib Pwlborfa

Brynfau'r Pennard

Caer Iwdon

Chapter One
The Marsh
(Vivian)

hispering the names of the dead, my fingers slip down the wood of my staff. My knees bend and I sink to the mud, like a snow covered branch breaking with the rot of age, its falling muffled, easy, and I sit where I land, in the stillness of late winter. The last of the sun is a spill of molten copper, floating with languidity on the heavy dark water. It glints with the dying light on the ridges and furrows of ripples, a moorhen scudding for the reeds. Then the pattern is broken as, in a fluster of feathers, she scuttles for cover, the russet of a fox disappearing into the twilight. I smile, *blessings of the close of day, Cedny.* Her head peaks back through the tangle of twigs down by the water's edge, and she gazes at me for a long moment, we share the serenity of home.

Closing my eyes, I rest my head against a branch of the old yew. It's still damp from the sleet, and where the bark is gone it is smooth as silky skin. The scent calls me to breathe in with a yearning for its embrace and I sigh, feeling its spirit fold more fully around me. Together we watch the night closing in. "Ywena," I whisper, "what of this day?" and my words melt into the twilight as had the sleet into the darkness of the muddy ground a short while ago.

The soft *shlip* of a paddle draws me to lift my eyes. A shepherd boy is slipping by in his flat bottomed boat, the bleat of a tiny lamb wrapped tight in the folds of his cloak. From

his silhouette, I think him the son of Defydd, and in the old
family boat standing behind the young lad is the form of his
father, dead more than ten winters now, and from his song I
know him well, the shimmering of his music seeping into the
marshes that were his home. I remember the day he died, in
some other futile skirmish, and I can hear still the women's
grief that was cried out over the fields of bloodshed, that was
offered with such rage and tenderness to the gods. His wife
was six moons grown with her first child. She called him Llafn,
hoping the sharpness of his name would keep him safe, and
indeed now the boy's boat does cut through the water with the
silence of a knife.

He won't look this way. There is nothing upon this island
they call Ynys y Cysgodion that brings comfort to the soul. A
place of shadows and gnarled ancient yews, and they half hidden
in the robes of the thickly tangled forest, veiled and dripping
with ferns and moss, which in turn hides the tomb barrows of
the ancient dead. I don't believe a mortal soul has trod upon
this dark-clothed tump of an isle for many a generation, except
myself and the few who take care of my needs. In the villages,
ever seething with superstition and tattle-talk, what or who
they think we are differs from hearth to hearth. Rumour has
it that I am the daemon mother of all marsh-widows, or the
washer of slain men's garb, the gatherer of the dead. Those who
attend me are dangerous rage-sprites who, dressed as pretty
maidens, draw young men into otherworlds of enchantment
and eternal yearning.

When someone is desperately ill, or a plague sickness is
brewing, or fighting has surged beyond the people's reason,
when the local healer or seer is wise enough to admit the state
is beyond her knowing, a priestess is called out from the isle
across the water where my work is done, Ynys y Niwl, an isle
most often draped in mist, where my community of priestesses
and seers make their home. But the messenger comes with
curiosity drenched in apprehension. As a child, hidden in an

old yew near y Ffynnon Goch, I would watch these strangers from the world outside. Having fought through the hungry marshes, seeking the elusive streams of flowing water, finding their way to the grassy slopes of Ynys y Niwl, they would scurry for the healing springs, unwilling to look around, hoping there to meet a priestess, or maid of the community who would carry a message to some soul who would help, someone who could unknot the ravelled threads and bring ease, someone who could see what others could not or did not want to see.

Only now and then do I go myself into the world, on days like today, when even those whom I hoped had more common sense are speaking of the sky falling down upon their cowering heads. Increasingly I find such journeys deeply wearying, for the world beyond my haven of islands is complicated with the fear and hunger that provokes human violence. In my mother's day, the druids worked for the people, keeping some order with the wisdom of their ancestral line, but too often now the local druid is tied up in tribal politics, and his own self importance. His own hand in play, he is now a part of the games of power. He helps no one.

Little bats dart out over the water, breaking their day's fast in the twilight.

Leaning on both staff and branch, feeling the old tree spirit rise beside me, slowly I find my feet and the cold night air. The faint clink of iron touches my ears through the trees. One of the girls is preparing the evening's broth that will warm my blood and bones, the other setting the prayer that will silently call me home to eat, but before then I know I must again seek counsel, and this night, with no moon, I am called to the barrow. I leave a kiss upon the yew wood, so grateful for its song that hums within and around me, and I turn to walk away.

Finding a path through the hazel, elder and thorn beneath the high trees, I sense the frailty of all that holds intact the structure of time. Stories tell that this land was dry when such tombs were crafted, and considering where they lie in this landscape of marsh and lake, on the edge of the western seas, I can see how that could be. As if moving through cobwebs, as my hands reach to steady the tread of my feet, I can't help but tear threads, and as I do so the forest slips away and for a moment I am striding up the sunlit meadows of this same hill, as I have done many times before, making my way with a deep-rooted pride to the tomb barrows of my people. Yet when I reach the clearing, it is in winter's darkness and, instead of pride, I taste fear. A sadness hums in my belly for all that has been lost, and all that will be lost in the years to come.

And the prayers surface in me like the rising of the lower stars, they that journey along the horizon before slipping back into the otherworld, songs I have heard every day throughout my life, songs that tremble with grief and love and wonder, curling up like smoke to drift in the wind. *Ancestors, I sing, in my breath I breathe your breath ...*

Built of great stones, set with mud and turf, some forty steps long, some upon this hill are still secure, sealed as they have been for more cycles than can be measured. Not even the young ruffians of the settlements around the lakes, too eager for the thrill of fighting, dare to disturb such places, so thick are they still with power and presence. That this one is partly opened only adds to the fear of my little isle. The huge slab of stone that closed it, having sunk a little into the sodden ground, leaves a gaping mouth, large enough for a creature of slight build to clamber through. Or an old woman. With my song lingering in the evening air, I make the prayers of honour and climb over the broken stone, crawling into the breathless dark of the low mud passage...

Around the fire, I sit on layers of fleecy sheep hide, wrapped in the furs that will cover me when I turn to sleep. Gwenlli fusses for a moment, making sure that I am warm. She uses no words but to me it sounds like chatter, and I meet her eyes. She lowers her head, softly clasping her hands before her. *I will leave you*, she whispers silently.

I bow and she tiptoes out, and I hear the gentle murmuring of her voice as she joins Creyr in the other round reed-woven hut that completes our homestead. Lifting tea to my lips, I watch a moth dance around the fire light, and let my mind drift to the pathways of the done day.

Tales heard at my mother's feet seep from darkness into memory, stories of the quiet hook-nosed warlord of Roma who, in the time of my grandmother, had conquered a thousand tribes and ruled fiercely the greater part of the vast landmass that stretches beyond the southern sea. The stories told how this man had gathered an army of many thousands with the intention of taking for himself every one of these Brythannic isles, but on the invocations of the priests the sky gods stirred up the wind, and with the gods of the seas and those of the shore, his fleet of invaders was broken to tatters.

His successors still rule the land beyond the sea, within what is called the empire of Roma, and though some tribes do rise up to regain their freedom, it is said that none succeed. Traders and saphers speak of it as a world set quite apart from this, a world where many don't fight the conquerers but willingly cede their lands, in exchange for promises of peace and wealth. And indeed, they say, it is a different life that is led across the southern waters. Some say it is easier, displaying their jewellery of amber and gold as if that were proof of serenity, goods traded with the empire in Gaul and beyond.

Pouring water from the jug, I drink, and run my fingers around the smooth edge of the bowl. A new breed of traders are now to be found at the markets of Llynwen and Pentreflyn, not local folk of the Durotrigians, but travellers who bring sharp tongues and foreign coins, selling delicate cups, fine glass, gems and cloth, and dreams. They speak of a new trench road being built, not half a day's walk from here, a track that will run from the sea coast in the south west across the land to the eastern sea, some ten days ride. They are calling it the Ffos Fordd.

I am afraid of this empire. My visions show me our lands overrun by lines of broken men given a wage to fight, like a plague of ants pouring over the meadows and seething through the forests. And when I am told that tribal kings to the east have welcomed Romans onto Brythannic shores, my fear further grows. For this time, priests were not called to invoke the gods for protection. This time, with their human greed, the tribal guardians simply sold their rights for their own personal gain. So has the greatest betrayal been wrought upon the Brythannic lands and her people.

Two winters have passed since the first Roman force stepped upon the islands' shores and my fear still grows. And all day, today, I have spent in the gathering halls by Llw Ffynnon, the deep wells shared by oaths of allegiance to the north of here, speaking with tribal chiefs and druids. The fighting up on the Bryniau'r Mendydd has taken the lives of six more young men; it was their names I called as the sun touched the grey canopy of High Bredd to the south west, aiding their journey over the waters to the lands of the dead. Yet still their people squabble with blades as ancestral vows are broken, rights are eroded, the land dishonoured. And each one believes that if the lead and silver mines were their own, trading these metals with the empire over the seas would bring them enough wealth to secure their own self-governance. I sat in the halls as each voice rose in the clamour of desperation, frenzied as clipped hens trying to take to the air.

Rumours, confirmed by the colours of my visions, were confirmed again by a son of Castell Coel, returning from travelling east through the winter. A new warlord of the empire, known as Vespessian, is coming with an army like ants devouring, plundering his course over the southern lands of the Durotriges. At each of the ancient caer towns, with fire and iron he destroys until the fort is surrendered, and the town given to him. Heading for the rich mines of Cornualle and the Mendydd, when he arrives he will take the land and all its wealth as his own.

Yet our people fight each other, boys killing with the rage of fear.

The fire is growing low with my thoughtfulness and I push myself onto my feet to gather a handful of wood from the pile by the door. Lifting the covers aside, I look out into the peaceful night of our small forest clearing, and up into the winter-black starry skies. A song rises in my heart, prayers of wonder and thanksgiving, and as I open my soul to the darkness of her presence, the sweet black water of certainty seeps into my body. It is a night without moonlight and I whisper the names of the stars as my grandmothers and theirs have ever done. Tomorrow at dawn, after welcoming the light and breaking the night's fast, I must go to Ynys y Niwl, to the sanctuaries of vision, and find just what this certainty is that flows through such chaotic change.

A tiny moth alights on a burning log too hot for its feet. Yet as I guide it gently away, I am acutely aware of myself with a broad humility. For here by the fire, I know too of some other change breaking over the world, yet I do not know what it is. As if standing in the forest, after the final blow of the axe has been driven into the tallest tree, I know the crashing destruction will come. But I do not know where or when.

In the barrow, I sought vision and guidance from the dead. Drawn through the web of lives, sacred thread to sacred thread, a face came to me out of the gloom. It was that of a tin trader of the land of Cornualle, his skin nut-brown, his ancestry of Iuddic blood from the far eastern reaches of Roman law. We have met before. And in remembering his face it was as if a door opened once again in my soul, yet through that doorway I saw nothing.

It was very many cycles ago. He brought with him, to Ynys y Niwl, a young man whom I believe was his sister's grandchild, a lad with a beard still soft and deep clear searching eyes. He intrigued me, this young man, for he left traces of energy in the air, as if his soul were heavier than his body, weighed down with an ancient grief with which I felt a deep empathy. He was clearly a seer.

In the barrow I saw this young man dying. His beard rough, his eyes older, his hair wild as that of a man who has lost the ability to understand, and with his arms outstretched, he cried out to his gods in soulful desolation. I searched for more, not clear why the image was given me, seeking whether those who took his life were of his own Iuddic people or men of the Roman power, but the most surety came from that sense of the tree falling. His death had somehow been the last blow of the axe.

It will take a while for the ripples to reach us, but they will.

And I wonder when the tin trader will appear again on Ynys y Niwl, waiting by the springs, for I now feel sure he will. I forget his name.

I stand again, too restless to be still, my soul heavy with a powerful sadness I do not wish to feel, and pulling on my hide boots, gathering the fur rugs about my shoulders, I wander out into the night. A little way from the old yew, whispering of star light and the gathering clouds, I drag one of our flat bottomed boats into the water. Using a long hazel staff to push off against the mud, I set myself afloat.

With just the *shlip* of the paddle breaking the quiet of the night, I follow the silent songs of the streams that wind their tangled narrow routes through the marsh, and before long my craft spills out onto the wide open and shimmering darkness of the lake known as Llyntywyll.

An owl calls and, letting go my human vision of the past and the future, releasing my soul into the cold stillness of now, I murmur my reply, *and I am here, I am here, and all is well* ...Then there is silence, the silence of the winter forest, and the hush of a cold breeze moving through the reeds.

Pulling the furs about me, lying down in the bottom of the boat, feeling it rock softly on the swell and my movement, I close my eyes and breathe out until there is nothing left in my body. And in that darkness and quiet, I make my prayers, opening my soul ... *my lady, my lady* ... *black water, ancient memory* ...

And I dissolve, through the wood, into the waters of the lake.

Chapter Two
The Flowering Thorn

(Eosaidh)

I am not accustomed to piloting so tiny a craft, a flat-bottomed dugout made from an oak of the Isle of Mist, and it rocks crazily under my weight as I struggle to get the feel of the paddle. For a moment I hover, leaning over the dark water, some of my precious provisions slipping over the side. The words I mutter are not the holiest of prayers, I fear. A flatboat is the only way to get across the marshes that lie ahead, but here in the open water off Bryn Llyffaint it is treacherous. I risk a glance over my shoulder. Already the island hill fort is fading into the moonless dark, the outline of our trading vessel lost in shadow. These last two days we have sailed northwest from Pendunn near Land's End, headed for the lead mines up in the Mendydd. The hill fort is an outpost of the Dumnoni, and a logical place to pull up for the night before the final leg of the journey. The crew will be expecting me to sail with them at dawn; the mines need looking into in the midst of this latest fighting. But there is no future for Eosaidh of Cornualle in the lead mines of the Mendydd, nor in the tin of Carn Euny, my home. Only a few allies among the Dumnoni will know of the secreted boat, the provisions for a camp, and the disappearance of a mine owner. They will tell no one that I have faded into the marshes of Affalon.

Though still in open water, it is quiet on the broad inland sea, and cold. I pull my furs around me, settling into a remembered rhythm with the small paddle. It is just past midnight. The Hunter is high in the sky, but scudding clouds and a fresh breeze from the northwest tell of bad weather approaching. Which of us, I wonder, will reach the island first? I left with the turning of the tide, by our best reckoning. With luck, I will travel the fifteen or so miles, find my way through the marshes at high tide, and make landfall by midmorning.

Looking away to my left I can see campfires up in the Mendydd. The tribes are battling for control of the mines, each hoping to be in a better position to bargain with Vespasian when he arrives with his legion. But I have lived long enough among the Romans to know the tribes have no hope. With a wry chuckle I remember that I have known Vespasian long enough as well. Even now he comes from the east, stopping only to conquer and pacify each town, village, and hill fort along the way. He is patient and thorough, and very effective. It has been nearly two years since the Romans landed along the southern coast. Vespasian's march toward us is patient, but inexorable. Soon he will be here, and there will be no winners among the tribes. The mines that have belonged to my family will belong to the Romans, and many of our people will be slaves. Not a noble ending for the great metals trader of the Mediterranean world, known once to Rome as Joseph of Arimathea, Minister of Mines in far off Iudea, trader in lead and tin.

For a moment, a wave of regret sweeps over me as if raised by the rising wind. I rest my paddle on my knees and let the boat slow to a stop. Without a keel, it turns in the wind. The far hills, the water, the reeds spin gently about me. Overhead, the Hunter disappears behind a veil of dark cloud; the night is gloom.

Slowly the bow swings back to the east, and I lower my paddle to keep it steady. There is nothing but darkness ahead. Somewhere out there the water will turn to marsh, and the marsh to sacred land. Somewhere out there is the village of the lake people, and the wooden walkways they have built across the marshes to their grazing grounds in the south. Somewhere off to the left, off the shores of the Mendydd, are the mysterious reed-ringed islands of Affalon; the most mysterious of all, the hidden island of the Lady whom I seek this night. But it is the Isle of Mist my eyes search for in the darkness, for it is there I have met her before, and it is there I am bound. For a moment my mind fills with the rich wonder of old and tender memories that seem more dream than real.

The seawater sloshes under the flat bottom of my boat as it slowly rocks upon the waves. Otherwise it is quiet out here, alone, on the water. I hear the slow rhythm of my breath, see the faint vapors of it in the cold air. Very nearly I hear the beating of my heart. Painfully, I remember that I am alive, and the lad is not. So I seek the Lady, in whose realm, I hope, to find refuge not only from the approaching Romans, but also from the loneliness of my own soul. I pull back on the paddle, and the boat glides forward once again.

I hadn't counted on how much time there would be to think out here, to remember. I remember the last time I saw the Lady of these marshes, years ago, long before the Romans finally decided to subdue this far-off corner of the world. The lad was with me then. He had come with me several times to the tin mines of Carn Euny and the lead mines of Pryddy. Miryam, his mother, had as always not wished to be parted from him. It was less a fear for his safety, I think, as a desire to cherish every moment of their time together. Even then she knew, with the heart of a mother, that the number of his days was short. We had stood on the docks at Caesarea, beside the Phoenician vessel that would take us to Massalia, the main port of the Gaulish tin route. I could feel the worry in my niece's heart for the lad, but it did not penetrate my knowing self-assurance. If he is to be a builder of more than Galilean houses, he needs to learn the metals trade! Roman forts and Greek temples make use of pipes and gutters as well as wood and stone. And it is our mines that are the origin of these metals for the known world, our mines in Cornualle and the Mendydd, which the Romans and Phoenicians call the Casseritides, the Isles of Tin.

And so we sailed to Massalia, and then up the Rhodanus and down the Sequana to the Great Channel, and on to the island port of Ictus. We crossed Cornualle overland to avoid the treacherous currents around land's end, and sailed from Pendunn to Bryn Llyffaint, and so to the mines at Pryddy. Ah, Pryddy! The little village that was summer home to us as well as mine head. The lad loved it there. One evening, our inspections finished, he stood on a bluff overlooking these waters. I could pick it out even now if it were day. The sun was low in the sky to our right. To our left, across the marsh, its rays lit the strange cone of a hill, the high tor of the Isle of Mist, with an unearthly red glow. I can hear his voice still, as clearly as I hear the swish of my paddle in this quiet darkness.

"Tomorrow, Uncle Eos," the lad said, "Let's take the flatboat over to that island. I have a mind to see that hill that seems to rise to the heavens!" And so we did.

The sudden scratching of reeds across the bow wakens me from memories. I have reached the edge of the marshes, where the open water narrows into the entrance to Llyn Cimwch, named for the abundance of crayfish in its shallow waters. Along the eastern horizon the first faint glow of light tells of the coming dawn, and outlines the thatched roofs and palisades of Pentreflyn, just ahead. I shake my head and wonder at the improbable stick houses set upon a patchwork of logs, clay and available debris, literally floating upon the bog. Hanging in the balance between earth and open water, and the tribal powers of the Durotriges and Dobunni, they are a curiously solid presence in the midst of shifting elements and events.

The scent of cooking fires means that many are already well into their day, and will easily spot me if I come closer. I have met them before, travelling between the mines in Cornualle and the Mendydd, so my only fear is of the delay of friendship. I skirt the village far to the north, staying to the edge of open water and avoiding the wooden walkways that disappear into the marshes to the south. These folk, too, will not survive the advance of Vespasian. For years the changing climate in these parts has meant rising water levels and more difficulty in maintaining the village. The Romans will merely complete what nature has begun. The lake people will soon seek higher, safer ground.

In the growing daylight I find a main channel into the marshes, and settle back into a routine paddling. Ahead I can see the tor outlined against the dawn, but the clouds that passed over me in the night have now passed over it, too, and soon will overcast the entire horizon. The wind has stilled for the moment of dawn; a cold mist rises from the reeds. The lower slopes of the tor disappear in a white shroud. I will not be able for long to use it as a guide. The lake village slips by on my right, and once again all is quiet, save for the swish of the paddle, the song of the flat bottom of the boat on the waves, and the calls of the waking animals of the marsh. I crash through a tangle of reeds and a startled heron takes flight just off my bow. On a rock, thirty yards off my right, sits an otter with a shell of some sort in his paws. I fancy he looks at me with a mixture of curiosity and mild annoyance. Who is this strange creature that rides on a log and disturbs the morning business of the marsh? Time passes as slowly as the reeds.

The tor and the marshes ahead are now fully enshrouded in mist. By a sense of filtered light, changing water depth, and the gathering choke of reeds, I feel my way toward the island that the lad and I visited that day, long ago.

I remember the hard, rasping sound as we beached our boat. The lad was first out, leaping onto the stones. With the sweep of a muscled arm he grabbed the gunwale and hauled us up onto the shore! Even now I marvel at his strength, wondering whether I will be able today, at my age, to drag this old oaken dugout out of the water even with two hands.

She was there at the springs when we arrived. I remember to this day the tenderness of the look that passed between us after such long absence. I remember, too, the strange look that passed between her and the lad, as if they shared some secret of destiny. She sent him on his way up the tor, warning him that there he would find the beginning of what he was searching for. If she knew what was ahead for him, or if he did, I never heard another word about it. The Lady and I sat by the springs and talked as we had years before. I told her my tales of the outside world. She led me on inner journeys of the spirit. What a strange and unlikely pair we might have seemed to others' eyes, a priestess of the mysteries and a trader in tin. I wonder would they find it strange, or scandalous, to know the whole story? But no one ever saw us together except for the lad, who thought us not unlikely at all. He never saw the tor again. On another high hill, outside of Jerusalem, he ran afoul of the Romans. He preached love and freedom, and they crucified him for it. Now, at the other end of the world, I flee the same Romans, and hope that Vivian can tell me the meaning of the lad's death.

A sudden lurch of the boat pitches me forward onto a pile of supplies. I have found the Isle of Mist, I am confident, but where I am on its shoreline, I have no idea. I stow the paddle and step out into the cold, shallow water. At the bow, with both arms and a bowed back, I struggle the boat onto solid ground. Before me the land begins to rise. It is one of the four hills of the island, but which one? The shore is lined with hawthorns, a tree known by the tribes for granting strength of heart. I cut a long twisted staff from one, and begin the climb. Perhaps, as often happens, the top will rise above the mist and I will see where I am. As I climb, the wind freshens once more from the northwest. The temperature drops with the wind, and the mists begin to part, the sky above remains gray and threatening. The last shreds of mist are torn away as I reach the summit, and instantly I know where I am - atop the long ridge of a hill that stretches out to the southwest like the neck of a great swan. Bryn Fyrtwyddon it is called, but I once heard a trader call it Wirrheal. In either case, it is the Hill of Myrtles.

Atop Wirrheal I get my bearings. To the west I can see the open water across which I have come, and Bryn Llyffaint in the distance. By now my crew will be scratching their heads, having no answer to the mystery of my disappearance. I utter a prayer to wish them well.

Just below me to the left a small rounded island rises out of the marsh. It is sacred, I know, to the tribes, a hill of the goddess of the land. I can see the remains of a huge bonfire in the meadow beneath it, left from the celebration of her festival only a few nights ago. There is a gentleness about her service that makes me wonder about the desert warrior God of my own people. Yet I often saw that same gentleness in the lad.

To my right rises the mysterious tor, the high hill that seems to connect the worlds. Below it is the smaller, rounded Hill of Apples. Between them, the steep, wooded cleft that is the Valley of the Springs.

There I am headed when a sudden blast from the approaching storm nearly knocks me from my feet, and I clasp the thorn staff tightly for support. Suddenly the sleet is upon me like a flying wall from the northwest, stinging in its horizontal rage across the hilltop! Nearly blinded by the onslaught, I duck for shelter into a thicket of hawthorn, leaving my staff propped against the largest of the trees. It is no drier here, but the tangle of bare branches provides something of a windbreak. I pull my furs over my head, sit on the ground, and bend low to form the smallest target for the weather. There is nothing to do but wait it out.

The wind howling around me raises doubts about the wisdom of coming here.As far as I know, no one lives on this island, though the Lady and her priestesses come often to seek the wisdom and comfort of the Holy Springs.Certainly the island shows little intention of hospitality towards me at the moment! Will it welcome me, a world-weary Iudde who knows more about the Roman gods than his own, or those that watch over these shores? Then, what can any man know of the gods? Every time we think we have Adonai figured out, he surprises us with something new.The Romans will never sort out their gods, adding to their number with each new region they conquer.Some in Iudea, and this is the greatest wonder, some in Iudea are even beginning to say strange things about the lad . . . But what can a man know of the gods? Partly, that is why I am here.

It seems well past noon when the wind begins to ease and the sleet comes to an end.I stretch stiff, cramped limbs and climb out of my thicket.The sun breaks from fleeting clouds, bathing Wirrheal in radiance.All about, the trees are covered with sparkling clusters of ice! I reach for my staff and it, too, is covered with ice blossoms.Blossoms! It is as if this whitethorn staff has flowered in midwinter, and all the hilltop with it! I raise the staff toward the sky for Adonai to see.And perhaps the goddess from her rounded hill, and whatever other gods there may be on this Isle of Mist.Like Aaron of old, it seems I have been given a flowering branch as a blessing and sign of favor, and of welcome.Together this flowering thorn and I turn down the eastern slope of Wirrheal and head for the springs.I pull some bread and cheese from my bag and, as I descend, eat a first meal in a new world.

The darkness of evening begins to mingle with the darkness of ancient yews as I follow the stream uphill to the place of watersmeet.Here two ancient springs flow together, joining their mysteries.The waters of both seem clear enough.But on the left the iron rich water of the Red Spring turns all it touches a bright blood-red.On the right, the White Spring covers the rocks and branches over which it flows with a fairy coating of white calcite.The Red Spring comes from the Hill of Apples, the White Spring from the tor itself.It is among the apples that I am likely to meet the Lady, so I follow the Red Spring to its source.Here I find the grotto of rocks, and the deep pool in which the spring rises, bubbles over, and spills out into its downward journey to the marsh.

The grotto is surrounded by yews.Beyond them, wild apple trees climb toward the brow of the hill.It is still, except for the churning of the water and the song of a blackbird high in the trees.In Erin, they call the bird the Black Druid.Three stars shine above, marking day's end.I drop my bag by the pool, and lean my staff against one of the old yews.The sleet-flowers are gone, but still it pulses with the promise of life.I lie down beside the pool, drawing a second fur over myself, suddenly realizing my exhaustion.The earth and rock beneath me are a welcome enough bed and sleep will come quickly, though what dreams will arrive with it I cannot guess.In the eastern sky the Hunter begins to rise again through the trees.The Black Druid ceases his song.I have never known such silence.

Chapter Three
The Scent of Apples
(Vivian)

Gwenlli is angry with me: I have not eaten. She rakes the paddle through the water as if it had no soul, her vision clouded by her irritation. Slightly tipping the boat, I lean a little from where I sit so that my fingers can slip over the silvery surface of the water. Now and then I break its dark glossy mantle, sharing with it in silence the laughter of tiny splashing ridges, feeling the power washing through my soul. Yet still the young woman pushes down the alder paddle in anger. I turn to her, "Be gentle, Gwen."

"But, my Lady, I was given instruction, I must be sure that you-"

"No, child," I shake my head. And turning back, I sigh. "You are thinking of yourself."

"My Lady, I am concerned, I am thinking of you."

"Think of the water, Gwenlli." My fingers leave dark ripples that float over the surface, drifting out to the sturdy winter reeds that edge this narrow course, thick brown stalks, a thousand lines, unmoving as we pass. "Think of the water," I whisper, and close my eyes.

A smile touches my face as, reluctantly, she resets her focus, slowly remembering the ways she has been taught, and I breathe the songs of connection as the boat becomes lighter. Before long, we are gliding smoothly through the deep silence of accord, human spirit touching wood spirit touching water spirit in peace.

Though much of the night was clear, by the time I was willing to release into the tides of sleep there was already the heavy scent of damp in the air, seeping into every pocket, every comfort, every breath, clinging with the claw-threat of frost. We woke to the marsh mist, in some places floating a man's height off the water, as if with uncertainty, unsure what to do. Yet, as we move now through the dawn towards the sacred isle, the mist is so thick it seems as if the spirits of the waters have exhaled their essence into the air, breathing out into the skies, for there is not a glimpse of life above us, nor beyond an arm's length in any direction: nothing but white mist.

And as the waters exhale, so do I, opening my eyes to the journey ahead, our little boat cleaving through, Gwenlli guiding its path through the maze of high reeds and mud. It isn't long before we find our strange harbour. Bare rot-blackened branches loom down through the mist like a hanged man, still as death without a breeze. I reach for one, Gwenlli another, and we pull ourselves in towards the old dead willow trunk where I can step off the boat and onto dry land.

The spirit form of a man seethes through the mist, his void-full eyes piercing all that he perceives. At his shoulder, another joins him, staring, silent, waiting. There is ancient recognition, but no words that need be said. I reach up a hand and again touch the mist-sodden wood, bowing to the dead, barely forming the words from the depth of the sentiment, *Thank you for your guardianship of this place, revered kin.*

It is with their help, fingers without substance, hands that cannot be held, that Gwenlli pulls our boat up onto the muddy bank. I make my way through the trees.

These mists have enveloped our islands for many cycles, for many generations. To those who study the mysteries, they are a sacred embrace, and in this belief have we learned how to call them to us, that they may protect all we retain through times of turbulence and death. So is this island called Ynys y Niwl, the Isle of Mist, for seldom is it without its veil, isolating it from the world beyond, holding our community in sacred seclusion. Yet at its heart, where the apples of my Lady's trees grow fat and sweet, where her students and priestesses have built their dwellings, where we gather for our rites, we have learned too how to clear the skies, breathing in the stars of our most honoured ancestors, drawing down their gift of light as a glow of unflawed certainty.

So it is that I sit now beneath the exquisite blue of a winter's early morn, the mists still hanging over the valleys and waters below. It is a blue sky yet more beautiful seen through the twisted grey branches of this ancient apple beneath which I sit, the grey-greens and soft blue of lichens and moss softening her still, like the fluff of a caustic old woman's beard. Her tangled roots have grown around the sides of this wide flat stone that is my seat, as if clasping it for her own, and before me, her sacred spring trickles from its muddy cleft in the incline, slipping over stones laid out for her path, and into a pool of what has been for aeons deep black water. My gaze settles into its depths.

Do all people, I wonder, consider the era of their lives to be the most aberrant, the most bloodied with death, the most violent with change? The druids of our land are losing their power, the old magic decaying with the corruption of their sacred vows, corroded with their thirst for positions of importance. The ancient rites of our people are left undone. I close my eyes to ease the sadness which is too vast to endure, gathering up the threads to weave tight my intention. Then whispering my prayer, *My Lady, mother of life, show me ...* I slip on the path of my gaze, down into the pool.

In pelting rain, the fury of a gods-driven storm, this is where they fight, on the sliding banks of a sacred lake, stamping, screaming, mud and water beneath their feet, hundreds of men, women, children, fighting, in the brutality of panic, my people, in rage and fearful chaos. And still the enemy comes, seemingly invincible, like strange beetles with metal shells, cowering protected from axe blows and daggers, emerging unhurt to fight on again, and again and again.

Then I see the leader of these metal-clad warriors, proud in his arrogance, riding high on a mighty horse, and out of the water his men are dredging up offerings, blades that have been broken and cast in sacrifice to the gods, our gods, in prayer, and each offering is given to the warrior on horseback, and he claims some, dropping them into a bottomless sack, and some he hurls back into the water with the disdain of deep ignorance. They are seeking some thing, but what? In the darkness of battle, I can barely see. Then a druid stands to call his curse and he is slain, then another, and another. And then I understand.

It is a long blade, and on its hilt is carved the great boar of my people. And as each druid falls, his blood spilling thick and red into the turbulent storm of this sacred water, the struggle to grasp this long unbroken blade becomes easier, until in one sleek movement the warrior takes it. As he holds it high, the eagle of Roma alights on his shoulder. And my sight is blurred by the tears of my rage.

For a moment I falter.

The call of a raven wakes me. I breathe and find my body has been starved of breath, my heart now racing. The surface of the pool flickers over my mind, then once more I am sinking into the soft suffocation of water, and on the wide wings of the raven, with blackest raven eyes, I find I am flying above a crowd, innumerable people all gathered together before a great temple hewn of stone, shining with gold. It's a strange land, of searing heat and dust.

Then I see warriors bringing that Iuddic lad, the one with clear sight, such bright and grieving eyes, the one of the tin miner's blood, bringing him before a chief of Roma. He is older than when we met, broken with exhaustion, beaten, bloody, pale and bruised. His grey-white face is wet with tears and for a moment I think he is already dead. Yes, he is dead, no more than an illusion in the arms of his captors.

The crowd is shrieking victory, and the great Roman chief offers that broken lad our long blade, the white boar's blade of the Brythannic Isles. And every spirit within my blood opens its soul to scream and, raven-voiced with rage, I too rise up to scream, a curse enough to rouse the force of every god of this sacred land ...

But he turns away. He does not take the blade. The dead lad turns away.

When I lift my head from my hands, I find a young girl is sat near me, waiting for me. She is shivering, cowering in the folds of her cloak.

"Did I frighten you?" I whisper.

She nods.

"Were you sent to find me?"

Again she nods, her cold pink nose poking through a chink in her cloak. I beckon to her that she come close and help me rise to my feet. She bows, murmuring the words of respect she has been taught.

"Come, help me."

And her little cold fingers wrap around mine, and she pulls as I stagger to my feet, letting the vision fall through me, finding its own place to settle in my soul. Then, out of the blue, as we walk through the trees, I remember.

"Eosaidh!"

The child looks up, "My Lady, my name is Tegan."

And I laugh, "Not you, child. My old head forgets many things, but from the mud of my memory I have just remembered the name of a tin miner: Eosaidh!" I rumple her hair through the cloak's hood, feeling the name like a fallen leaf now silently floating upon the water of my soul. "Now run along and tell Gwenlli I need bread and cider, and a good chunk of hard goat's cheese. And apples. He is hungry, this Iuddic tinner, he's hungry and cold and waiting for me ..."

A reed-woven basket in my hand, I make my way to the path beyond the orchards. Walking out from under the winter-bare branches, I step again into the soft white embrace of mist. The path rises, until it reaches the base of Bryn Ddraig, and I follow its course down the other side into the valley of the sacred springs, where the people come to collect the healing waters.

While I'm still at some distance, a young woman spies me. Before I can blink, she is running towards me.

"My Lady," she bows, breathing hard with fear and coughing, "my child is sick, my Lady, I beg you!"

I touch her arm and see the child she holds in her heart, a body rotten with damp. By the springs, amidst those gathered, I see a few of my priestesses, one a bone-setter, one a herbwise, and I keep my stride, smiling gently to assure the woman she will be given help. Then before another soul in desperation reaches for my aid, I pull the hood of my goat wool robe down over my face and whisper a prayer to the mist that I might pass unseen.

The herbwise bows as I slip by, our fingers almost touching.

It is beneath the old yew that I find him, half lying on the cold ground beside the splashing stream of iron-red waters that are y Ffynnon Goch. Eyes closed, he breathes the deep growl of a lifelong miner, his cloak clasped about him with a rough cold hand. And I watch him as he slumbers, a flood of images moving through his dreaming mind. Slowly, through the storms of many years and much sorrow, my soul starts to remember this man I have known before. Yet as I watch, I find myself both troubled and moved by the depth of the change that is obvious within him.

Eos, I whisper.

Then I remember the mist-spell that has lent me invisibility. As i step from its cloak, his eyes open, and I murmur, "Eosaidh". Forgive me, I am late."

He blinks, "Vivian?"

So few call me by name, I am unaccustomed to the intimacy. The word reaches into my soul and I am aware of the urge to take half a step away. He blinks again, his shade still a little uncoupled from his body, as the flood of time washes through him with its flotsam of memories. I lift the hood of my robe, and his eyes, waking, search mine. There is an intensity, an urgency, that was but a glimmer all those years ago, and I watch as he realizes the intrusion of his gaze.

He struggles to lift himself, resentful of the winter's ache in his limbs, and clears his throat as he reaches to grasp again his dignity. "I am still asleep," he says, and again looks up, with an uncertainty I sense unfamiliar to him. Empathy touches my heart, and I bend my knees to sit on the stone by the spring beside him.

"It seems we are both older than when we last met," he smiles. "Yet, I think the years have been kinder to you."

He runs the fingers of both hands through his hair, brushing off the yew needles and other debris of the night, plucking a few from the nest of his beard. And when he feels himself a little more adequately composed, he bows, saying softly, "Shalom, my Lady," and he offers me his hand with the greeting.

It takes a moment for me to respond. As he gains the coherence of wakefulness, in his voice and his face the changes rise into evidence. It is as if he has been on the road for a dozen cycles of spring and harvest, wandering in search of something he has yet to come close to finding. And as I lean forward to take his hand, in its rough cold weight I am filled with a sense that he has come to a halt. Without his quest resolved, he has laid down his pack, here, on Ynys y Niwl, before me.

I feel two streams of water meet within me, a flood of caution and one of strange relief, their currents pushing against each other, leaving eddies of disquiet. I can do nothing but acknowledge this effect of his presence. I let go his hand, and I smile.

His face flushes in response.

"It has been a long time, Vivian."

"Yes, Eosaidh. A very long time."

And our words drift into stillness, held by the timeless breathing of the yew. It is a stillness I need, that I might find my feet in this moment between all that has happened and the looming storm of the future. I hear the voice of a child, a spirit yet to be born, crying out in fear and rage, *It's him, he's bringing it, it's coming with him!* pointing to this old man with tired brown eyes, and I whisper, *No, child, he brings only the story.* And I know that is the beginning: I must hear the story.

It is he who breaks the silence, "Vivian?"

"Eos, I'm sorry," I murmur. "I brought you some food," and I push the basket between us, lifting out the bread, "I'm not good at these things any more, I forget -"

But his hand touches mine. "Lady, it is not your place to serve me." He smiles, "we have graver things to be good at than baskets of food."

I look into his face, wondering if he feels this weight of apprehension in me. Yet in those dark brown eyes what I see are the colours and clamours of a thousand villages, of camps and stories, of markets and fighting, of a life without me in the great towns of Roma across the southern water, the noisy dirty caers of other lands I have seen only in visions. It is like a baneful dust upon his body and soul, a pungent scent, at once repelling me yet also provoking a curiosity to understand.

"How many cycles have passed since last you were here, Eosaidh?"

"It has been almost twenty five."

"So long?" I shake my head.

Holding lengths of time is another craft I have little skill for. Beyond these islands and the endless flow of the water, the world travels at a speed that lies outside my grasp. It seems only to get faster. In this tinner's face, through the clutter of so many brutal worlds, in his eyes, there is such a craving for peace. He reaches for the loaf of bread and breaks off a piece. His hands are shaking.

The shimmer of the dead draws my focus to his side: the young lad of his blood is there crouching beside him. With arms bare, sun-browned, he is of the same age as when we met, twenty five cycles gone. His face is soft, his beard barely grown, yet the depth of grief in his eyes is more acute than I remember. He bows gently to me, with a blend of sadness and purpose, and I too bow in greeting, opening my soul to hear what he would say.

Care for him? he murmurs.

Will you tell your tale ...

But with a smile, he says, *It has been a long and wearying journey. Care for him?*

I can feel the tinner gazing into my face, wondering what I am thinking, as I myself wonder what I should say to his kin. With that gentle smile upon his face, the spirit fades, a flicker of light in the well-depths of his grief.

I look down into the water and sigh, so full of emotions.

"It has been a very long time," I whisper.

He bites into the bread and, as if weighing the moment, I lift an apple from the reed basket. In all the dull dark colours of late winter, the bright green seems as a treasure in my hands. Our eyes meet.

"Yes, my lady, it has been a very long time," he says softly.

And suddenly there is so much sadness, I turn away, resentful of his intrusion.

His voice is gentle, "I have not seen nor tasted the apples of Affalon for so many years. Are they as sweet as ever?"

"They are as sweet," I say quietly, and pass him the one in my hand. Smiling with a tenderness, as if with wonder and relief, he lifts the fruit to his nose and breathes deeply its scent. Then he cuts into it with his trader's knife, closing his eyes as he bites, drawing in its soulful nourishment with all that he is.

"Why did I stay away so long?" he whispers.

And again I turn away.

For a while the world is put aside as, his blade thrust into the cheese, he tears himself another wedge of bread, finding the hollow of his hunger. With the vigour and the manners of a traveller, he eats in great mouthfuls. And it is only after some time that he comes to chase the thoughts that are sliding through his mind, and I wait until his words rise into sound.

The edge of his hunger a little dulled, he pauses his meal and with concern across his brow he says, "I saw scores of campfires up on the Mendydd last night. The clans are fighting for control of the mines, hoping to be in a good position to bargain with Vespasian." He pulls off another wedge of bread, cutting a slab of cheese. "My Lady, Vespasian does not bargain with clans. When he arrives he will seize all the mines, and enslave every owner he does not kill."

He fidgets with his knife, looking down, pushing the blade into a shard of bark. "He and I were nearly friends once. But no more. Now I am in as much danger as the others."

He offers me the bread and cheese, but I have no hunger. He eats, more slowly now, then reaches for the jar of cider. Pulling the cork, he breathes in the scent of the fermented apples and spice, and once again I have the sense of his road-weary decision to cease his travelling. A flicker of winter sunlight finds its way through the yew canopy, touching his shoulder. He looks into my face, concern laden with resignation.

"The Romans are upon us, Vivian. The world is changing."

"I know."

He wants me to say more, but there are no words to speak aloud.

"Tell me why you are here, Eosaidh."

He looks up, for a moment unsure. Perhaps the words which I had meant given into sound were spoken only in thought. He heard them, nonetheless. The bread and cheese in his fingers has taken on a weight, and he sighs, throwing it gently into the mud and dead leaves, then turns his eyes to the skies above, as if seeking strength from his Iuddic god. It is a god of the islands that blesses him, however, with a golden light that barely warms the skin, yet still soothes the soul. Half a smile crosses his face as he sees the cleft in the thick cloud letting through, as it does, the vision of a pale winter blue and sunlight, but it is a smile drenched in sadness.

"I cannot go back to Cornualle. The Mendydd mines are closed to me, and I fear there is a Roman price on my head. The only safe place I know is here. The Isle of Mist is well hidden and uninhabited." He looks into my face," I hope to evade Vespasian here," then lifts the jug to his lips, drinking down the cold cider with a thirst. Yet his thirst is for comfort too. Avoiding my eyes, perhaps he hopes that I will accept his plea and offer him shelter. He is not a stranger to these lands and must know few are allowed to stay. I watch him, waiting for him to speak his truth.

"Why are you here, Eos?"

He is silent for a long while, the splash and flow of the spring's song holding our presence. When he speaks, his voice is low, his soul heavy with grief.

"The lad..." His eyes question me, "do you remember the lad?" I nod and he continues, "The lad is dead. These fifteen years. At the hands of Rome. And now those hands are closing in around me."

The basket of food is forgotten, and cloud covers the morning sun.

He looks up, waiting for my response, but sees in my face that I already know.

He sighs, "Vivian, I need your soul-help." This time as he talks his eyes change, tears rising behind the old shield of his strength as he reveals the wound to me, the rent in his soul. "I know you have seen his death in the depth of your being. I, too, must understand what happened with the lad, for I fear it is something greater than this world."

He searches my face, and I gaze back, So you too sense its potency. I wonder how far this feeling has spread, like a plague upon the heels of the Romans' killing. "You must tell me all you know," I say quietly.

He swallows, pushing a hand across his face to wipe from it the tenderness and tears. "It is a long and grief-laden tale, Lady."

"And one you must share."

I watch the images move through his mind, like birds across a sky at dusk.

"The lad you sent to the top of this tor those years ago, to find his destiny ... he met that calling on the crest of another tor, at the other end of the world." He reaches to takes my hand again, an act borne upon the presumption of a connection made too long ago, and one most in these marshes would find unthinkable. A part of me longs to pull away. His hand is rough and cold, and seems somehow to remind me of my own limitations.

"Vivian ..."

I gaze at his fingers, overwhelmed by an exhaustion.

"May I stay now and tell that tale? You will not want to bear it all at once. It comes with many questions that have troubled my heart all these years."

Our eyes meet, and in silence we look at each other, the mist rising through the trees, the scent of rain in the gentle lift of the wind, both wondering at the details of each other's thoughts.

"The rain is not far off," I murmur quietly. "Come, we must find ourselves shelter and warmth for this tale."

Chapter Four
The Lad's Tale

(Eosaidh)

The west wind off the sea is heavy with the threat of rain as I follow the Lady of Affalon up a narrow, wooded track. Singing waters of the spring fade into the sighs of yew branches in the wind, fallen needles of past cycles pad our footsteps, and the mists of the sacred isle embrace us. I have not been this way before, it is strange to me, and I am not certain where we are headed. Vivian sings quietly, as if to the mist, and the mist responds. To our right the high summit of the tor fades, emerges and fades again, always in a different place. I find myself becoming disoriented as we walk. Finally the tor disappears altogether. The dark yew forest closes in, all but the lower branches now lost in a gentle gray-white. A chill rain begins to fall as we reach the crest of the path and begin to descend. We must be on the north side of the island, but my eyes have no frame of reference, and I am lost save for the presence of the Lady. She continues her soft song, a song that begins to warm the rain, to lift the mists.

At the top of a ridge we pass through a barrier of blackberry brambles, still bare, with no promise yet of budding. I can smell the smoke from hearth-fires, mixed with the rich scent of tilled earth, and pastured sheep, though there is no sight or sound of them. So the isle is not uninhabited, as I had thought it to be. A smile crosses my face as I chastise myself. "You can spot a

Gaulish village or a Roman camp a mile away, Eos," I muse, "but things are different here. Things are not always as they seem."

We continue our descent, dropping below the rounded hill of the Red Spring, sheltering from the west wind. The rain continues to fall, but Vivian's song seems to have tamed it so that it refreshes rather than chills. We cross the last of several streams, picking our way carefully across slippery stones. Suddenly we are in the orchards of Affalon. The mists lift, and all about us are trees slowly emerging from their winter's sleep, their branches appearing yet barren as midwinter. Above, the sky is a deep, brilliant blue as the noonday sun brings only a chill promise of approaching spring. I look about, but the tor is still hidden in the mist. I cannot be sure where I am on the island. Then, to my surprise, I see the cluster of huts.

A roundhouse, no more than five arm-lengths in diameter, stands at the center of several smaller structures. Smoke rises from the roof holes of three, as well as from an open fire ringed by stones nearby. All are simple structures, made of slender poles, mud and straw; a wild and uncivilized place by Roman standards. Several chickens scratch and peck through the golden straw strewn about. They mingle contentedly with a few wild geese. A doe and two yearlings forage at the clearing's edge; their winter coats still dark, their eyes showing no sign of worry at the nearness of human activity. They gaze at us for a moment as we approach, then lower their heads once again to the sparse grasses at the base of the apple trees. A young girl, of perhaps sixteen summers, looks out from the roundhouse, her eyes like one of the yearlings, and quickly slips back inside.

"She cares for me," Vivian says, "She will heat some water for tea."

Though Vivian walks easily through the open doorway, I must stoop to enter. Indeed, I find I am only able to stand upright near the center of the single room, beside the hearth fire, where a kettle is already at the boil. The floor is strewn with hides. There is little else to indicate the purpose of the structure, whether it is dwelling or meeting hall. Almost without movement Vivian sits, and indicates a fur to her left. I sit with less grace, removing my damp cloak. The rain seems not have clung to her. The girl brings me a length of warm, woolen cloth, and I dry what parts of me I can.

We have not spoken since we entered, but I feel the Lady's eyes upon me. She speaks to the girl in words I do not understand, though I recognize a name. Gwenlli nods, pours steaming tea into two bowls, and offers one first to Vivian, and then to me. The warmth is a blessing to my cold, stiff hands. I settle into the fur beneath me and taste the gentle sweetness of the tea. Its scented steam curls about me. Blackberry leaves, I think to myself, and goodness knows what else. It seems a magical brew, clearing my brain and strengthening my body. Gwenlli withdraws to the edge of the floor hides, seats herself, and begins working with a drop spindle. She will not leave us alone here, I know, yet her concentration on her spinning will give our conversation full privacy. Vivian looks at me over her tea with expectant eyes. Though she does not speak, I hear again the words, "Eos, you must tell me now everything you know." It is a few moments before I am able to begin. When I do, it is slowly, and quietly, as I search for words.

"It was in the spring, in Jerusalem, now fifteen years ago. He met his death on a Roman cross."

Already the difficulty of speaking the tale is apparent. The look on her face tells me the Lady is not familiar with Roman crosses. I sigh, and give thanks for the blessing Adonai has given her. Then it occurs to me she knows nothing of Adonai either, the name of my people's God. I explain the horrible instrument of torture and death, upon which the executed die slowly, from exposure, suffocation, and bloodletting.

She lifts the back of her hand to her forehead as if reeling from the image. "Ever do men construct more brutal ways of taking each other's lives," she whispers. I can sense her disgust, but after a moment she shakes her head slowly and looks up. There is such sadness in her eyes. "And what did the young lad do to provoke such a violent passing?" she asks.

"He had become the wrong person at the wrong time, for the Priests and for the Roman Governor alike. He had begun calling people to a revolt of the spirit at the very moment Rome most feared a revolt of the populus. A message that in any other time or place would be one of love became, there, in the turmoil that was occupied Jerusalem, a catalyst for rebellion. His mother and I tried to steer him clear of the authorities, but the more we begged him to heed us, the more zealous he became."

The last time Vivian had seen the lad, he was a carpenter and a mason, come with me to the Mendydd to learn how to use lead and tin in the building trade. His arms were strong, his hands skilful, his eyes bright with an artist's ability to see a finished product in a piece of raw oak. I close my eyes and try to see him again that way, rather than the image of death that comes crashing into my memory.

Without being asked, Gwenlli appears at my side pouring more tea, and just as quietly returns to her spinning. Vivian watches me closely. I can feel her gaze in the center of my being as though she were listening to the words I am not saying, feeling the grief in my soul. I go on.

"In his thirtieth year he gave up all pretext of carrying on his father's building trade. He took up the life of itinerant preacher and healer in the Galilee. He called people to embrace the reign of Adonai in their lives, and encouraged them to love and care for one another, even as our ancient prophets had exhorted. He was well thought of, but not well followed, except for a small band of Galilean fishermen. For three years he preached and healed." The look in Vivian's eyes changes, and for a moment I sense she is seeing him in some way I never have. "He could see things the rest of us couldn't, Vivian. Things that were holy, things that were frightening."

Vivian is still. With the smallest of movements she sets down her bowl. She stares into the fire. "Many are teachers and healers," she says. "This is not what brought his death."

"Perhaps if he had not begun to challenge the Priests . . ." My voice trails off as I see the lad on the hillside overlooking the sea, speaking to the people. I hear him again in his rebuke of the self-righteous:

'Why do you see the splinter in your neighbor's eye, but do not notice the tree in your own eye? You hypocrite, first take the tree out of your own eye, and then you will see clearly to take the splinter out of your neighbor's eye.'

I am silent again for many long moments as I see his face in the Galilean sunshine, and feel the calm breezes off Genesseret through my beard. Those times in Galilee were filled with promise. Perhaps he would have become a great Rabbi, had he let sleeping dogs lie! But he seemed determined to challenge the powerful for the sake of the weak. It was a grave risk. In the end it killed him.

"I suppose it was at Caesarea Philippi in the northern Galilee where the beginning of the end came. For three years he had been traveling through the villages preaching the love of the reign of God."

Again, Vivian's face bears a subtle change of expression. This phrase is not part of her theology, I suppose. Though she does not ask, I offer, "My people believe that the One God is like a Father, offering unconditional love to his children." She nods in understanding, but a shadowed look tells me something in the idea is troubling to her. With embarrassment I remember she serves the Mother. A Father God is not familiar to her. I begin to worry that perhaps she will not connect with my tale after all. I struggle to go on, less sure of myself.

"He met with some success, but most knew he was the builder's son from Nazareth, and paid him little heed. Then he went to Caesarea, the old Greek city of Panias. I heard tales that he met there with the folk of the shrine of the Great God Pan." Vivian stiffens and a tremor runs through her body. She looks down to the earthen floor, and moments pass in silence as her stillness returns. This is not going well. But another gracious nod bids me continue.

"Perhaps he was seeking their advice. Perhaps he was just sharing what it meant to be so involved with the Holy, who knows? But his followers say he changed after that. He became obsessed with going to Jerusalem to confront the leaders of the Temple, there to become a sacrifice for the welfare of the people. It must have been at Panias he learned such a thing. There is no precedent among our own people. 'I must go to Jerusalem,' he told Petros, 'and there be arrested, and beaten, humiliated, and killed.'"

I am watching Vivian closely now, unsure of the effect my words will have. Her eyes are looking far off, to another place and time. She seems to be withdrawing into herself.

"Petros tried to dissuade him," I continue, "but he was all the more determined."

The tale is longer in the telling than I realize. No longer is there daylight at the doorway. Gwenlli lights an oil lamp that hangs from a roof pole. Vivian sits in absolute stillness, no longer looking at me, but the energy within her draws the hardest part of the tale from the depths of my heart.

"He was not in Jerusalem a week when the arrest came. After the pretence of a trial, in which they could not decide whether his crime was Roman treason or Iuddic blasphemy, they settled on a charge for which the Romans could sentence death: they said he wanted to be King! My God, Vivian! He was a craftsman, a healer, and a teacher. He wanted no throne!"

She turns again and looks deeply into my eyes, seeing with me. My body shakes with rage as I see the lad, bloodied, standing silently before Pilate. The rage turns to heart-wrenching grief as I see the cross raised above the Jerusalem hillside in the afternoon sun. The grief turns to emptiness as I see him drop his head, and give up his spirit. I cannot go on with the tale.

Rising from the furs, I knock over my tea and nearly stumble into the fire. I begin slowly pacing the sparse floor, the image of the lad's death working its familiar torment in my mind. I stand in the doorway, hands on the doorposts, looking out into the gathering dusk. For the first time in a long while Vivian speaks aloud, her voice quiet as the whisper of the wind in the trees.

"You must tell me all of it, Eos."

"Here is the most difficult part," I answer. "I took him down from the cross myself that day, shortly after he died. With my own metal shears I cut the nails holding his arms and legs to the hard wood, and lowered him into my own arms. There was so much blood. So much blood, and his body seemed to weigh almost nothing. His mother was there, my little niece. I laid him across her lap. Miryam held him tenderly, the pity breaking her heart in two. Never have I seen such sorrow. I wiped his blood from my hands, and touched her shoulder. Vivian, she looked at me with the eyes of death, and my heart broke with hers. Joachim, the lad's follower, helped her up and led her away. I took up his body, and laid him in my own tomb cut out of the hillside. I saw him there on the cold earth. I myself helped to roll the great, heavy stone into place, sealing the opening. I myself returned him to the bosom of his ancestors, to the earth from which he came."

In the quiet darkness of the tomb there would have taken place the final judgment of his soul. There his body would have rested until the resurrection at the Last Day, when God's Anointed One will come to deliver Israel, and all the dead will rise again.

"But on the morning of the third day after his burial, the stone was found rolled back, and the tomb empty. The lad's followers and the authorities accused each other of stealing the body, to what purpose I cannot guess. The Galileans among us gave up and returned home. I went back to Arimathea."

I return to the furs by the fire and sit again across from Vivian. She watches quietly, always watching, with tender but inscrutable eyes.

"In a few days astounding tales came out of Galilee, impossible tales that Petros, Jacob, and Joachim had seen him there, alive!

They had shared breakfast with him on the shore of Genesseret. His followers became more enflamed than they had ever been in his lifetime. They proclaimed his resurrection, and called him Messiah, the Anointed Son of God who was the Savior of Israel."

A deep sigh escapes Vivian's lips. I cannot tell her thoughts. At the sound, Gwenlli looks up, and comes over to fill her bowl of tea, and put another small log on the fire beneath the trivet and iron kettle. I had not noticed how cold it is becoming.

"I truly did not know what to think of the lad," I say, "who had stood with me on the Mendydd and learned the trade of tin. Can an ordinary man be the Son of God? But I threw my lot in with his followers, for they were in need of help. The authorities cracked down with renewed vigor. Many innocent people were chained and thrown in prison. I was removed from my Roman post as Minister of Mines and imprisoned, myself, for two years."

Vivian's face turns to mine at this.

"When I finally secured my release, I found those still most in danger and began planning an escape. A year later I sailed with them from Joppa on one of my family's Phoenician trading ships. Miryam, the lad's mother, was with us. And the Magdalene, who the lad loved."

Vivian speaks again, surprised. "He loved?"

"She was always at his side. They often spoke of love. It is hard to know for certain how his followers lived, but it seemed to many she was his wife."

"And this girl," Vivian asks, "What was she like?"

"Her name also was Miryam," which in the tongue of my people means Star of the Sea. She was a Magdalene, a priestess. She was young, and strong, and there was a fire in her eyes and a power in her spirit." Why, I wonder, is the Lady so interested in the Magdalene?

"We sailed for Massalia in Gaul, where they settled. I followed the tin route across Gaul and the Great Channel home to Cornualle, and there for years tried to put Jerusalem behind me.

But always there was the nagging in my soul: What is the meaning of it all? What could I have done to prevent it? Why did the Priests and the Romans find him such a threat? And always, always, is it possible that an ordinary man can be the Son of God?"

Without speaking, Vivian stands and leaves the roundhouse. Gwenlli follows silently into the darkness outside.

I sit looking into the flames of the cooking fire. The tale is nearly told, the Lady has gone out into the night. All is quiet except for the crackling of the flames. I feel the silence sweep over me, the stillness enters my bones, the sound of my breathing rises in my ears. It overcomes the crackle of the fire. Have I offended the Lady? Have I been too presumptive of her understanding? Has the tale caused a distress I could not foresee? I look around the single room. Its simplicity bespeaks a life that does not deserve - may not tolerate - the violence of Rome and Iudea, and the battles of Eastern gods. The feel of the Lady in this space is something physical. It seems to me I am out of place, disjointed. Perhaps I do not belong here at all. I close my eyes, and wait.

Presently, Gwenlli returns with an iron pot and sets it by the kettle on the trivet. She pours grain into it, and herbs, dusting off her hands. I watch her anxiously, hoping to find the hospitality her actions portray. Where has the Lady gone, I wonder. As if in answer, Gwenlli looks up from the fire, her young face framing eyes that burn with intense feeling. As if to comfort me, she says, "My Lady will return." Satisfied with the pot on the fire, she takes up her spindle once more.

I am watching the simmering grain, its aroma filling my senses, when Vivian returns. She touches my hand gently as she passes by, to sit again where she had been before. As she passes, she leaves the scent of burning herbs and cold, dry air. She sits in stillness, as if she had never left. This is a magical woman, a magical place. For all I have heard of Affalon, never have I understood the depth of its meaning. There is a sacredness here as great as the Holy of Holies in the Jerusalem Temple. Yet it is different. It is the sacredness of women. Perhaps, I suppose, of the Goddess who is honored by them. It is something beyond my knowing, beyond my understanding.

It is now fully dark outside the doorway, Gwenlli is stirring the simmering grain on the fire. Vivian is as still as stone, yet it seems I can hear the beating of her heart. Her eyes tell me to finish the tale.

"Two years ago, the Roman legions landed on the southern coast. Last week I received word that Vespasian's army has swept past the old stone Temple on the great plains of the Belgae, and is occupying scores of their villages. Those which do not capitulate are burned. He will be here soon. The Mendydd are in turmoil. Even Cornualle is no longer safe. Our mine holdings are all but lost."

I look at Vivian with eyes that cannot decide whether to plead or demand, though my heart tells me either choice would be an error. Her expression is grave, and confirms that fear in my heart. Yet what she is really thinking I cannot begin to guess. I have sat across the table from Roman governors and Phoenician traders, and struck bargains that required the insight of a seer. Yet I cannot guess the mind of this mysterious woman. I know she will accept nothing but complete honesty. I hope that I have given it, as far as I know how. She leans toward me and again looks deep into my eyes. She is reaching into me, reaching to find the last crumbs of truth, to touch the very emotion that has raged like the sea within me. How does she know of that which has yet lain unexpressed? Only now do I feel it myself, as it rises up within my inmost being.

"And you thought of me," she says.

"Yes, I remembered you, Vivian, my old friend of the mists. 'I will go to her,' I said. 'I will go to her, and perhaps I will find answers.'"

"Perhaps." She looks down, listening deep within herself, as if gazing into the dark waters of a pool. "Sometimes, Eos, there are no answers. Or none we would accept. But perhaps you will find peace."

Vivian looks up and murmurs to Gwenlli in their own strange language. Gwenlli rises, stirs the pot once again, and bows to her Lady before leaving the hut. Leaving us alone before the fire. The scent of stew drifts into the air, but neither of us pays it heed. Vivian turns to me and looks into my eyes with a sharp clarity I have not seen in her before. Her eyes are deep and black, seemingly bottomless. For a moment, in the shadows of the oil lamp and the flickering fire, in the twilight of the hut, doubt again moves over my soul.

"Do you have anything that was his?" she asks. Does she know? Can she know? I know in that moment I should be truthful, but fear clouds my judgment and I hide the fact of the cup hidden in my little boat, pulled up on the shore beneath Wirrheal. There is a silence like a fragile bridge spanning a high divide, which she holds in place with her eyes.

"I have seen much of this in visions, Eosaidh. His pain. His death. And he is dead, though I have seen, too, how many would have it not so. Both those who loved him, and those who feared him. Eos, many wish to use him still, and use him they will."

Her words are asking whether I, too, am planning to use the lad, for what ends I cannot yet guess. The question hurts. But it is not, after all, only her question; it haunts my own mind as well.

"Lady," I respond. "Whether he is dead or not, that I do not know. I have seen much death in my life, but perhaps I have never understood it for what it is. Not because of the words of his disciples, but from my own experience of these fifteen years I know he is not dead in any sense of the word that I have known." I pause, and gaze into the fire. "Nor is he alive in any sense known to me."

I look back in her face, and realize she does not know, in this moment, whether I am friend or foe. What can I possibly be bringing to this sacred hearth that threatens her world? And yet, I know in my heart that it must, and must threaten me as well.

"There is something in this that is not of this world, Vivian," I say at last. "I know not what it is. It may be danger, or it may be hope. You are the last friend to whom I can turn, to find the answer."

"Is that what you think I am? A friend?"

My voice drops to a whisper. "I am no threat to you, my Lady."

Her onyx eyes flash as black a night and her rage hits me with a crippling force, as though she had thrust the end of her yew staff through my gut! Mentally I reach for my own hawthorn staff, which is leaning by the door. I would be even now swinging it in self-defense, but it is beyond the reach of my arm. In my head I hear her angry words: *What could you ever know of this?* For an instant I consider drawing my blade. It feels as though I am being confronted by forces of darkness. The oil lamp gutters, and the hearth fire retreats within itself. A raging wind howls in the silence, but whether it is a wind of this world or some other I cannot say.

Then, as quickly as the storm began, it disappears. Vivian turns away, and I can see the anger drain from her and fade into the air. The flames of lamp and fire revive, and the darkness dissolves. I relax my tensed body but a little, my hand still on the blade at my side, one eye on the Lady of Affalon, the other on my staff beside the door.

Moments pass. Eternal moments.

When she speaks, it is with a quiet, gentle voice that bears no resemblance to the rage just past. A voice that seems to be a part of the mud and reeds of this hut, a part of the fire and the twilight of shadows. A voice that is one with the slow, dark waters of the rivers and marshes that surround us. It is then I understand we are strangers to each other, for I am of the open sea of Cornualle, and the desert sun of Iudea. And in realizing she is alien to me, I understand the threat I am to her.

"If you do not leave tomorrow," she begins, seeming to decide upon her words as she speaks them, or perhaps listening to one who gives words to her, "if you do not leave tomorrow, then a place will be found for you. Here, on the island. And if you stay, you will not leave the island, nor the valley of your dwelling, not without my consent. You will be told where you can walk and where you cannot. Food will be given you, and you will spend time each day at work, helping with the heavy tasks."

I weigh her words silently. In these last few moments I have ceased in my own mind being a supplicant. We are, I now understand, key actors in the meeting of worlds. She has powers I cannot guess at. But now I know that I do as well. Different powers, but powers nonetheless. I cannot guess whether that was partly the aim of her rage, but it is indeed partly the result. From this moment onward, our relationship has changed, changed from those meetings so long ago, in a younger time. Changed from the last few hours of this day. Does she imagine I will be quick to comply? I think not. I think she is demanding integrity, not subservience. But can I accept these terms? Gwenlli is staring at her Lady in disbelief from the doorway, amazed that I am being allowed to stay. Vivian turns to her and whispers something, and she looks down, waiting. Then Vivian looks straight at me. Somehow in all that has happened, we are both standing, facing one another across the hearth.

"Know that my words are for your own protection. If you cannot agree, you must leave at dawn."

I walk slowly to the door and retrieve my staff without answering. From this moment on, the thorn will always be at my side. I turn to look at the Lady, whose eyes are again calm, and still. Outside, a gentle rain is beginning.

Chapter Five
Apple Blossom
(Vivian)

ere, let me show you."

"But it will die!" His voice is desolate.

"Hold out your hand, little one."

He uncurls small pink fingers and onto his palm the old man places the little honey-brown worm. The child's mouth opens out into a grin, quickly followed by a breaking peal of giggles. "It tickles, it tickles!" he squeals. His sister watches with a gentle smile. "You have to be still, Marni, you don't want to frighten it." Eos looks at her with a gentle curiosity and respect.

"No, lad, you mustn't frighten it."

"No," he whispers and, holding out his hand with determined solemnity, he looks up into the tinner's face. "But it's still going to die. Isn't it?"

"Yes, little one. But it has spent its short life in a warm heap of food, growing fat and long and wriggly," and with his fingers he tickles the child again, who wriggles and giggles. "And when a creature lives a good life, it becomes not just food to nourish the body, but food for the soul as well."

Wide eyed, the little boy nods and, turning, searches the orchard, "And for red robins and glas chits and black marsh chits and ... and ..."

Saillie laughs, "Not glas chits, silly, they eat barley grain and meadow seeds!"

Eos smooths his hand over the boy's mess of hair, "Let's see who comes."

And I watch, comfortable in the knowledge that the little gathering does not know I am there, some way up the hill beneath the broad canopy and heavy blossom of another old apple tree. To see him in such gentle relationship it is funny to imagine this man as the important and wealthy trader that he was, travelling the world, able to read and write, to speak so many tongues, a man who has shared food with chieftans and leaders. In his solitude here, cutting his own wood, sitting with the children, sometimes I catch a glimpse of that side of him, like a shine polished into a stone that has moved through many rivers. And I remember how much he has lost.

I breathe the sadness of lives lived and feel the warmth of spring. The sunshine is richer today, reflecting in the golden yellow of the cowslips and daffodils, flowers that peek through the fresh flood of new grass beneath the trees, and with eyes closed, for a while I listen to the chatter of the birds, feeling the innocence and excitement of the children's sweet pleasures: a bowl of Siona's chicken worms from the store and an old traveller to show them how to hand feed the nesting robins.

"My Lady!" The voice stirs me and I open my eyes, but before turning to the girl who has called, my gaze meets that of Eos who has looked up the hillside at the sound of the voice, and found me. There is stillness between us, the heavy silence of words that can't be spoken, words that have not yet found their sound. Has this shadow been upon my heart since his arrival, almost two long moons ago, or has he simply given it a clearer form?

Then the girl is beside me, "My Lady?"

I turn, "Yes, I am with you."

"I don't wish to disturb, but we have found toothwort flowering by the alders at Farydd Brook, for the first time in many cycles."

"On the alder?"

"I have not myself seen. I was sent to bring you."

I sigh, "Yes, I am coming."

Her basket is filled with prickly woodruff and periwinkle, muddy radish and green motch, a dozen winter burrs riding the skirt of her cloak, her face flushed with health and learning. She glows with spring's new life and I smile as I take her arm, though in truth it is hard to feel a part of her new cycle. I glance again at Eos, who still gazes up at me though the children are pulling at his robe.

Six nights have passed since last we spoke.

"Yashi, Yashi," Marni tugs, "can we feed another one?"

With fingertips I touch the tender green of the honeysuckle and, for a moment simply breathe, the look in his eyes touching my soul. The soft song of the honeysuckle washes quietly through me, these old climbers that bring the first spring leaves to the orchard, some opening out on old grey growth, some on the stretch of soft new tendrils, winding as they do around the apple's branches, never pushing yet gently holding on so perfectly tight. I sigh and turn away.

"At Fern Brook, did you say?"

"Farydd, my Lady ..."

Though the days are now a little longer than the nights, and some are so blessed with the warming sun, the dusk is still clothed in a biting chill. Furthermore, as this night embraces the island, I am distracted by an uncomfortable cold within me. It is Gwenlli's hand on my sleeve that brings me from my scattered thoughts; I've been fidgeting with the fire and, with her touch and a silent bow of her head, she pushes me from it.

Yes, child, I smile, feeling both her care and her admonishment.

I wanted to return to my own dwelling on Ynys y Cysgodion, but conversations about foxes and chickens, about toothwort and young hawthorn leaves, have kept me here too long. Resigned to another night spent on Ynys y Niwl, I sit down upon the hides. Picking up the small dish of peat-black oak, given me by a travelling druid from Erin's land, I sigh, recalling once again my last conversation with Eosaidh.

In the black water I had seen a vision of fighting in a temple, though how I knew it was a temple was not overtly clear. It seemed a stark building, holding sacred only the emptiness of a human soul undisturbed, a human soul alone. No bird song or music of the breeze, no river's flow or fruiting tree, the temple was crafted with the wit of human invention, and within its hard stone walls a crowd of men were shouting, their voices echoing around pillars and off the sharp lines of stones with corners, the ceiling heavy above them, dark and flat. Their souls seemed to me just as the ceiling was: untouched by the bright wands of sunlight that scoured the bare and dusty floor.

And in that place I had asked to see what was honoured, and no soul was revealed to me, yet I became aware of a power that loomed with an oppressive force, as if watching every move and taking every breath. As I closed my eyes, the inner eyes of my soul that allow me this gift of vision, instead of clearing my sight I descended from that place into the very sand beneath their feet. Yet the sand was not of the earth but of the skies, and it drove through the wind like snow in a blizzard. There was no air to breathe, no way to see through the storm, and my eyes became enraged with the stinging salt of sand. Choking, again I stepped back from the vision, this time freeing myself from its clasp.

White petals of apple blossom were floating on the water as I opened my eyes, giving the sweetest touch of welcome to my soul so bruised. I bowed in gratitude, oh blessed spirits, I thank you, yet I needed at once to stand, to stretch my legs and breathe, breathe the cold clear air of these Brythannic islands. With my hands upon the apple bark, my soul entwined with their old grey roots deep in the mud, I sought out the serenity of understanding. Each time I had journeyed to comprehend what the tinner brought, this sand had choked me, and yet I was no closer to finding resolution. How I longed to find resolution, but that day I had felt only the surging tide of frustration.

So did I rise and walk, and as my feet took me striding through the orchards, chickens and wild birds scattered before me, even the goats in the low meadow bleating from the trail of indignation that was laid with my every step. And with every step that indignation rose higher within me: for how dare he bring this god to our islands' shores! It is one thing to honour the gods of your people when upon the road and travelling far from home, but another to call their power to another's lands! I knew it had to stop. I had to stop it.

At the top of the hill, I stopped to catch my breath, wearied from my pace and the swell of anger, and there remembered the words of a travelling sapher. Taking the floor at a gathering of druids and priests, speaking of the Iuddic faith, he had declared that to them there is only one god, "For the Iudde say that all others were long ago denuded of their grace and are now no more than mist and delusion ..." Was this the god that Eosaidh honoured? A god that considered himself above all others, or even to have conquered others? The idea flickered through my head like a dragonfly upon the lake, unable to find a place to settle, or any depth of understanding.

I leaned against the old oak on the hill's rise and closed my eyes. Struck by lightning some time during my childhood years, it had been such a beautiful cave of soot and scent and solitude to me as a young girl. Now, its ruin a haven for a thousand creatures, I honoured its spirit and breathed my soul to find calm. Questions were colliding in my mind: why was it that I felt so deeply disturbed? As if my soul - and the soul of my people and the land - were being struck, excruciatingly slowly, by some force of lightning, I lay fallen, like the oak, with the vulnerability of my roots exposed. Yet nobody else had noticed. I ran my fingers over a ridge of dry grey bark, and felt the oak spirit move through me.

"Would you guide my thoughts?" I whispered, "oak brother?" I stepped away, feeling the spirit's quiet direction. *Look at me,* he murmured, *look.* And in the beauty of his rotting body, glowing in the spring's soft light, he who had sheltered and comforted me almost every day throughout the whole journey of my life, I saw a glimmer of hope. *Yet,* I turned away, *yet, brother, must we die?* And I gazed out over the beauty of this sacred land.

From the highpoint, looking north, I could see the orchards, the thickly forested hills, the precious green meadows that ran down to the reeds where this blessed island's shores dissolve into marsh, everything humming with the waking breath of spring.

Few paths through the marshes are visible from near or far, yet I know them so well, as I looked out I could feel where each current flowed into clear water. I knew just what the mists were hiding, and my heart moved to each island that rose through their soft white cloak, even as far as the ridge of the mainland, the Mendydd hills, and the rivers that flow from the tribal wells at Llw Ffynnon.

I could feel the humming of lake communities on the edge of open water, fires burning in roundhouses set upon their unstable spreads, the elders reciting their people's stories to the children in the damp air. And I could see still with my grandmother's eyes the lake village she knew so well, on the southern edge of Llyn Hydd, a community now scattered, its spreads now submerged beneath the slowly rising water.

Every curve of land, softened by trees and cloud, every colour and flow of water, each thicket of thorn, bramble and nut tree, each blaze of yellow gorse and blur of reeds and marsh withies, every story told in the firelight, everything before me I knew better than my own body. In water and mud and bark, in cloud and tree not yet clothed in leaves, I saw before me the flesh of my gods. Every whisper was a note in the songs of my ancestors, a part of their stories which must ever be told.

And furthermore, as I sighed that day, I was conscious of everything before me, each curve of hill and shore, each ripple of water, being an extension too of my own ageing body. For on that day as on every day, as I gazed out over the world, I could feel every touch, every axe blow and every prayer, every paddle that pulled through the ancient water.

How could he know this?

I turned and sighed, looking down towards the walkway that stetches over the marsh, lost in the mist that now covered the island's low south west, the white haze lingering on the waters, barely stirring beneath the warm breezes that moved softly over the hill top.

Taking the track heading west, to avoid the crowd gathered by the springs in the valley, I walked through the forest and down, heading for his dwelling near the lower slopes of Bryn Fyrtwyddon. On any day, it is a beautiful walk and, even amidst the seething of my soul that day, my thoughts found peace in the shimmering of the spirits waking and stretching, sap rising and leaf buds pushing from dreams into new green-tipped life. Yes, I almost found enough calm to meet him gently.

The cracking blow of his axe reached me before I could see him through the soft mist as I came to the edge of the forest. His back towards me, his tunic cast off, dressed only in the creased wraps of his leggings and his old Roman boots, he swung the blade down into the fallen wood. And even beneath the anger, I was aware that in my old heart I smiled softly as I watched, for though he wheezed, wet with the sweat of his exertion, he looked strong and well. Tending to his own needs, and giving to the community, heaving water, logging wood, had brought him health in these past moons. I felt a wash of relief.

He had not seen or heard me through the mist-soft and muffled air and, as I stepped from the bare forest canopy, I made a decision. Instead of approaching him, within a veil of silence I walked to the small hut he had built himself a little way from his own roundhouse. As it faced east, away from the focus of his working, I was soon hidden behind it.

I knew it was not honourable for me to intrude, but the visions of the sand god's rage would not leave me, and a seething loyalty in my heart propelled me on, loyalty to my land and to my gods. I had seen this small building and never asked him about it, nor had he offered any words of explanation, yet its purpose was obvious and increasingly so as time wore on, for the colours and currents of the air around it were clearly changing: no longer the russet, grey and green of the island, here the air was bleached.

In the tenderness of truth, however, I was aware too of a clawing deep desire to reach some intimate part of this old man's soul. It was longing that lay as a fog within my mind, concealing a deeper grief I did not want to feel, and I pushed it away as my hand touched the carefully hewn wood of the doorway.

Something was nailed to the frame: a tiny box, upon it inscribed a six pointed star. Some invocational amulet honouring the ancestors, I assumed, those whose spirits dwelled in the stars of the dark sky. There was no softness in its magic, however. My fingers felt for its essence, but the current seemed one only of words and habit. Was it there to keep me out? I didn't feel that to be its purpose, yet it did not welcome me.

Over the hide that draped the door was a worn woven cloth of an unnatural blue, albeit faded by the sun. It was a dye not local to my lands. Trimmed in fine silver, the wear on this edging showed its age and I wondered if it were a possession of his bloodline, and how often it had been hung upon a temple door, in how many places across the world. As I pulled it back, with the heavy goat hide beneath, I felt I were stepping not into his own heart, but into the heart of his people. Though no spirit was with me, I did not feel alone.

Though the hut was no more than a woman's height from wall to wall, I was immediately sickened by what I felt inside, for it seemed to me as empty as the dwelling of a rich man unloved. There was little light but that cast by a small lamp, burning as if it had been so for a long time: the smell of pungent grease hung thickly in the new thatch and daub. In the scent was an incense of unfamiliar herbs and resin, and the burning bowl beside the lamp showed where it had been smouldering. I touched the blackened debris and brought my fingers to my nose: frankincense and cinnamon, some ground leaf that seemed to hold within it an earthy spirit of another land, and a musty red spice I did not know. These were laid upon a rough wooden altar, set carefully upon logs, and this upon a rug of coarse woven wool, dyed with a similar blue.

Beneath the altar I saw a simple polished wooden box.

Is this where you hide it, Eos?

I closed my eyes, conscious of the extent of dishonour in what I did, wondering just whom I was protecting with the most vigour: the young lad whom the Romans killed, who remains so alive in his heart, or my own land and my people? Or myself.

Yet, I opened the box and found nothing. In it was a scroll, and upon it were lines of Greican letters. For a moment I wished I had learned this tongue, used by the druids and travelling priests. I lifted it out and sought out the invocation written into its ink, the current of prayer, yet it felt like the little box upon the door: filled simply with stories, the spoken words of a people declaring their identity. It had no value to me and, replacing it, I closed the box quietly, hearing still the slam of his axe as he worked the wood outside.

Where, I wondered, was the source of this energy I could feel? But for some stale flat barley bread under a cloth on the altar, there was nothing else. It seemed the hut itself, by its very intention, was the source, radiating the beliefs of his people, like a beacon on the green slopes of my island.

I closed my eyes, retrieving another vision so often seen in my soul: the cup of blood. If I knew just what this cup was, it would be easier to find, or to understand its power and relevance. Pausing in the half light of his temple, I reached out across the waters of my mind, seeking, feeling again the certainty that Eos had brought with him some object that brims with the life of that murdered young Iuddic priest of his blood.

So did I call, within that temple and against my own judgement, *my Lady, show me what I need to see here.* The effect was immediate. Hurled from that place, my soul battled again the storm of sand, filling my lungs as I struggled to breathe, and I screamed, *Who are you?* The change was as immediate, the sand disappearing, leaving me standing in a shaft of blinding light. I knew I was not alone, for I was one amongst a crowd who stood close, holding to each other, yet the loneliness was crushing. I had never felt so alone. I looked around me, assuming I was the outlander, expecting to see ease, but I saw loneliness in every face, each soul holding onto the people around them, and above, always this presence, searing, watching, blinding. In the harsh power of that light, horrified, I called within my soul, *my Lady, what is this?*

The soft earth took my weight as I found myself again in Eosaidh's hut, opening my eyes to perceive my grandmother beckoning me to the doorway, *Come, leave this place, leave now, come ...*

Seething at my own inability to understand, seething at his presumption to construct a temple to this isolated god, here upon my land, this god of dust and heat, of human insolence and disdain, I gathered myself up, and breathing in the power of the land I strode from the hut out into the afternoon's light, down to where Eosaidh was still chopping wood. While still a good few paces from him, the words rose from my soul.

"What right do you have to invite your god to my land?"

Startled, he dropped the axe and reached for his tunic, hastily pulling it over his head as he turned towards me, "Vivian?"

I stopped a few yards from him, pointing back towards the hut, "Are you so blind as to not realize the damage that you do?"

"I didn't bring him to your land, Lady." His face was all confusion. "He was here already."

"He was not!" His words are incomprehensible.

"He has always been here! As has your goddess. Lady, all gods are everywhere," he raised his hands in explanation, but his words were simply salt and dry elder on the fire of my rage.

"You are so very wrong! This is a land of water and apples. There is nothing your Adonai can bring but dust and hunger. Do you not understand the danger you bring? Such power here can only bring devastation!"

Wresting the axe from the log between us, he swung it through a high and sweeping arc, bringing it crashing down into the wood with a ring that echoed out across the island and shuddered through the marshes. Startled, several herons took flight from the along the water's edge, circling out of sight around the western end of Myrtwydden, but he did not stop to watch their flight, instead dragging the axe again from the wood to bring it crashing down. A lapwing rose up from the cusp of the forest, crying out its *peewhit, peewhit,* seeking to distract whatever intruder there may be from her nest, a handful of crows lifting onto their wings with chattering indignance, and my heart pounded. I stared into his soul, but for some time he only continued to cut and split wood as though I were not there, taking out his wild anger upon that downed elm which, unlike me, could not respond. Sweat shone on his brow as the anger in his heart blazed through the straining muscles of his shoulders and arms. One final, great swing buried the axe head almost completely, and he turned to me, barely able to control his voice.

"Lady of Affalon, hear me! I speak Greek, Latin, Aramaic, Cornish, and the Brythonic common tongue of these islands.

I have travelled the length and breadth of the world, and the lands that surround the central sea. I have seen the worship of the Tyrian Ba'al, I have been at Herod's Temple to the God of my people, I have seen the Temple of Diana of Ephesus, the Gods of Athens and of Rome, I know Cernunnos of Gaul, and Manannan who inhabits the Cornualle seas. Whether these be many gods, or all manifestations of the One, I know not. But I do know the wide world is bigger than you imagine, and that there is more to the Holy than this collection of islands on the edge of civilization."

I shake my head. "And why do imagine that I care anything of the lands beyond here? What are they to me? This mud is my soul, this mist is my breath, as it was the body of my mother and her mother before her."

"But you know nothing of the world, Lady!"

"What do I need know? That beyond these lands, the world is peopled by common thieves risen to steal my mother's body? Why do they come, Iudde? Because you travel the world to display our wealth, digging deep into the sacred earth for more of this shining treasure that lures these bloodsoiled magpies of Roma! Who can your god be that call to the magpie? !"

"I did not come here to start a war of the gods, Lady. I came here because we once were ..." He lifts a hand to his forehead, for a moment closing his eyes. Then again he finds the strength to look into my face with frustration. "I came here because I need a friend who understands my agony. Instead, I find only cold welcome and conflict!"

As I stood before him crying out in my rage, it was as if my soul had gathered up every little island of the marshes beneath the folds of my cloak, such was my desperation to protect this place from all he brought. Were we friends now? Were we ever? I could see the memories flicker through his soul yet in that moment I closed my mind so as not to remember. Already he had provoked more weakness in me than anyone had done before. I whispered prayers to the goddess of the land and felt her holding me, breathing me.

In my voice there was ice.

"How can you honour a god that shows no honour for other gods?"

"How can you, Vivian? The Lady you call Mother -"

"You know nothing of her!"

"I know she is the one you believe nurtures the hills and apples and waters of Affalon, but you have hedged her about with so many laws that even on this holy isle I cannot find my way to her."

"You would not know where to begin."

"But you will not teach me!"

His words lingered in my mind ... *I cannot find my way to her.* I looked into his face and wondered, Would you want to? Are you seeking her? But the words found no sound. Instead I looked down and spoke quietly, hearing the ice still sharp in my tone.

"I protect her from thieves."

"I am no thief!"

Our eyes met again and he looked away.

"Besides," I added, "you must be used to laws. Your religion is thick with laws."

"True, but the Torah of my people is the teaching of Adonai, not his fences. It is the way to find him, not to hedge out foreigners."

"That is not what is taught of the Iuddic tribes, Eosaidh. Your people are scattered for their land is already broken, torn apart by the warriors of Roma. But this land, tinner, this sacred land is not yet lost! Do you not see how I must protect it? And yet you come, as a friend, and tear a rent in my cloak of keeping!"

He shook his head, breathing to control his rage. The spirit of the blade-hacked elm shimmered in the air between us like sharp bronze dust. He pulled the axe from its fallen trunk, wiping off the head, and slung it across his shoulder. Sweat glistened on this forehead and, drawing his sleeve across his face, he gazed at me, his eyes filled with anger and pain.

"Eos," I whispered. "I ask you simply to take down that temple."

"It is not a temple, Vivian."

"Whatever word you use to name it, it hurts."

He looked down, pausing for a moment. "Yes. It all hurts."

And with that, he turned his back on me, picked up his staff of thorn and strode purposefully towards his dwelling house.

Our conversation was over.

"Food, my Lady." Gwenlli's gentle voice draws me from my memories. Seeing my face, she no longer offers me the bowl but puts it carefully on the bench beside me, the tender concern in her eyes softening my heart.

"Bless you, dear child."

She pours water into another bowl, adding a spoonful of dried herbs and petals.

"You are grown tired this moontide, my Lady."

"Yes," I sigh, "I know."

She is quiet for a while, sitting at my feet, stirring the tea.

"You've not spoken to him?"

"No."

"Fianna says that he is thinking of leaving, my Lady."

Her words, so softly spoken, kick into my heart with an unexpected force.

"Has she been talking to him?" I say too quickly.

"Only because she cares for the children. He loves the children and has been a great help to Fia when there is much to do. My Lady?"

Tears are rising in my throat. That she notices makes me feel like a child. I close my eyes, wondering how stupid I have been, how stupid I am now. And how stupid I can yet be. I have not felt so lacking in answers since I was younger than this sweet girl. Taking the spoon from the bowl, she carefully places the tea in my hands.

"I must speak to him, Gwenlli."

"In the morning, I'll send -"

"No, Gwenlli. Now. It is only just dark and he will not be sleeping." I pass her back the bowl and start to clamber to my feet, but she holds me.

"No, my Lady. You are not strong enough to go."

"Of course I am!"

"No." Our eyes meet, and I see a strength in her I have not seen before. She bows, "Forgive me, my Lady. As I said, with respect, you have grown tired. I will send Morfrenna to see if he will come." Setting the tea upon the bench, within a moment she is gone.

Footsteps gather outside, the whispering voices of the girls and Eosaidh's soft growl, then spirit-light footsteps as Morfrenna creeps away, and Gwenlli lifts the hides of the door, saying, "My Lady, he is come. Would you see him now?"

My heart is beating too fast and I nod, closing my eyes to find again the stillness and strength of the earth beneath me, my Lady of the dark mud, feeling my roots lying deep within her soul. When I look up, his figure fills the doorway and I bow my welcome.

"Shalom," he murmurs and bows in return.

"Forgive me for -"

But he shakes his head, "I was half way here already."

"You were?"

"Forgive me if I have broken more of your rules, Lady." I close my eyes, turning away from his antagonism, but his tone softens, almost apologetic. "In truth, I was by that old black oak, high on the ridge, at the base of the tor, watching the sun setting above the mist. I suppose I had been waylaid by my thoughts when your scout came searching for me. I fear my presence was more than a surprise to the young thing," he smiles, though with sadness.

"I am glad you have come," I say softly.

Our eyes meet, full of hurt and questions.

"As am I," he murmurs.

"Sit," I motion to him. "Come and sit."

Gwenlli puts another log on the fire, filling the kettle from a jug. I whisper to her in the old language, "Leave us, dear one, just for a while?" She questions me with her eyes, but I insist, "I'll be alright." She bows and leaves, though not happy to do so, and when the hides are down again, Eosaidh looks at me with curiosity and concern.

"Why did you send her away?"

"Don't ask such questions, Eos."

He sighs, "Vivian, you are a complicated woman."

"We are complicated, Eos." And I add, "Both you and I."

In the moments that follow I wonder what it is we are to talk of: the issues that have made my belly churn and my head hum like a swarm of hiving bees, or the pain in my heart that I see in his eyes. I close my eyes, seeking guidance, and hear my grandmother's voice, *Vivi, you are human, find your humility.*

I open my eyes to see her sitting by the fire, her eyes wet with age and tears, and her smile serene with empathy. *Go on,* she whispers. I breathe in deeply, with acknowledgement, and turn to the tinner. He is gazing at me, filled with tenderness and uncertainty.

"Eos," I murmur, "I have not behaved with honour."

"Honour." He gazes into the fire, but his mind is not with the flames; I feel his soul close, his breath in my heart. That he senses the poignance of my words moves me deeply. He does not speak, but instead remains close. For a while he closes his eyes and I watch his tenderness beside my own as we sit in silence.

Then quietly, he speaks the word again. "Honour. What is honour, Vivian, but the proud attempt of the mighty to preserve their way of life."

"It is more than bloodshed, Eosaidh."

He looks into my face, "I know. But perhaps it is not honour we should be seeking. It is understanding."

"Nothing should be done without honour," I whisper. "But I do seek understanding. I wish deeply to understand you." For a moment, our eyes meet. A log slips on the fire and he reaches to steady it, allowing me to find my voice again. "Yet with such violence, so many now pouring through these lands ... Eosaidh, it was the druids' gathering at Llw Ffynnon, a few days ago at the moon's quarter. They gather at the wells with the councils of the local tribes, and I sat through such stories of fighting. The tribes are imploding, destroying themselves from the inside, splitting with the stress of fear. So many are dead, Eos. And news from the south," I look up into his eyes. "It won't be long."

"No, not long. Even now Vespasian is in Exmoor and drives toward Cornualle." He looks to the covered doorway as if, through it, he might see the advancing fires of Roma's ant-like invasion. "As long as he stays to the south, we have some time, at least." I wonder for a moment how he knows this, whom he has been meeting without my knowing, but I set aside the fear knowing that to raise it again will bring only conflict between us.

I sigh, "Eos, I do seek to understand you."

His face expresses only gentleness, "What can I say to guide you?"

"Your god, Adonai: where does he come from?"

For a moment he gazes at me, with a frown through which he struggles to find his words. "He comes from nowhere. He is from everlasting to everlasting."

They seem to me words repeated from the mouths of his people's teachers.

I shake my head, "Eos, your words are without meaning."

"They have meaning to me," he says.

I look into his face, "Are you able to share that meaning?"

For a while he thinks hard, rubbing his beard, then shrugs, "He is the eternal one of Heaven."

"Heaven?"

"Yes, Vivian. But we met him at a moment in time, in a very earthly place. Sometimes we call him Immanu-El: God Who Is With Us. For we were slaves in the far land of Egypt, and he brought us out."

"I have heard saphers speak of Egypt -"

"Saphers?"

"The travelling priests," I say, but his face is still blank. "Do they use another name in Cornualle? They are travelling thinkers, they talk of ideas . .."

"Ah, philosophers," he nods, understanding.

I quell a surge of impatience, "But what is Heaven?"

He laughs, placing his hands on his knees and rubbing away the stiffness. "I am a tin merchant, Vivian, not a theologian!" But seeing I don't lay aside the question, he thinks for a while, and says softly, "Heaven ... I think, heaven is the eternity in which Adonai dwells, the mountain top from which he comes to his people in their need."

"So heaven ... is the open skies?"

"The open skies and beyond the skies. It is upon the crest of the far hills and in the valley of springs. Heaven is where God dwells. The skies are his throne, the green earth his footstool. I remember the lad saying to me once, 'Uncle, the kingdom of heaven is within you.'"

He searches my face, wondering if his words are making sense to me. Yet in his eyes, he reveals too that they make little sense to him.

"But Adonai dwells in the silence as well," he adds. "In truth, though, for many years he has been silent to me."

"Silent or silence?" I ask.

"Silent."

He pauses for a long moment, his eyes downcast, and my frustration at not grasping his meaning is deflected by this wash of desolation. When finally he looks up and gazes into my face again, the empathy in my heart rises through me like a flood. "Silence I could understand. There have been nights on the sea, or moments in the depths of the mines, when I have come face to face with the mystery of the silence of God. But that silence was alive with his presence. In the years since the lad's death I have been searching for meaning, and Adonai has been silent to me."

Perhaps, I wonder, you were no longer able to hear.

For a long while we sit without speaking, though our minds are in different places. As he remembers his murdered kin, my soul slides through the deep water of wondering without words. Yet, as I rise to the surface, I still have no clear sense of his Adonai.

"Forgive me, Eos, but I hear no answers."

He frowns, seeking words once more.

But it is I who speak, "You have no idea who he is, do you? I hear you speaking only the words of your teachers, but they are poetry describing something that you cannot yourself explain. He is everything and yet he is nothing. What is he made of? This is mystery to those who live their lives with hands in shit and barley, but you, Eos," I shake my head, "not you, dear soul. Your mind is awake! Yet in your words I hear you tell of an imaginary chieftain. Is this Adonai? The high chief of your people?"

"No," he sighs, rubbing his beard with the roughness of his hand. "He was, once. 'Adonai, God of Hosts', we called him. Leader of the the heavenly legions, deliverer of Israel. But it has been a long, long time since Adonai has brought his hosts to our aid. All the hosts are Roman now, and the chieftains speak in Latin, not Aramaic. Even here, in far-flung Cornualle where my family has been dispersed for generations, the Roman hosts are coming."

I smile with a sadness at his wandering soul that would confuse Conualle with these islands of the marsh, so far from Conualle. But he turns to me, with no realization of what he has said.

"The lad did not call him 'High Chief'. The lad called him Abba, Poppa. He would gather little children around him, hold them on his lap, and say,'This is what Adonai is like, he is like our Father. He is our Da. 'Vivian, it would have moved your heart to tears to see the compassion in his face, the gentle way he held the little ones."

"I know," I whisper. For a while again we find silence. His heart is full and I watch the tides of his emotion as they wash through him, gazing into the glowing embers of the fire. When I break the stillness, it is to ask him to attend to it. He stretches his legs, apologizing for not having done so before. And we smile at each other, with a tenderness I am relieved to share.

When he sits again, pulling his robes around him, I ask the question that is troubling me.

"Eos, he is father to his children, your Adonai. That I can hear. Yet who is your mother?"

The father I can understand, the raw power of a father's rage, blade-sharp and ever distant. That I could feel in the temple of sand, in the emptiness and straight stone-hewn walls, in the oppression of being watched by one who judges. This is a father's role. But there was no giving of the mother in that place.

He looks deeply into my eyes and something moves over his soul, a recognition that makes me wonder what he has seen.

"What do you see, Eos?" I whisper.

He looks down, then again into my eyes, and the fire's light sparkles in his own, wet with rising tears, but he does not turn away. "I saw Miryam," he murmurs, gazing into my face, "the lad's mother, my niece, that day when I cut his body down. The way she held him, so tired and with such love, holding his broken body. In your face, I saw Miryam ..."

"The lad's mother," I say softly.

"Vivi," he whispers, "I will show you what you have been searching for."

Chapter Six
The Cup of
Enaid Las

(Eosaidh)

It is hours before dawn, and I have not slept. Sitting on my cot in the darkness, I pull my sleeping furs close to keep off the chill. It is sometime in the first week of the Roman month of Aprilis, sacred to Venus. That fact, and the bright light of a moon approaching the full flooding through the open door, tells me without a calendar that it is the approach of the Passover, when we Iudde crossed over from slavery to freedom, from death to life. It is the lad's passover as well, for it was at this time, so they say, that he, too, crossed over from death to life. On my lap, wrapped in a sheepskin, is a small box made of the acacia wood of Iudea, tied with a leather strap. A few moments ago I drew it out from under the cot, where it has been since I built this hut two months ago. In the box, packed in sheep's wool to survive the journey, and wrapped in a fair linen cloth, is the cup. Only I have set eyes upon it in all the years since that last meal, but with the rising of the sun this day, I will show it to another.

As I remove the sheepskin covering, the scent of acacia fills the air. I am amazed at how it has lasted all these years. I untie the strap, and slowly lift the lid. Outside there is the silence of the night; the moon climbs in the sky, framed now in the open doorway. A shaft of moonlight falls across the cot, bathing the old box in its cool brightness. Almost with reverence I pull back

the soft fleece and fair linen, and there, absorbing and recasting
the moonlight, lies the cup. Made of translucent glass, its rich,
cobalt blue color is the shade of the deep heavens. Gently, I lift
it from the box, and hold it quietly in both hands. The image
of the waxing moon shines within the bowl, diffusing through
the glass so the entire cup seems to glow a royal blue. The glass
is nearly like a scrying bowl I once watched Vivian use. As I
gaze at it I remember, and images form in my mind...

We were in the upper room of my home in Jerusalem, gathered
with the lad and the Twelve for the Passover meal. As the
supper was ending, he poured fresh wine in the cup, and raised
it above his head giving thanks to Adonai. It caught the light
of the oil lamps as it does the moonlight now, and reflected it
back to us as if it were a giant sapphire. The lad spoke: *It is as
if this wine is my life's blood, poured out for you and for everyone,
for the forgiveness of sins. From now on, whenever you drink wine,
remember me.* Then he drank deeply, and we passed it from
hand to hand, each doing the same. There were many of us
there that night, yet the cup held enough for all. I remembered
the words of Torah, *For in the blood is the life.* He was offering
us his life. No greater love, he had once said, does a person
have, than to lay down his life for his friends. In all the years
since, those words have echoed in my heart. *No greater love. No
greater love.* The next day, on a Roman cross outside the city,
he died.

Now, holding the cup in the moonlight of Affalon, that love
comes flooding back into my being, and I think I understand.
It is a human face the lad has put upon Adonai, and the
tenderness of a human heart.

"Uncle Eosaidh." It is a solid voice, and not of my imagining.
I look up, and there he stands, in the doorway, framed by
moonlight. He is not a day older than when I saw him last.
These fifteen years have aged me in spirit as well as in body;
so much older, so much more tired. But he has not changed. I
should be afraid, but I cannot be. How can I fear one so close

to my heart, even if he is no longer of this world? "Uncle Eos," he says, "You have kept it."

Instantly I stretch forth my hands, offering him the shimmering blue glass, but he makes no move to take it. "The cup has passed to you, Uncle," he says, "It is yours to bear now."

Holding it again close to my breast I say to him, "I wish to share its presence with the Lady of Affalon." The lad smiles. It is a knowing smile, and I wonder at its meaning. "I have kept it safe all these years," I tell him, "and have shared it with no one. Yet I cannot help feeling that its destiny is with many."

His countenance turning serious, the lad says, "Uncle, there are many sheep and many different folds. There are many trackways to the Green Pastures. Each is the path of Life. Yes, take it to the Lady, and she will show you more, though the work of this cup is nearly done."

Perhaps it is the slow shifting of the moonlight through the doorway, perhaps it is more than that. The soft glow of light in the blue bowl of the cup begins to grow. Brighter and brighter it becomes, until the light in the cup fills the room with its brilliance, blinding me to all else. I can no longer see the lad, but still I hear his voice. "I am the Light of the world. All who walk in love's light are my friends, and I am theirs. Bear this light, Uncle. It will not fail you."

Slowly the brilliance fades to the soft glow of moonlight infusing the blue glass. The lad is gone. A white hart walks slowly past the doorway, pausing to look in at me, for a moment enchanted by the blue glow, and then moves on. I wrap the cup again in its fair linen, place it in the soft fleece, and close the acacia lid. It is time to go.

Last night we arranged to meet at the Red Spring, early, before the others arrive in search of healers and seers. As I set out across the meadow, I glance over my shoulder at the east slope of Wirrheal. Near the top is the thicket where I sheltered from the storm my first day on the island. One thorn tree stands tall above the rest. Its crown seems to glow with the ghostly white of the first blossoms of May, but it is only the moon in the bare branches. The sky is showing first light in the east; dawn is coming.

Thorn staff in my right hand, the acacia box clutched under my left arm, I turn towards the valley of the springs. The moon begins to fade above as I enter the valley, following the brook up the steady incline to its wellhead source. A gentle mist has begun rising from the marshes. I cannot see her in the new light, but I know Vivian waits for me at the well. I enter the small grove of ancient yews that surround it, and she is there, leaning on her staff. Gwenlli sits quietly on the rough-hewn bench near the wellhead, a basket on her lap with a stoneware pot that steams gently in the cool air. Vivian sits beside her, and Gwenlli offers her a small earthen cup of hot tea. She touches Vivian briefly on one shoulder and the two women exchange looks I cannot hope to understand.

I lean my staff against one of the yews, set the box down on a mossy stone, and stand looking at the Lady of Affalon. Memories of last night's vision come flooding back to me. Vivian, Miryam, and the Magdalene. I, who have never married, have had the friendship of more than my share of mysterious and powerful women. It occurs to me that I have understood none of them, though I have respected and loved them each in the depths of my heart. Each of them carries within herself some measure of the power of the cup, each of them a bearer of life in the world. Only days ago I would not have thought of such a thing, yet now it seems so clear.

It was the Magdalene who first spoke to me of such things, on the boat, on the way to Massalia. The night was new, and the Evening Star shone brightly in the western sky, across our starboard bow. I was sitting on a coil of rope watching the star rise and fall above the waves with the pitch of the boat. "She is beautiful," said a woman's voice behind me, and I turned to see the other Miryam, the Magdalene, watching the sky as I was. "Aphrodite she is called by the Greeks, " she said, "By the Romans, Venus. She is the goddess of Love." The Magdalene sat on a cask of olive oil across from me. "Mostly, she is simply a woman. Men forget that even ordinary women are bearers of life." I smiled. Sarah, her own young daughter, was asleep in the cabin. "Sometimes I think she is Asherah, she who walks on the sea." My own name, Miryam, comes from her. It means 'Star of the Sea.'"

We sat in silence for a time. "You have brought the cup with you," she said at last. I did not answer. "It bears his life within it, you know, even as I did. Even as little Sarah does, sleeping below."

"We all bear his life," I said, but I did not know the meaning of it.

"Yes, in different ways we all bear his life," she answered. "Care for the cup, Joseph," she said, "and I will care for Sarah." I suspected her meaning, but I did not ask. To this day I am not certain whether she, too, was a vessel for the lad's life. That moment was so many years ago, and I have not heard from the Magdalene, or had word of Sarah, since. Suddenly I can feel the ache of age in my bones.

Gwenlli speaks again to Vivian, and I am awakened from my dream.

"Forgive me Vivian," I say, "my mind was wandering. It seems you remind me of so many women."

Vivian stands, taking a step towards me, and searches my eyes, seeking the vision from which my words have emerged.

"I am a woman, Eosaidh. Do you now begin to glimpse understanding of what that means?"

If Vespasian himself were to stand before me and roar "I am a general, man! Do you know what that means?" I would not hesitate to answer. But now I am silent. Again I see the Magdalene on the boat to Massalia, holding little Sarah in her arms. Then, suddenly, she is Vivian, lifting a glowing cup of cobalt blue glass. "No, my Lady," I say, "I do not understand at all. Can you help me?"

For a moment she gazes at me, deeply, into my eyes. "You must trust me, Eosaidh," she says. Trust has not been easy between us, and it does not come easily now. But I nod quietly. Her eyes are coldly penetrating, compelling. She looks through my own eyes, into my mind, into my being. For the first time in my life I am aware of my own soul, as she gently touches it with her gaze, touches and holds me. I am rooted to the spot. Vivian takes a few steps closer, our eyes still connected. I am aware she is using the magic of her craft, letting me feel what it is to be her. Suddenly she is directly before me, though I am no longer aware of movement. It seems as though her cloak opens and envelops me, her warm skin touching mine, and I realize I, too, am naked and unable to move, caught in the spell, her energy flooding through me like crystal clear yet black dark water. Only for an instant do I feel her touch, for she passes the boundary of my own skin, and I am enveloped in her flesh. Expecting the hot, masculine response to this greatest of intimacies, I am surprised to find something very different. For I am aware of receiving rather than penetrating. My loins have a sense of roundness as if they were meant to embrace life rather than spew it forth. A gentle swelling above my heart is filled with the awareness of motherhood, and the presence of milk. Muscles that had become hardened with labor are softer, subtler, gentler. My heartbeat grows quicker, though the racing in my mind calms. Slowly, I stop analyzing, and begin simply to feel. I cross my arms over ripe breasts, and hug to myself a heartlonging for life. I am aware of a gentle swelling of my abdomen, a straining of the muscle wall, and I feel movement inside. Slowly, in awe, I move my hands to my rounded belly, and feel the hard kick of a child within me. I know the feeling of oneness with a new life being brought into the world. I look out through the eyes of a woman, and see the poetry of the world about me. I am a mother, and I feel the strong, gentle arms of the Mother of All wrapped about me, wrapped, myself, in swaddling clothes and lifted to her breast to drink.

I hear the music of her voice in my heart. *Eos, Eos, how I have longed to hold you to my breast as a mother holds her young.* I give in to that voice, and sink into the deep, soft warmth of an embrace so tender it breaks my heart and mends it again. All is darkness. All is silence, except for the quiet steady thrum of a beating heart.

Suddenly I feel a sickening blast of blind rage. The angry mother shouts within my mind, *How dare you? How dare you take my child?*

Every muscle in my body seizes and prepares to fight. My mind is torn with the conflict of warring emotions. The warm gentleness of nurture, the blazing anger of attack, and the cold, dead horror of despair. It is too much. My head reels and the world spins around me. I drop to my knees in the grass, retching up bile from the emptiness of my stomach.

And then it is gone, as if she has taken a step back. And we are once more wrapped in our robes, and the world around the spring is returning to my senses. The experience must have taken no more than a few moments, yet it lasted for ever. Slowly, I rise to my feet. Still she gazes into my eyes. Still her eyes are hard. She has given me a profound gift. But it is not a gift of tenderness. It is a gift of reality.

I hold my hands before my face. They are once again the hands of a tinner, though a moment ago they had been soft and fair. I can feel again the weight of muscle in my arms and shoulders; in my spirit there is the struggle and conflict of birth and death. I look at the stern power in Vivian's face, and begin to speak, "I never, I could never . . ."

"Such things do not offer themselves to be held by words, Eosaidh," she says in a voice that is cold and calm. "You have brought me here to show me something. Show me, for the day is passing." But the experience is still full in my soul and I try again to reach her.

"Thank you, my Lady. Thank you, Vivian."

She nods. "Show me what you have brought," she says.

I reach down and pick up the acacia box. "On the day I arrived, Vivian, you asked if I had with me anything that was his".

Gwenlli's hand grasps Vivian's cloak as she whispers to her in the old language. Vivian murmurs a response, turning back to look into my eyes as the words slip accusingly from her lips. "And you denied it."

"Until this morning the treasure this box holds had meaning only for me. It is my memory of the last meal we shared, on the night before he died. These fifteen years I have shown it to no one. I have spoken of it only once, with the Magdalene as we sat on the deck of a Phoenician trader and watched the setting of the Evening Star." I raise the box to eye level, sense the smell of acacia wood, and in my mind's eye see the soft glow of blue glass within. "Now I am aware it has meaning and power beyond my imagining. The power of Life, and the power of Death. But mostly the Power of Love."

Her expression is cold, and her words as still as ice. She does not share my anticipation, and her face betrays growing anger. "Be careful, Eosaidh of Cornualle," she says. Her eyes grasp the box with an intensity as though she had taken it into her arms, though I still hold it.

Suddenly I am shaken. The coldness in her gaze and words chills my heart, and, holding the box tighter to my body, I make a sudden decision. "More than anything you have taught me, Vivian of Affalon, you have taught me to be careful." I pick up my staff, and step back from her. Full daylight has come. "I have been repairing my old boat," I say, "and there is much work left to do." Slowly I turn from the women at the well and look down the path that runs along the stream, winding its way down the hill toward the vale before Wirrheal. The few early spring flowers growing along its edges bring no joy. Clouds from off the western sea cover the sun; I feel older than ever before. Sighing, I take one step, then another, and the leaving begins.

I am a dozen steps down the path when I hear footfalls behind me, and a tentative voice, "Eosaidh?" I know it is Gwenlli before I turn. When I do, I see the worry and the nervousness in her face. Looking over her shoulder, I see Vivian standing at the well. Her face is hooded. I cannot see it.

"I have been thinking of leaving for some time, Vivian. Fianna knows. I have spoken to her about it as we cared for the children." Gwenlli turns and looks at the Lady, saying something in their old tongue. Slowly Vivian nods her head. "I have been here two months," I say, "and still you do not trust me. I can understand now why trust is a challenge, but I cannot understand why that challenge has not been met." I take a few steps back toward her. Gwenlli steps aside on the path to allow me to pass.

Quietly I say, "Vivian." She looks at me, a fold of her hood falling aside. I can see her eyes, but I cannot guess what she is thinking. "Vivian, we have been friends. Do not let the gods make us enemies."

She looks at me strangely. I wonder whether she is thinking, or feeling. Then I remember the spell, and I know that both are the same for this woman of the marshes.

"This word, magdalene," she whispers, "means priestess?"

"In a manner of speaking. It means 'She of the High Place.'"

"His magdalene bore him a child?"

"Not his priestess, Lady, for the lad desired not priests or priestesses, but friends only. Miryam Magdalena was high priestess of the Temple of Mari, the Great Mother - She who is called by some Asherah; by the Egyptians, Isis; by the Greeks, Aphrodite. There are some who said the Magdalene was his wife, and Sarah, his child. The truth of this is among the many things I do not know. But, I suspect it is so. There have been many more unions between the followers of Adonai and of Asherah than my people have ever cared to admit, as is attested to in their own scriptures."

But the details about my people aren't the focus of her attention. Her eyes fall on the box I hold so securely beneath my arm.

"Did she use it? At the Temple of Mari?"

The sunlight is reflected off the waters of the spring, blinding me. In the light, I see a woman holding the cup. She lifts the glowing blue glass, offering a prayer I cannot hear. It seems that it is Vivian, but how can that be so? Might it be the Magdalene? Might the lad have shared the cup with her? That, too, seems unlikely. But I am newly aware of how much I do not understand. The vision fades, and there is Vivian again, standing beside the well. I cross the remaining space between us, dropping my staff at my side. Gwenlli is there, and takes it up before it falls to the ground. With both hands, I hold the acacia box before Vivian.

"I do not have knowledge of that, Lady," I answer. "I know only that it was the lad's, and held the wine he called his life's blood. Perhaps, Vivian, you will take the cup, and tell me."

This is the first time I have used the words 'life blood' and 'cup'. A light flashes in Vivian's eyes as if she is seeing again a vision she has seen before. Her body seems to relax, and she utters a long and peaceful sigh. Her gaze remains fixed to my own eyes, but she is seeing beyond me. Gwenlli says nothing, her nervous energy palpable as she stands beside me holding my staff. She bites her lip and watches her mistress, waiting.

Slowly Vivian lifts her hands from the dark folds of her cloak and silently takes the box from me. Never have I given this treasure into the hands of another since I first removed it from the upper room that night so long ago. Never would I give it to any other human being, save the one whose hands hold it now. Yet I sense the solemnity with which she receives it. Why is it so important to her? How can she know anything of this holy cup? It is a moment of extraordinary trust that I offer her, and I sense she is aware of that moment with all of her being. Each of us allows the other's trust to live.

When she turns her back to me and moves to the spring, it is harder for me. I follow as closely as I dare, not wishing to be far separated from the cup. She crouches down, stumbling a little, provoking Gwenlli to move quickly to her side, helping her to her knees by the sacred waters. I step forward to her shoulder, on her right, with Gwenlli on her left. Gwenlli hands back my staff, and kneels. Vivian rests the box on the ground and, untying the leather thong, turns the lid back on its leather hinges. She places both hands upon the open box, uttering an invocation in the old tongue. Slowly, her fingers push aside the lamb's wool, and she pulls back the covering of linen cloth. For a moment she pauses when it is before her. Rays of the morning sun strike the glass. A blue glow fills the space before the Lady, and rests upon her face. Gwenlli whispers to her. She looks up at the young woman and nods with a smile, a smile that seems to reveal both relief and sadness. High in the yew over our head, a raven calls, spreads its wings, and flies off. Vivian takes a slow, deep breath, then lifts the cup into her hands, bowing her head in prayer, whispering to the waters, waking the sound of their journeys in my mind, splashing, rushing, turning and diving, as if they are responding to her quiet call.

She turns to me, looking up into my face. As though she were describing it to me, I can feel she is filled with love and tenderness, the wholeness of a woman's task, the deep satisfaction of giving, sharing, holding. I have seen this look before, many long years ago, as the lad and I were returning to Cornualle from the Mendydd. As I lay awake on deck in the night darkness, I saw her face, and her arms extended outward, as if giving the lad something precious. I never saw the gift, but I never forgot the look on her face. And I am looking at it again now.

When she speaks, her words are as soft as the comfort of love, "Thank you, dear Eos, blessed soul, for returning this Cup of Enaid Las."

Returning? I drop my staff in surprise, letting it fall to the ground beside me. There is a lightness in my head, I seem to lose connection with the solid earth beneath my feet. Returning? She knows the cup! Has it come from Affalon? Can it be so? Returning? I would utter the word as a question to her, but before I can speak, she lifts the cup high and breathes in with the power of the sudden gust of a wild storm. I see the look in her eyes, and realize that she is about to smash the glass on the stone of the wellhead! No!

I am on my knees before her, between her and the hard, wet stone. My hands reach out, taking both of her arms with a firmness no one would dare use toward the Lady of Affalon. There is a gasp from Gwenlli, who reaches for something inside her cloak. But Vivian, in a steady, unearthly voice says, "No, Gwen. It is all right." Gwenlli removes her hand and slumps back, sitting on her heels. Vivian still holds the cup at chest height, and I hold both her arms. We look into one another's eyes. "Vivian," I say, "Not yet. Not until I have heard the tale." I can feel her tremble, and let go of her arms. She clasps the cup to her breast.

"So here is the true reason I returned to this isle." My voice trembles even as she does. Slowly, I raise my hands again, joining them with hers around the cup. We hold it between us, both looking into the soft, blue glow of its bowl. I look up to her face again, into her eyes, and she raises her eyes to mine. "It is beyond all reason, Vivi, but this cup binds us both. Tell me the first part of its story, for I know only the last. What is this cup? And how did it come to the lad?"

Together we are kneeling before the spring, its blood red waters overflowing the pool and tumbling down the narrow valley toward the sea. Around us are the ancient, towering yews of Affalon. Around the old trees, beneath the eastering clouds, another mist begins to rise upon the isle. In the quiet we listen to the tumbling waters, the whisper of the wind, and the gentle rhythm of our breathing. In the silence it is Gwenlli who speaks.

"Shall I make a fire, and boil more water for tea, Lady?" she asks.

Chapter Seven
The Stone Womb
(Vivian)

ad I doubted my vision? Yes. For, in truth, I had not believed that any but the young lad would hold it with sufficient reverence. I look up at the old tinner and acknowledge fully the love that has kept the cup so safely in his heart, "Thank you, dear Eos, blessed soul, for returning this cup of Enaid Las."

His mouth drops, his staff clattering to the stone rim of y Ffynnon Goch, and with it I find assurance that he did not know of its origin: the boy never told him. It matters not. I close my eyes and the prayers flow through me, as spirits rise around me, the waters lifting through my soul as rain from the ocean, gathering up into the songs of the old dead like vast black clouds, tearing open the web of life with the sky gods' gift of fire, thunder roaring through my soul as I cry out the words of a spirit returned, the torrential storm of rain about to come -

But before the invocation finds sound, the tinner's hands are upon me, holding me firm. For the briefest second, rage fills me, but before I can struggle, a voice fills my mind with surety. *Not yet*, she says.

"Mother," I whisper.

She crouches down and lets her fingers touch the red water, a cool flush of spirit moving through my soul as she does, and she looks up into my face, *There is time, Lady*. Behind her my grandmother smiles with a beautiful strength that flows so clearly upon the ancient blend of our blood and the waters. And with her I see others, women of the old council, sisters of the sacred lakes. There is an undiluted calm.

Then I feel Gwenlli's soul and the taste of her blade. Her instinct to protect me is strong enough for her to wound him badly and I must respond. Time has slowed. I hear my voice aloud, saying, "No, Gwen. It is all right," as much for the tinner as for the girl. Hearing her sheath the blade, in the flow of one quiet long breath I find the beat of my heart once more, and look into the soul of the old Iudde. His eyes are moving fast, searching mine for reason.

"Vivian," he says, "Not yet. Not until I have heard the tale."

With my soul, I nod, and he perceives it in my eyes, breaking the tight clasp of his hands around my arms. I don't know if he knows what he has just said, for his words were only in part his own, and in part the flow of my mother's in the air that he is breathing.

His voice trembles, "Now I know the true reason I returned to this isle." He lifts his hands and gently places them around mine as I hold the cup, amplifying the power already pulsing through me. I am shaking. He looks down and whispers, "It is beyond all reason, Vivi, but this cup binds us both."

The words crash through me. My soul in its entirety longs for nothing but to be released into the waters, to slip down into the depths, to join the souls of my ancestors on their journey to the otherworld, and in my longing is the longing to take this man with me, to fill every atom of his being with dark water, sparkling with the breathless life of the gods, utterly undivided. But his mind is cold, he has no idea what he says, nor what I am feeling. His hands slip from mine, and he sits back on his heels, suddenly a meadow's breadth from my soul. Across the well, my grandmother is the only spirit who remains, her face now whispering to me of the sadness of love and understanding.

"Tell me," he says, "tell me the first part of its story, for I know only the last. What is this cup? And how did it come to the lad?"

I look down and find my breath, murmuring a prayer for strength.

"Shall I make a fire, and boil more water for tea, my Lady?"

I turn to Gwenlli and smile, aware of my exhaustion, "No, child. Bless you." I speak in the old tongue of the marshes, "I need to take him to Croth Ddraig Las."

"My Lady -"

"The old ones are with me."

"My Lady, you are needed."

"And I will be with you yet a while, child. Long enough."

She looks down.

"Please arrange for Creyr and Fianna to come to Penn Willows."

She bows and gathers up all she has brought, giving to Eosaidh the woven bag of provisions that were to have broken our night's fast. They speak together, but I barely hear their words, he questioning what is to happen and she evading his questions. With the full weight of love I feel for my land, I replace the cup in its protective covers and gently put it back into the box of foreign wood.

I had kissed her forehead and smiled, sharing with her all the certainty that I could afford, but the look in her eyes has stayed with me. She does not question through a lack of trust, but she does not understand. That her feelings are shared by others on the islands of our sacred community only adds to my concern and, for a while, as Eos and I take the track through the southern meadows of summer grazing, I listen for guidance, my feet wakefully touching the land.

We share few words on the journey. Stopping more often than I would wish, we now and then share a smile at how old limbs move so slowly, but I know that he stops for my sake and hides it to spare my pride. Where the track is muddy from the spring rains, he tries to help me, but he carries the basket in one hand and his staff in the other, and I smile and make my slow footsteps, singing to the land when my mind becomes distracted and my feet slip needlessly in the mud. On the stone wall that marks the edge of Henddol, we sit for a while and share some bread, watching the starlings chattering, and the grey tickits in the gorse. Half a dozen baby hares play in the grass, their bodies alive with the scents and sounds of the sloping meadow. Amidst the blackthorn, hazel and marsh willows, an alder stands tall and I lift a hand to show Eosaidh.

"That's where we're heading, Eos."

He shields his eyes from the sun, now lifting through clear skies to our right.

"And what's there, Vivian?" His voice is washed with a blend of raw tenderness and affection.

"A flat boat," I smile. "We then make our way through the Bitter Marsh."

His face shows all that he is feeling, "You are tired. Do we need to do this, Vivi?"

Again, he calls me Vivi.

I wrap my cloak about me, "Let's find the boat."

For a while he drove the boat, using the greased alder paddle and the strength of his body, but, with my heart so tender, each splash was a jolt upon those subtle bruises. Having crossed through open water, as we near the marsh again, I take the paddle from him despite his protestations, and turn the boat in the water so I am driving from the back. When at last he accepts, he too turns his body to watch the course that lies before us.

Singing to the spirits, tears slide freely down my face, and I am grateful for the water's soft and familiar embrace. The marsh sprites are curious, mischievous, tapping the sides of the boat, asking about Eos, *who is he, who is he?* and my songs play over the thick waters in reply. He says not a word, listening and watching, knowing that he'd not know how to make it through the tangle of paths alone, each as narrow as the boat, criss-crossing and hidden, disappearing through reeds and swamp weeds that whisper as we pass.

At Y Gors Chwerw, I ask him to hold the boat still and he shudders, holding onto the reeds, turning to ask without words *what is this awful place,* and in the old language I murmur prayers to those who linger, souls caught in the slow water, trapped by the deep cleft in the earth beneath the marsh, spilling the bitterness of ancient bloodshed and the earth's own grief like oil into the water. The songs of the dead rise around us as we move again through the dank and gloomy air and my voice rises with them until they are still. Eos shivers, his soul showing the anxiety his head hopes to hide. He sniffs, rubbing his nose on his sleeve, trying to be rid of the stench of rotting, and I paddle as silently as the water allows me, heading for the tall dead rushes.

As we come close, he notices the bent willows and I smile with affection as his broad shoulders relax. Handing him the paddle, he digs into the earth beneath us, drawing the boat as far onto the shore as he can, then clambers out, dragging it up the mud. The three willows are ancient but, grown poorly in the bitter water, they are cracked and lean over upon each other, like sisterly crones, haggard and contriving malice.

"Settle, spirits," I whisper. "You know who I am."

Walking uphill into the forest, I am aware of Eos looking around with wide eyes, taking in the gnarled and twisted trees, dripping with lichens and mosses and ferns, none much taller than himself. A green woodpecker's laughing call makes him jump and we exchange a smile.

"It's not far now."

It is heading down the other side of the hill that I stumble, my legs hopelessly tired. He drops his staff and takes my arm, stopping my fall, and it is in that closeness that he first spies the oak, its leafless spring canopy rising out of the gnarled and twisted forest. I lay my hand upon his, and point to the oak's roots, "Look."

The gods are with us. The sun, not quite at its midday height, is not too high in the sky for the magic to be lost. From where we stand, the stone beneath the roots is glowing a perfect deep-water blue.

"Come," I whisper and, taking his arm, we walk to the edge.

The sound of trickling water evokes his curiosity, and he takes a few steps ahead. Then I watch as his soul is filled by what he sees: naturally hewn by the flow of ancient water, the cauldron of rock, held by the embrace of the hillside, three feet deep and as broad. Opposite the flow, across the hole in the stone is the slab of blue glass crafted to fit, leaving enough space for the water to pour through beneath, trickling its way down the hill towards the marsh.

I remember the first time I was brought here, by my grandmother. I was no more than ten summer's old, yet I couldn't believe that so much of my life had passed without me knowing such magic. As I watch Eos taking in its beauty, my pleasure is blessed again with the innocence of the child that I was.

He turns to me, filled with questions.

"Is this..." he struggles for words, "a temple to your goddess?"

I smile for his words explain so much of his misunderstanding.

"This is a gathering place of my gods, Eos."

Putting his staff and the basket on the ground, he looks down into the cauldron, the glass painting its walls such a rich blue, the water absolutely clear, sparkling silver and blue in the sunlight. Drifts of yellow buttercups shimmer in the grass around the edge and, above, the old oak stands like a warrior in his stillness. I walk to his side and look into his face, his forehead ridged with thought.

"Not one goddess, Eosaidh." And I show him each one, speaking the name in the old tongue and in the language we share: the earth who give birth, the waters that flow, the sun that touches, and the wind that meets us here. I tell him of the ancestors who listen within the stones, holding the stories of every gathering, and the spirits of the trees who gives the songs to the wind for those who would hear. And there are some I don't speak of.

And he listens, at times nodding and at times gazing at me, as if I am speaking of things he has never before understood, and he breathes in deeply.

"May I?" he murmurs, not wishing to make a mistake and pay for disrespect.

"Don't touch the water inside the bowl, but otherwise, do as you will."

The bleeding ground above the oak, near the spring's source, he will not approach, so well crafted are the spells that protect it. I can think of no other dishonour that he might do while within my sight and, as he walks around the bowl, scrambling down the hill to the base to see how the water flows out and into the stream, climbing up the other side, I watch him, feeling the trust that this requires in me, yet not sure what it will mean. He crouches on the grass, feeling the smoothness of the limestone beneath his fingers, and the shimmer of blue in the rock catches his eye.

"There's copper!"

"A little," I whisper.

"That's how it holds the colour so well!" He shakes his head, smiling broadly. "The water must have flowed strongly here for many aeons, yet how it was crafted into such a perfect shape ..." And wide-eyed, again he shakes his head, the miner in him absorbed and awake. And in his clumsily old limbs, I see too the young boy, eagerly learning his father's trade, studying the rocks, seeking out treasure.

"It is naturally made?"

"So my people say."

I set myself down on the earth and lift the wooden box from the basket. Noticing what I do, he stops to watch as, carefully, once again I unpack the Cup of Enaid Las, laying it down on the short spring grass.

"It was born here, Eos," I say softly. "Not crafted here, but conceived here." I feel him listening with every part of his soul, no longer smiling, but aching to hear every word that I can offer. "It is not the only cup of its kind, but each one is made for a special purpose, or passed on for good reason - not only in their conception, but the way they are made by the glass fferyllt in the lands of the Dobunni, then brought back to this sacred place, to be blessed and filled with power."

I reach to untie my boots and, awkwardly, he isn't sure what to do. He turns away, gazing down into the water as I pull off my leggings, undoing the clasp of my cloak and letting it fall behind. I pick up the cup, holding its precious soul in my hands, and again he looks into my face, searching.

"They never empty, Eos. For the soul of each cup is born through the songs of this ancient sacred place. The cup is ever filled, ever renewed. It holds within it the powers of regeneration," I look into its depths, feeling the ageless grief. "It holds eternal life."

"Vivi ..."

"Eos, let your soul come with me."

Lifting my robes, I slip down the smooth stone into the bowl. The ice cold water hits my feet, my legs, freezing my blood, and the patterns of my mind shift instantly. I look up at him but am unable to speak; his eyes are fixed upon me, asking a thousand questions. I turn away from him, *Come.* And closing my eyes, I release into the songs of the spirits that dance and rise up through me with such a glorious power, my soul suddenly filled with the music of their stories, tales from deep in the dark womb of the earth, sparkling in black water, surging up like a flood of life, until I am able to feel the gods themselves, like the sharpest blades of a thousand moments cutting through my mind. And with each breath I take, a new life is born.Life, such life, and the songs of the birthing water rise through me.

And through the exhilaration, the ecstasy of such emptiness and fullness, I craft the words of my intent, bringing my mind to feel my fingertips pulsing around this cup, and within it I can feel every drop it has ever held. I reach into its essence to seek out memory, flying like a buzzard through the clouds of a gathering storm: the waters of a thousand sacred wells, the tender touch of seeking, the cold touch of waking, Roman wine shared, soft lips upon its rim, and love shared, such love in hope lifted to the gods of love, then lips cracked and bleeding, the cries of hope and freedom, all held so tight within this soul of blue glass. And when I open my eyes, the cup filled, lifted high in my hands, the water alive like a bright sun of blue, shimmering blue upon the deep lake of the heart, its light flooding out across the world, my own heart calls the songs of my people, my heart calls to Eos ...

But he has stepped away. He is staring at me and in his eyes there is fear.

I turn from him, quickly rolling over into myself, breathing deeply, pulling back my spirit,whispering my prayers until I can again find my body and a world that he might understand. Placing the cup on the grass, my hands shaking, though I struggle to lift myself out of the sacred water, he does not come to help me. I dry my feet and pull on my leggings, tying on my boots, wringing the water from the bottom of my robes. *You silly old woman,* I murmur, *silly bloody old woman.*

When I look up, he is still staring at me.

I clamber to my feet.

"Come, let us go. They will be waiting for us at the willows."

"No," he breathes in deeply. "Vivian ..."

I watch his mind tumbling, seeking out words.

For a moment we gaze at each other.

"What did you see, Eos?"

He walks to me and picks up the cup from the grass. For a glimmer of a moment it feels like any other drinking bowl. The Enaid Las is still within me, and though he is yet a few paces from me, as he holds it towards me, inviting me to place my hands around his upon its curved blue bowl, I feel his hands deep within me. Whispering a prayer to my goddess, I resist my desire to push him away, *He feels you, my Lady, he is feeling your power* ... His hands are trembling, but he stands himself tall, his broad shoulders squared and strong, his eyes never leaving mine.

"What did you see?" I murmur.

"I saw an old man and an old woman drink together from the cup, Vivian." I see the vision is still within him and he is breathing it to find strength, yet this is a man who does not have visions and each word is taken like a footstep on thin ice. And each word touches me like snow melting into water. "Together they drank, and together ... they became young. As they drank, they were surrounded by a brilliant blue flame. It seemed to fill the entire grove. And as the light grew," he breathes in deeply, "the two seemed to become one, though they remained always two, as though they danced around one another." He takes another step towards me. "All around them there were countless people, shining as bright as the sun, singing the most beautiful song. Vivian, this cup holds more meaning than ever I might have dreamed."

We are so close, the cup between us, I feel no separation. I long to step away, to free myself from his need, his hands around the cup that is a part of my own soul. *My Lady, must I bear this?* Shades of the land are pulling at my robes, moving through my legs, spirits in the breeze, saying, *What does he want, what does he want?* I lift my hands and place them upon his, feeling the intensity between us grow, knowing that, just as I long to release myself, so I long too to dissolve myself, my eyes closed, my head falling back, and in perfect surrender, letting his mortal soul drink from mine.

"Eos," I whisper, "is this the mother you seek?"

I hear his voice in my head, *You are ...*

He looks down.

"Eos, when the boy was here, your kin, all those summers ago, when you brought him to these islands, we knew he was coming. Many of the old ones had felt a seer drawing near. Some spoke of the waking of the crow god of our people, some believed it was a child who would emerge from the waters, bringing death. Some said he would bring life, a new river of life. When I saw the boy, your kin, I knew: he was the seer we had felt. In his eyes were the tears of the ancestors."

Our eyes meet. I am so aware of how close we are; the drum of his heart is in his breath. I move my fingers over his, feeling the roughness of his skin.

"My people were not convinced. It was hard to accept that a young man from so far away could make such a difference. He was not a warrior of Roma, nor would he ever be, that was clear. Would he be a slave, used, tricked by the empire? My sisters agreed, this is what would be." Again, I look into the tinner's eyes, his beautiful face now lined with both questions and grief.

"There was not time to gather a council," I look out to the far waters and sigh. "It fell then to me to do what I must. Within those few days when you were here, staying in the village across the lake, I made sacrifice to the gods, calling for guidance. The vision was clear: the seer would become a Iuddic priest and with him would come death."

Eos closes his eyes, sorrow washing through his heart. "How strange that such a desire for peace would bring such violent death. In the end he believed that through his death, the shalom of life would come."

"I know, he taught peace, Eosaidh. But what did he know, when he walked these wet shores? His home governed by the thugs of Roma, warlords who did not value the lives or the customs of his people. Your people. And, as Brythannic chiefs are doing now," my gaze looks to the south east, "his own people surrendering to foreign rule and law, dishonouring their gods in return for promises of power and wealth. That's all he knew, Eos. He longed for peace, to ease the weight of grief that was within him. But what did he know of peace then? As a boy, you brought him to me as a blade not yet fully tempered by the smith. And who was to be his smith? An angry warrior of Roma? An unthinking or bitter teacher of your people? Another child dying of bloodwease or hunger?"

An image of the boy shimmers in my mind, standing on the high tor of Bryn Ddraig on Ynys y Niwl, his arms lifted up into the wind, his palms open, breathing in with all the power of his hope. "All," he had cried out, his voice thick with the accent of his own tongue. And he'd looked deep into my eyes. "All must change," he'd whispered. And I'd looked around, over the rivers and marshes, the islands with their little settlements, the ridges of forest, but the reach of his arms had not even begun here, and their extent had stretched beyond my understanding of the world. And I had smiled with sadness, holding in my hands the softness of his face, "How do you know that what you want is best for the world?"

His deep brown eyes had filled with such determination. Lifting his fist to his chest, breathing in deeply, the boy had said, "My father. He is here, the god of my people." And in that moment I had seen him like a spirit of the wind, claiming a substance that he did not possess. Yet I saw too that, like a wind, his course could not be changed, and the scent of death was in that wind.

Slipping his hands from beneath mine, Eos gives me the cup. He lifts a long black lock of my hair that has fallen over my face, bringing my mind back to the moment.

"You gave him this cup?"

"It was," I pause, aware again of the trust I give, "it was crafted for my own son."

"You have a son?" He is shocked.

"He was apprenticed, back then, to a druid of the Dobunni."

"And you gave the lad his cup?"

I breathe in, hiding my grief, allowing my mind to reach around the cup. I had not expected to see it again, and to do so had not been necessary - until the flood of dying energy had again touched my soul, when Eos had stepped onto the shores of the sacred isle.

"There was no time. I did not believe I would see the lad again." I look out over the marshes to the open water. "He could see, Eos. I knew he would find depth in the teachings of your people, that he would see within them and become a priest to your tribe, but words spoken to the people don't provoke change. The rebel's words may be precious to a people under siege, but once angry rulers have spilled that rebel's blood, the people quickly forget. Your boy's words had more power than most, yet what we saw in him was simply a great deal more blood spilled as a result." I shake my head, "So much death."

"I was there, my Lady. I saw the death of which you speak with these old eyes. With horror I saw the many deaths that followed. And now, too, I feel the death that rises up in the Mendydd, and among the tribes to the south where the same Romans who killed those of my blood now destroy those of my adopted land." And with gentleness in his great arms, he draws me towards him, and wraps me in his strength. I close my eyes, letting him hold me, barely able to recall letting anyone do the same. For a moment his head touches mine and I feel him breathe in my scent.

"I have tired of merchants and soldiers and kings, Vivi," he says, quietly. "I loved a woman once only in these long years, and it has been long since I have felt the touch of her tenderness upon my face. Yes, I have longed for the one you call Mother. I have seen her in the lad's young mother, in the Magdalene, and now, in you, who are also Mother to the lad." His words shimmer in the air, held by the spirits of this sacred place, and though I try to listen, they sink into my body before I can grasp them. I hear him whisper in my mind, *Why do you let me hold you, Vivi?* I open my eyes and I do not know.

"The cup, Vivi," he says, and I look up into his face, "it is more than just the glass from which it is fashioned, isn't it?"

I wonder how much he can understand of what I say.

"It is a cup of rebirth, Eos."

Chapter Eight
Whitethorn and White Linen

(Eosaidh)

For the third time I try to reset the axe head on its ash handle, and for the third time I fail, dropping it on a toe and wincing in pain. I utter an oath of disgust. I am annoyed at myself. *Eosaid, you fool! You are an old man. It is all this May sun can do to warm your bones of fifty-seven summers.* Yet my mind keeps wandering to images of the Lady of Affalon when I ought to be concentrating on my work, like a youth addled by springtime!

A full cycle of the moon has passed since we traveled to Croth Ddraig Las, and it is once again at first quarter. She hangs high but dimly in the sky, a ghostly presence in the waning afternoon sun. I have wasted most of the afternoon here on the slope of Wirrheal, under the branches of the great thorn. But the scowl on my face is belied by the chuckle deep in my heart, for the time has not been wasted. That it could be, I learned from Pilate when a tin shipment was late arriving in Jerusalem. "You are wasting my time, man!" he shouted at me. He was a haunted and hurried man. So much to do, and so little time in which to do it. It seems such is a Roman trait, or at least a military one. I look off to the south, and imagine I can hear Vespasian shouting the same thing to his lieutenants. On the Isle of Mist it is not possible to waste time; there is no time to be wasted.

So here I sit under the thorn, its overspreading crown of white blossoms above me, the axe head forgotten. Occasionally a blossom drifts down and lands softly in my hair, or upon my shoulder. I think briefly of the thorns crowning the lad's brow, and wonder how these here can be so beautiful. The cry of a kestrel startles me, and I look up to see the bright white feathers under its wings flash against the blue spring sky. Nearby, in the branches of the thorn, a pair of wrens look for a nesting place, their warbling song giving thanks for the coming of the warmer weather.

Below, in the meadow that lies between Wirrheal and the marshes, Fianna is leading her young charges home from an excursion around the island. They have been looking for spring herbs, and had stopped at my resting place to gather young whitethorn leaves for teas. Young Elwyn made a face and stamped her foot when I told her I knew the tree was good for heart ailments. I suppose I should have let her tell me herself. I will never understand women, I am afraid, even the youngest ones. Will I ever hope to understand the one who, in these days, causes such a disturbing ailment in my own heart?

In my mind I drift back to that moment when she lifted herself from the cauldron. She did so with difficulty, but I could not bring myself to help, her leggings and cloak lying beside us on the grass. I looked the other way and pretended to be immersed in thought. *You old fool!* I said to myself. *You're an old man, and an old fool.* And I studied the copper embedded in the rock until she had tied on her boots again. She had given the cup to the lad, the cup that had been fashioned for her own son! She had seen his vision, and known his need, and given it to him those many years ago. *It is a cup of rebirth, Eos,* she told me. I thought about the tales from Galilee, and the old Cornualle myths,and wondered if the dead could truly live again.

I stepped forward, taking her in my arms, drawing her close. Her head rested upon my shoulder, just below my chin.

I could smell the scent of moss and bracken in her dark hair, feel the fragile strength of the marsh reeds in the frame of her small body. Slowly, the world began to spin around us, and I was transported into a time and an embrace from many long years ago. For a moment I sensed the joining of youth. But we are grown old, and the world has changed, and this embrace held a deeper meaning than youth can bear. She was warm in my arms as the world turned and dissolved around us. With part of my mind I was surprised that she allowed me to hold her. But mostly I melted into her being, and felt the loving presence of life stirring within us.

As the moment passed I looked into her face. "The cup, Vivi, it is more than just glass, isn't it?"

"Yes, Eos. It is a cup of rebirth."

In the sound of her voice I knew the cup was, in the world, a sign of the mother. Vivian is herself the cup, as is Miryam who bore the lad, and the Magdalene, who brought young Sarah into the world. Gently, with reverence born of deep love, I bent and kissed her forehead. She looked at me with a heartrending union of love and pain in her eyes for the space of a moment, before the spell was broken.

With a sigh she said, "They will be waiting for us, Eos, at the willows, Creyr and Fianna."

She was still holding the cup.

I looked from her dark eyes to its blue brilliance and back. "It binds us each to itself and to one another," I said. "We can neither of us claim it now. Yet when you first saw it you were about to break in pieces. Why was that so?"

"For its task was complete," she answered simply, "Else why would it have returned to its source? The law bids me then release its soul back into the water."

I thought it strange that in the midst of such mystery she would speak of law.

"I still do not understand, Vivian," I said, "What was its task, and by what law is the Lady of Affalon bound?"

For a long time she looked silently into my face, wondering, I suppose, how what seems to her so simple appears to be so hard for me to understand.

"I could not remove the current of death," she said. "His life was set upon it. I searched with the seers of the island, I spoke to others after you were gone, but it was agreed that nothing could be done. If sufficient power had been found to pull him from the current's flood, the force would only have changed its direction, spinning into itself, causing yet more devastation, and in a manner that seemed even less comprehensible. Do you understand, Eos?"

I did not understand, but I nodded my head, that she might continue.

"We sent the Cup with him, hoping against hope in its power of life. To some here it seemed pointless, for what effect could it have on us if the boy's presence amidst his people, in lands far away, generated tribal wars within the empire of Roma? And even I began to doubt as the years passed by." She turned away from me, looking over the blue cauldron at the presence of the great, old oak. I can remember the singing of the water as it filled the silence. "I began to wonder," she said, looking at the oak and not at me, "whether my visions had been affected by what happened between us, between you and I."

I drew her close again, with one hand gently cradling her head against my shoulder.

"The task of the Cup was to serve its keeper, to offer its power," she said.

We were silent for a long time. The day was ending, and light was beginning to fade.

At last I said, "From that time on, Vivi, his life was changed. He became love itself, and though he died violently on a Roman cross, it is said already that in love he defeated death, and offers life to the world."

Vivian sighed deeply. "Perhaps then, we changed the rivers of history, with the Enaid Las, because of that day we spent together."

Perhaps we did.

I should have spoken more of that day, but instead I asked her about the law. She had been so distrustful of the laws of my people written in their parchment scrolls. Yet she had said the law bid her destroy the cup.

"It is the law of nature, Eos. A song is held for a purpose within its container, and then it cries out to be released that every whisper of its soul can find a new song, a new life and a new purpose. The work of the seer is to know nature's laws and serve them."

I thought perhaps I understood. God and Torah, after all, do not exist above or apart from the world, but within and among all that is. Even our own prophets had told us the law was to be written on the soft flesh of our hearts, not on tablets of stone. I let this gentle thought sink into my own heart. A peace spread through me from her words.

"Then the cup's task is not complete, Vivi," I said. "For it must serve the ages. If the lad's death is to weave love and not hatred into the history of the world, Enaid Las must continue to serve those who will follow."

She pulled away from me abruptly and searched my face. Through some magic of that place trust had been shared. Yet I seem always to be losing her trust. Again, in my spoken words, some thread was pulled or broken.

"Follow him? No, Eos. Its task is done. His task is done. Breaking the cup will free him! Do you not see? He is still bound to it, and it to him. Each flush of magical renewal spills out the waters of death. One does not replace the other, Eos. They are ever tied together. We must break this soul cup."

Thinking she did not understand me, I tried again. "Vivian, perhaps his task is not done. Perhaps his offering of the cup that night in Jerusalem was not the end of his mission, but only the beginning." I left her side and began to pace, partly from excitement, partly from the frustration of explaining Jerusalem to Affalon, partly from fear of losing the precious moment we had just shared. It was all coming apart again.

"Vivian, the lad was not the Messiah. That much is clear. He did not liberate Jerusalem from Rome. The gift he offered that night was not freedom, but life. Those who follow will not be following him as though following some great leader. They will be following the path of life."

She looked at me as though I was as dense as the marsh mists, and in truth I had no real confidence in my own words. I came back to her. She was still holding the cup. In that moment I realized as important as the cup was to me, the woman standing before me was more important still. "Vivian," I said softly, "I do not understand the ways of Affalon, nor the ways of soul cups. The cup is precious to me, but it is yours and you understand its magic. Tell me what you must do. I only wish for the lad's death to have meaning."

I paused, thinking to make one last attempt to preserve the cup that had held his life's blood. "Could we hide the cup, Vivian? Could we place it somewhere in secret where it would never again be poured out, but where its presence would anchor the time and space of the world to its gift of life?" I did not understand how she could let it go; she did not understand how I could cling to it.

Then she smiled at me "Would this not capture a moment and hold it, would it not deny its freedom to live, to change and grow?" She reached out and gently touched my face with her hand. "I know you need his death to have meaning, for without it the brutality would be too much to bear. This precious cup washed his life with hope, and with a great flood it gave hope through the days of his dying. Its magic lingers, that power of hope, of life ever renewed,allowing those who loved him to see his spirit guiding them on. But hope that is not allowed to change becomes a terrible curse, Eos. The soul of this cup sang of life rising out of death, because that was his path. Now, Eos, now it is time for you to sing of life."

She looked so tired. Her eyes closed with a quiet sigh, and she was silent, sitting by the edge of the cauldron. She placed the cup gently on the grass, and gently I placed it back in its box, wrapping it in the linen and wool. The sound of the lid closing was the only sound in the wood. Even the bubbling waters were silent. It was beginning to get dark. "Come, Vivi," I said, "darkness falls. Creyr and Fianna wait for us."

We returned to Penn Willows in heavy silence, bearing more in our hearts than it is possible to bear. Concern showed on the faces of the two young women who were waiting. We had been gone longer than expected. Swiftly and silently they went to the boats and took up the alder paddles, not daring to ask the questions apparent in their eyes.

Vivian touched my arm. I started to give her the box in which the cup had again been so carefully stored, but she shook her head. The stench of the dark, bitter water was heavy in the dense evening air. Creyr stepped to Vivian's side, helping her into the old boat that would take her away to the island I will never see. There was a deep moment of not wanting to part.

"Keep it, for now, dear one," she said to me, "I have an idea." Again she touched my cheek, and smiled with her eyes though she was horribly tired. I hated myself for the strain I had placed upon her. Then she stepped into the boat, and was gone, and I stood looking after her into the gathering mists.

"Come, Master Eosaidh," Fianna said softly. "It is late, and will be fully dark before we reach the old alder on Ynys y Niwl."

A glint of sunlight off the open water to the northwest catches my eye and brings me back to the present. Bryn Llyffaint stands out clearly in the westering sun. Can it be such a short time ago I left there in the dead of night to seek this island? It seems a lifetime. Were I higher on the slope of Wirrheal I would be able to see the hills of the Silures, purple and soft in the distance. Beyond them, far from my sight, the mountains said to be the home of the fferyllt. The home of the cup. Those who work the tin and lead of Cornualle and the Mendydd tell of these magical craftsmen in the far mountains, druid alchemists who work spells into the blowing of glass, and wisdom into the elements. The sun is warm on my face, and I am weary, and again my spirit wanders, across the water and the far hills, to the slopes of yr Wyddfa.

I see in my mind the hidden city of Emrys, on the high escarpment of Penmaen, and within it the stronghold of Broich y Dinas, called by many Dinas Affaraon, the Fortress of High Powers. I know no person who has been there, though tales abound, so I use only my imagination to see the towers and flying banners emblazoned with the dragons of the fferyllt. In a courtyard hard against the mountain wall there hangs a cauldron over a blazing fire. Around it are the chemists, stripped to the waist against the blazing heat, pouring into the cauldron their secret proportions:fine white sand from the outer isles, and copper from the hills, and other things I know not of. Within the cauldron is the rich glow of blue, molten glass. A Lady, beautiful and terrible seems to appear from the flames, wearing a deep scarlet robe. She stirs the cauldron with a great paddle and then, wondrously, reaches into the molten glass and lifts out a blue cup fully formed and glowing with life. "I am the renewal of life," she says in a voice that is at once a gentle mist and a raging torrent. A squall of snow swirls off the summit of the mount, obscuring the scene, and I realize with a smile that I have once again clothed the simplicity of these lands in images of my Romanized mind.

"Master Eosaidh." A gentler, nearer voice awakens me. It is Gwenlli, who stands before me under the thorn on the side of Wirrheal. "Pardon, Master Eosaidh, but my Lady awaits." She has come. She has given me this month to live with the cup, to decide my part in its fate. Now she has come, and I know the soul cup must return to the elements. I sigh quietly, gathering up the axe head and handle, which I will have to join on another day, and lean against my staff to rise.

Gwenlli is patient with my slowness. So young, yet she has learned well from Vivian to understand the necessities of age. I follow her down the hill to my roundhouse, and there is Vivian, sitting on a stone beside the open fire. I have not seen her this past month except in my imaginings and dreams, and my heart quickens. Today she looks nearly as young as Gwenlli. Some strange warmth soothes the ache in my bones. I stand a bit taller. *Eos, you old fool!*

"I am ready, Vivi," I say. She smiles and nods, as I duck into the hut to retrieve the cup. Reaching under my cot I draw out the box of acacia wood. In the silence of my own space, I take the time for one final visit with this last remnant of the lad. Sitting on the cot, I hold the box on my lap and undo the leather thong that holds its lid closed. The wood which once was oiled and smooth is, I notice with wonder, worn with age. The strong scent of acacia it once possessed is more a memory than a reality. When did it get so old?

Gently I push aside the lamb's wool. Once it was as soft and white as the summer clouds over Galilee. Now it, too, is old. The lambs from which it came are gone from this world, their descendants now nibbling the grasses of Iudea. Only the linen cloth still seems fresh and new. Then I touch the smooth, blue glass, and lift the cup from its soft bed. I hold it before me, once again seeing the lad. No longer the laughing youth who walked the Mendydd with me in the spring sunshine, whose strong, rippling muscles shone with sweat and tin as he learned the mines, he stood before us as he lifted the cup. Even then I was moved by its blue luster, and wondered at its power, though I had no idea of its origin. His face was lined with worry, but in his eyes was the deep peace of knowledge and conviction. *This is as if it were my life's blood, poured out for you and for all, for your forgiveness.* He drank from the cup, and passed it to the Magdalene. As she drank, she turned her eyes to him, large and brimming with tears. And he returned her look with a tenderness beyond words. She passed the cup to Joachim, and he to Jacob, and then to Petros, and then to me. The cup did not contain life; it was life itself. The wine was rich and warm as it went down. Even now, at the far end of the world, I can feel the new life that spread through my heart, and mind, and soul. Even now, in the dim light of my hut, the blue glass glows gently. But I see there is a chip in the rim, and a fine crack most of the way through the stem. The cup is returning to the elements on its own. I may as well become part of that returning. I watch from a distance, strangely detached, as my old hands wrap the precious treasure and close the lid one last time.

The soul of this cup sang of life rising out of death, because that was his path. Now, Eos, now it is time for you to sing of life. Yes, Vivi. Yes, I know. I emerge from the hut, staff in one hand, acacia box in the other. Silently, Vivian rises and gently touches my face. Gwenlli leads us into the valley between Wirrheal and the tor, Vivian following and then me, as the pathway leaves the meadow and enters the wood.

We make the mile long journey to the Red Spring in silence, immersed in our separate thoughts. Can she feel my eyes upon her as she walks ahead of me? I am certain of it. I find myself thinking about the son she mentioned, for whom the cup was first made. I marvel at the way such unconnected people are in fact so closely connected one to another, across the wide stretches of the world. And I wonder when it will be Vivi's time to sing of life again.

We cross the lower brook which carries the waters from the springs across the meadow to the marshes. In an ash high above a blackbird sings his evening song, the rich melody ringing in the treetops. The sun disappears below the low rounded Hill of Apples to our left as we enter the deep cleft of the valley and turn uphill. The waters in the brook seem to answer the birdsong in the trees, harmonies dancing with each other and echoing off the hillsides. We reach the place where the waters of the White Spring from the tor join the waters of the Red. Vivian stops for a moment, stoops to the earth and dips her hand into the place where the waters join. She sips from her palm and, turning, offers some to me also. Then she touches her wet fingers to my forehead, making some sort of sign. Quietly, we move on up the hill to where the old yews tower above a stone wellhead.

We hand our staffs to Gwenlli, who stands holding them together, the yew and the thorn that once nearly came to blows. And, together, Vivian and I kneel before the ancient well. The overspill and the rocks in the brook below are covered with bright orange-red, though the water itself is crystal clear. In the early May evening this water from the deep earth gives a chill to the steep valley and is almost painful to the touch. But it is the pain of life. For a time we kneel in silence, listening to the waters, our own breathing, the beating of our hearts. A raven drops from the yew and lands on Vivian's shoulder. She speaks to it softly in the old tongue, and it gently nuzzles her cheek before flying off. The red of the spring bed reminds me of the lad's blood at his death, but then the same red would have been part of his birth, also.

Vivian turns and looks at me. The time has come. I trust this will end the grief that has held me all these years, to rebirth it as tender memory. I open the old box and remove the cup.

"Leave it wrapped in the linen, Eos," Vivian says.

As if sharing the wonder of a newborn child, I gently pass the tiny bundle to her. For a moment it seems to be a child, our child, that I pass tenderly to its mother. It is the changing time of dusk, and the air hangs heavily over the spring. It seems that the great yews bend down over the wellhead, over Vivian and the child. But the light is fading quickly. There is a mist about the wellhead making it hard to see. She cradles the cup within the linen cloth, in her arms, clutching it to her breast, lifting it to her heart. And then I can no longer see it. It seems as though Vivian herself is wrapped in white linen.

She dips her fingers in the well water, singing a sad and haunting song in the old tongue. Before my eyes she seems to blend with the yews, sometimes old and bent, sometimes young and wrapped in swaddling cloths, barely apparent in the strange mist, singing, ever singing. With both hands she reaches down into the well, and her song changes as if she is calling, calling to someone or something unseen and perhaps unknowable to me. The clear waters of the spring darken to red. Not the red-orange of their iron ore, but the deep, claret red of new blood. The mist about her shines with its own light so that I can barely see her within, can only hear the song of drawing forth. Then there is the sound of many waters, and it seems as though Vivian rises from the well itself, drenched with water and blood, her song as the birth cry of an infant, and she stands over the well. The mists roll and swirl about her, the scent of yew grows strong in the air, the last light of day fades, and tiny lights like stars shimmer throughout the grove.

But as I look, it is simply Vivian, kneeling, holding the linen bundle before her as if receiving it from the well. The song has become a wailing, screeching through the air, the mists twisting and howling, the bolts of Taranis hurtling from darkened skies. With a shrill cry she raises the bundle over her head, a great lightning flash freezing all in place at the top of the arc as thunder crashes and an infant cries out in the fear of birth. For an instant time stands still. Then, with a final cry, she drops her arms and smashes the cup against the rocks.

For a moment, it is our child lying broken and bleeding on the ground. Vivian is silent. I cry out to her, but I do not know what I am saying. Then she turns to me, and the mist fades, and the yews draw back, and I see a darkness in her soul, Morrigan, the one who soldiers call the Washer at the Ford. In her tortured face, I see death itself, and my heart beaks. I cannot bear it, so I lower my eyes to the ground. The little bundle is silent, unmoving. But it is not the size of a child; it is the broken cup. When again I look to her face within the hood of her cloak, it is Vivian.

She closes her eyes for a moment, facing me, tears running down her cheeks as they are mine. She hands me the bundle and says, silently, in my mind, *Release him*.

Gwenlli is behind her and helps her rise to her feet. I can see the movement is very hard. The rite has taken a great deal out of her. Her hands are shaking, but her face is set with strength. She steps, clearly in pain, to where I am still kneeling, looking up at her. She bends down to me and kisses me with deep tenderness, covering my mouth with hers, sharing her breath. I am overwhelmed with the nearness of her scent, and the tenderness of her lips. *Release him,* she says again, without a sound. And she leaves.

I sit back on my heels, and then move my legs under me so I am sitting cross-legged on the ground, holding the bundle of broken glass. It is silent except for the singing of the water, and the night creatures of spring. And it is dark, fully dark. I do not know what I have seen. Certainly a glamour hid most of its meaning from me. By the stars, nearly half the night has gone. I feel as though I have been a father, lost a child, and become an ancestor within these moments. Looking at the broken bundle on my lap, now barely visible in the light of the rising moon, I know finally that the lad has gone. I let out a deep, heartfelt sigh, and at last I know that I can let him go on this earth, that he may be reborn in my own soul.

Slowly, I unwrap the linen. There are the small shards of blue glass, no longer a cup, yet still glowing softly in the moonlight. There is a tear in the corner of my eye, but it is a tear of life, not of sorrow. For the last time in my life, I fold the linen over the beautiful blue glass. This time, I tie the corners in a knot, making the bundle secure. Slowly I bend over the lip of the well. I can see the hint of my face reflected in the dark waters, and the stars behind me. Gently, I lower the bundle until it touches the water of the Red Spring. *Yeetgadal v'yeetkadash sh'mey rabbah* I intone, may His great Name grow exalted and

sanctified, *b'reekh hoo L'eylah meen kohl beerkhatah v'sheeratah.*
Blessed is He beyond any blessing and song. I let go, releasing
him, and slowly, achingly, lovingly slowly, he sinks into the
waters of the well, gently fades from my view, and is gone from
this world.

For an eternity I sit by the well, until the darkness begins
to fade and the hint of first-light appears in the east. A flutter
above me catches my eye and I look up to see Vivian's raven.
She has been watching all through the night. With a rustle of
feathers she lifts onto her great black wings, flying up and out
of the valley, bringing word to Vivian that it is done, that the
cup has returned to the elements. It is done.

Chapter Nine
The Ancient Fire
(Vivian)

e wishes to see you, my Lady.

Fianna's face reveals nothing. She is trained well in the island's craft and, in my unwillingness to hear her fully, I don't look into her soul to see what she is feeling. Instead my eyes move over the quiet hum of activity, half a dozen women absorbed in their tasks as the feast is prepared. Around them in the soft sunshine are bowls of roots and grains, dried plums, and baskets of young greens, the first of our own growing. A gathering outside the old storehouse is sewing robes, one of the older girls stitching feathers onto a length of cloth, a young child playing quietly with feathers still in the basket, carefully ensuring none escape into the breeze.

I smile.

Sianed looks up from her work and sees me. She is a skilled priestess and I watch her strength and calm as she approaches and bows with respect. I reach out a hand and we touch, feeling the earth beneath us, sharing a silent prayer of thanksgiving. She smiles, and murmurs silently, *Yes, my Lady, it will be a feast worthy of our ancestors.*

And those who come after us.

She nods.

Her daughter appears beside us. She must now be fifteen summers; there is laughter in her eyes, and the soft glow of thorn blossoms in her cheeks. She bows, "My Lady," and looks to her mother for affirmation which Sianed gives with the slightest movement. The girl's words are like bubbles from a clear-water spring. "My Lady, my brother has traded for us at the market of Trigentes, and we have dried vine berries from Gaul for the festival, and persica from lands even farther away."

Apologetic, Sianed speaks her words into sound. "My Lady, I was not sure it was wise, but my son was so pleased to find the fruits."

I nod, *I like this as little as you do, but this is how it will be in our children's world,* and I bow acceptance, "Thank him for me." I touch the child's shoulder and feel her life in my hand: it is like the warmth of a hearth fire newly lit in the morning.

"Thank you, my Lady," the child says. "He has also given us a small bag of what he called 'armenasca'."

Her mother continues, "I believe he could not have used only what I gave him - he must have traded with some of his own people's stores from Penn Brey. With respect, he offers them as a gift to you, my Lady."

"We shall have a wonderful feast," I say softly.

As I turn to move away, I see Seren's eyes. She is the oldest member of our community, Fianna's aunt. With gnarled and slow fingers, she sifts through the heap of dried beans on the cloth in front of her. *Listen,* she says, and returns to her beans as Fianna appears again at my side. This time her face does not hide her feelings.

"My Lady, you have barely seen him since the rite."

"There is much to be done," I say.

"Not here, my Lady, there is nothing you need do here." Of course, she is right. I have spent enough time with those involved in the morrow's ritual, and my presence is not needed here, where others have responsibilities. Seren's voice murmurs in my soul and I look into her eyes. She is a handful of years old than I, a teacher to the children most of her life and a herbwise whose art was sought after throughout the islands. Our eyes meet for a moment. *Are you afraid?* she murmurs, and returns to sorting the pile of brown beans.

Fianna's face expresses sadness.

"The rite tore his heart open, my Lady."

I seek her soul for what he has told her, but find nothing. If he has said nothing to this gentle soul, so rich and full with the songs of motherhood, I realize he has spoken to nobody of what happened at y Ffynnon Goch. Over the past six days, we have seen each other only in passing, across meadows, between roundhouses, busy with our own tasks. I have eased my heart by believing he will forgive my distance, being fully aware of the great deal of work that must be done for the festival we hold at the whitethorn moon. But I know I am fooling myself. What am I afraid of?

Seren's voice echoes my own, *Are you ashamed of what you feel?* She does not look up at me and I ignore her words. But Fianna I cannot ignore.

"Please," she whispers. "He is hurting now."

As I step beneath the canopy, with a hand I reach up to touch the flush of new leaves on the lowest branches of oak. The forest is so alive, washed with a translucent green, each tree and shrub stretching out with soft twigs of growth that sing to the sky gods, calling out to the sun.

And in the soft light beneath the now thickening canopy, my heart is lifted by the scent and sight of the bluebells. A sea of flowers, they are as deep a blue as these early summer skies before dawn, and around them and beneath them the curiosity and celebration of so many countless creatures, exploring and searching, scurrying and listening. And in every glade touched by sunlight the whitethorn is in blossom. I breathe in deeply the rise of all these beautiful songs, yet strangely it all now seems like a memory, a life and a world that I used to be a part of.

Using my staff to balance and guide me on, I make my way to the pool and, pondering my tiredness, I sit down on the fallen log that has been my seat for a dozen cycles. Before me, the water is perfectly still. Its surface shimmers into ripples where a fallen leaf moves across its gloss, but the watercreepers and tiny flies leave no mark. The rich cream weight of the elder's blossom hangs over the water, reflected in its darkness. I hold my head in my hands, and in the peace of my solitude I let the tears come. And they come.

Yet I am not alone. For with my tears come my grandmothers, their grandmothers, and those before them, and as silently I sob, my tears falling into the water, their spirits move in the wind, their voices whispering the songs of grief, their tears joining mine in the waters of this forest pool, waters which will sink into the earth, flowing out into the seas, to fall upon the land as rain and be raised in the cups of ritual, to be supped as cool blessings and again to fall as tears of grief. And the trees listen to our song and the wind carries it through the mists of time, each tear drawing from me the pain of my people, each tear allowing me to feel the depths of my body.

And I am not alone. His step cracks a fallen twig in the way that only a outlander can. I look up. He is some way from me, but I see him cringe, concerned he has disturbed me, and I gaze into his soul, wondering which spirits have brought him to find me. As he comes closer, I see his face becomes increasingly lined with worry. He strides with big feet around the pool towards me, sinking to his knees before me, looking into my eyes.

"Vivi, you are crying!"

I don't pull away. He takes my hands in his, searching my face for signs. For a while I seek out words, but none come through the waters of my soul that I can lift into sound. In fact, to my surprise, the tears keep falling.

"What has happened, my love?" his voice trembles with urgency. But the words are hard to understand. What has happened? In the grove here, held by my people, I have held their grief. Where would I begin to explain what has happened? It is but life that has happened. I feel as if the lake of my soul has been transported into the midst of a wide open sea, and I am losing my ability to delineate the edges of me. I look into his eyes. I want to say, *I am flowing out into the sea,* but know that this is not the answer to his question. He stops a tear with a finger, his rough skin upon the wrinkles of my cheek. "What has upset you, Vivi? Can you tell me, can you share this burden, Vivi? I can't bear to see you cry."

And I lift a hand to touch his face, smoothing the snaggles of hair from his eyes that now water in love and empathy. *Oh Eos,* how I wish I could draw you into my soul and show you what I see. And though he does not hear my words, I know that he feels them, for he lowers his head onto my knees and he sobs. And my grandmothers watch as I hold his soul, and he reaches into mine, not quite able to find me.

When words do find their sound, I am surprised at what I say.

"It was my son's cup."

He lifts his head and looks into my face, wiping tears roughly from his cheek. "Yes."

"He was about the same age," I murmur, and in his eyes I see the realization sliding into his awareness, his expression changing from sadness to dread.

"No, Vivi ..."

"He left the island, as boys do, with fourteen summers behind him, to apprentice with a druid, a wise man and an accomplished priest. No doubt you would have heard his name in the settlements on the Mendydd." But I have not the energy to say it aloud. I gaze out into the forest, the spirits of my grandmothers still around me. "He was to return, one summer festival, when he had gained his druid staff. I was to give him his soul cup." I look into Eosaidh's eyes. "But I gave it away."

When I don't continue, he asks, "What happened?"

"It was the spring after you were last here. He had been at the college on what the druids call the Mother Isle. For no reason that was understood, his strength was leaving him, and the seers on Ynys Môn decreed he must return to me. They knew something had happened to cause the sickness in his soul. But it is such a long way."

"I have heard of the island," he whispers. "It must be ten days ride or more."

"The journey took the last of him. He died in my arms, his soul depleted."

His face is pale. "You gave the lad your son's life."

"I did not mean to."

He touches my face with a hand, and our eyes meet, no longer wet with tears but with the emptiness of exhaustion, and he says with such tenderness, "Vivi, I am so sorry." And in my mind I hear Seren's voice, *Let him hold you, Lady.* I look up as if to find her, but the only spirit in the grove is my grandmother, and she smiles. *Yes, I murmur, I will let him hold me,* and I let my head softly fall to his shoulder. He breathes in through the sadness, with such love and relief. And as his arms move around me, I feel him bringing me back, and I almost laugh at the sensation: in the strength of his embrace, I can feel my edges once again.

For a moment, I am distracted. I draw the unexpected presence from the pocket of my robe and a smile breaks across my face. Sianed's daughter must have given some to Gwenlli, who sneaked a few into my pocket, knowing that I had not broken the night's fast with any appetite. Dried fruit from the Roman trader. I breathe in the sweetness but slip it back into my pocket. I have forgotten their name. Eos will know.

The sun was setting as we walked up the hill from the forest last night, and we'd stopped at the ridge and watched its last golden moments flood across the skies. I had closed my eyes and murmured prayers, but he'd squeezed my hand, "Say it aloud, Vivian, I want to hear your voice." And my heart had skidded through my soul, and I wondered how I could possibly allow myself to feel like this, but I had smiled and turned again to the setting sun, and spoken my thanksgiving to the young lord of light, "you who move through my soul with the songs of ancient fire," and he had turned to me before I was done, closing his eyes and putting his cheek to mine, whispering again my words, "ancient fire, Vivi, I feel this ancient fire."

I breathe in, dragging myself back into presence.

The gathering is strong. In the bright sunshine of the meadow we call Dolgwyl Waun, I look around me. There are folk here from ten tribes or more, stretching out in every direction, from across the marsh islands and into the hills beyond. Whole families are here from the closest settlements, mothers holding children with more running at their feet, the older people leaning on walking sticks, watching. There are groups of youngsters of fifteen to twenty summers, filled with anticipation, chattering and waiting, and by their manner I see some have come from the further villages, accompanied by a few fighting men to protect them upon the road, their tribal marks upon their arms and faces in woad. And some look upon me and the other priestesses of the island with a curiosity given courage by the strength of the nearness of their tribe, and in some I see fear, in others deep gratitude. A few try to catch my eyes to offer a smile of reverence, and others avoid my gaze as my eyes survey the meadow.

And each and every person is dressed in their finest, hide cloaks and furs of wolf and bear, fine woven linen and old clothes washed and mended, and so many feathers and shells sewn in, and flowers in their hair, both girls and boys, heavy elderflowers, and the delicate whitethorn and stitchwort, and head dresses crafted of hazel, ivy and dragon's weed, and bangles of bronze and silver, torcs and other neck pieces. And my heart is filled with the hope that is written in their faces, that is sewn into each robe, and hums in their blood as they wait and watch, and the last logs are placed upon the pile ready to light in the centre.

Walking away from the wood, I move to the great stone. The stories tell it once stood tall as part of an ancient temple, but now it lies in the grass, six strides long and embedded in the mud. Behind it is an old whitethorn, her thickly blossomed canopy reaching over the stone as if to protect its spirit from further disturbance, like the whisp of a fey young woman leaning over a great fallen warrior. My heart reaches to them both.

And I wonder where Eos is. Perhaps, I sigh, he is keeping a distance, ensuring his god does not object to his presence at the rite. I can feel him close but cannot see him, and yet again I command myself not to search the gathering.

The crowd have hushed and I turn to the centre, and feel the earth beneath me and the spirits' songs in my heart. Caldreg has stepped forward, two of his apprentices behind him. Since old Mordreg's dying, this is the second year he has been chief druid at the rite. As a passionate speaker for his people I know him well, for we meet often at the council up at the wells of Llw Ffynnon, but seldom do we share ritual. I know he is competent, if still weakened by the arrogance of his lack of years, and I watch his face, wondering if his vision has grown any deeper. I know his sister's man and her two sons were killed fighting Romans in the south not long ago.

I walk towards him and we meet between the fire and the stone. He takes my hand and, as he brings it to his forehead, I feel the energy of his land and his people humming within him. I am glad, and I acknowledge his connection, *Lord Druid.*

My Lady of the Waters, he bows.

His eyes are a clear deep blue, alive with passion yet not muddied by it. He is a long moon cycle younger than I, and his body feels strong and firmly set upon the ground. He has a solid confidence that makes me think of Eos. As the thought slips through my mind, Caldreg's eyes wake and question mine.

Ah, so you do see, I whisper.

What has woken your soul, Lady?

Who it is does not concern you, druid.

He bows, *We have a rite to be done. And for it,* he smiles, *you and yours are mine.*

As are yours mine, druid.

There is silence around us. We turn together to the edge of the circle, acknowledging the young man with the torch who has been awaiting our sign. Naked but for a cloth about his waist, his body marked with the woad of his tribe, he has been questing visions for three days and nights, sleepless and without food, and as he walks forward I see his soul ragged with exhaustion yet as exquisitely alive as the fire which he has brought to the rite. I walk up to him and run my fingers over his chest, whispering the prayers as I craft the signs on his oiled skin, and he tries not to look at me, breathing deeply, feeling the magic seethe into his soul.

Then with a snarl that explodes into a yell, he rams the torch into the heart of the woodpile and within moments the pile is ablaze. The drums begin all around us, their pulse moving through my body as they have these sixty five cycles and more. Lifting my eyes to the top of Bryn Fyrtwyddon, rising here at the south of Dolgwyl Waun, I see the druid's boys and I raise my staff. A great holler comes from the hill and, a moment later, the beacon upon it is lit. I think I see Eos on the hillside, watching, but I turn away, fearing I will lose my focus, instead filling my mind with singing the ancient prayers of gathering, wakeful to feel when the next beacon is lit. That one is not within our sight, but others are, and as the fires rise up from hilltops, the drums get louder and the gathering in the meadow begins to dance and cheer and holler, knowing that other fires within other valleys will be brought into flame as the threads of our people come together once again, celebrating the first warm moon of summer.

As Caldreg and I begin the necessary prayers, the gathering slowly quietens. He sings an ancient invocation, calling to the spirit of the great stone. I sing the prayer of the earth, and the children run forward to smear the mud of their islands and fields upon the stone's smooth grey sides. Caldreg sings to the fire, and burning branches are brought over by two of his people, embers shaken over the stone, tiny orange gold lights disappearing in the sunlight, leaving a sprinkling of black ash and spirits dancing. Young priestesses bring water, as the song of my goddess rises through me, and offerings are made to the stone and the land. And so does the rite continue, with barley sheaves and apples, with whitethorn and honey, with salt and milk and iron, as the gods of our people are each acknowledged, their songs sung and the offerings made. And at times the gathering sings with us, with drums and dancing, and at other times there is solemnity, the children wide eyed, the adults feeling the power of the circle.

And when the last prayer is made and the dancing has been wild and free, Caldreg walks to my side and almost smiles for the first time.

Is my Lady in love? he asks with his clear blue eyes.

It is not your concern, druid, I murmur in reply.

But the fellow is not present, he says. *Or at least, not amidst those gathered here. Is he hiding? My Lady, you have not given your heart to an outcast ...*

Your disrespect dishonours your people, druid, I whisper, adding, "Be careful."

He turns from me, finding it hard to hold in his smile, and rubs his beard with a fist.

"Shall we call the young ones?"

"Yes," I murmur. Mischievous imp.

Barely need he make the invitation aloud before the young people of the gathering are moving forward to the great stone, and from there, as the drums find their rhythms and the music is crafted by flutes, horns and lyres, they make their circles. The young girls, Sianed's daughter amongst them, laughing, nervous, excited, alone or hand in hand with a friend or two, dancing around the fire, their hair flying out in the breeze, simple short robes tied with ivy and reed braids, bare feet and faces filled with sunshine and expectation. The boys are the same, in the simplest cloths tied about their waists, any bare skin decorated with their tribal marks, some with furs across their shoulders, their boots tied tight, their chests full of hope and pride. And each one, filled with apprehension and curiosity, is blessed by Caldreg or by me, then sipping from the meadhorn and skipping off into the circle to dance once again.

Sitting beside me on the grass, Gwenlli offers me the bowl.

"Drink, my Lady."

We share the cool water in the shade of the oak, quietly watching as the celebrations continue. Along the track from the walkway there is a constant stream of people, carrying baskets of food, cauldrons, drums and infants, dogs yapping, children running at their heels, a few leading goats laden with urns and leather bags. All around the circle, cooking fires are burning, music and rhythms filling the air, children's cries and laughter, and the scent of roasting meat.

I breathe deeply: it is the only time in the whole cycle of the sun that meat is eaten on Ynys y Niwl, and though my soul flinches, a part of me also celebrates the strength of the people. If there is meat then there is hope.

In the circle, Caldreg is presiding over business deals, trading arrangements and land rights negotiated between tribes over many months, here to be sworn and witnessed by the gods and the community. Such oaths are not a part of my work, and for that I am grateful, for the tension shudders through the air, albeit with the men's daggers left by the great stone - except one, the druid's long blade upon which the deals are sworn.

To one side, Sianed and another priestess are speaking with a group of women, each one with children or infants in their arms. No doubt discussing peace and grief, children lost and born, remedies and communities, it is a circle I once ran, very many cycles ago.

And then I see him, and my old heart begins to race. He is standing beside Fianna, in his hand a garland of flowers that has been dropped by one of the little girls. They are talking together, with laughter and smiles, watching the children running around Sianed's circle.

"Take some more water, my Lady," Gwenlli says softly.

Her voice startles me and I am embarrassed, taking the bowl with thanks and drinking, then stupidly forcing myself to look elsewhere. But she has been beside me too many cycles. She takes the bowl from me with gentleness, saying, "He is a good man, my Lady."

"He is a distraction," I murmur, feeling the weight of the words in my soul.

"But, my Lady, perhaps -"

I put my hand on her arm to stop her from speaking. I know what she will say and I know it is hard for her to say. It is hard to hear: perhaps, at this time, as my soul tires of life, his presence is not a distraction. Perhaps he is a guide.

"Perhaps," I say aloud, and I find a smile and sigh. "Come, let us ask him the name of this Roman fruit." I hand it to her, and she helps me to my feet, then brings it to her nose as I steady myself, biting a little of the wizened brown flesh.

"Chewy," she murmurs with a frown, and we share a smile.

Making our way through the noise and commotion of the gathering, before either of them are aware of our presence their conversation is close enough to hear. No longer light with laughter, their words are serious and quiet with sadness. His voice at first lifts itself on the flow of my heart, then the meaning plummets through me like cold river stone. "She had no child that lived, other than her son?"

"Not one," Fianna is saying, shaking her head.

"How many did she lose, Fia?"

"Manann was her fifth child."

I stop.

They are still not aware of my presence.

Gwenlli takes my arm and leads me away from the gathering.

"The sun is low, my Lady. It will not be long before the heart of the rite. Let us make sure that you are fully refreshed and prepared."

One drum is marking a slow steady beat.

With the fire at my back and my hood hiding my face, as I have done so often, into the dusk I call my song. Using the language of the marsh, I know few but the old people and the women of my community will understand but that is not important. Nor is it now taught by the druids of the marshes and I feel Caldreg, his soul open to me completely, listening with his essence, not reaching for understanding yet seeking the current of power that he can follow.

And I sing. And in my song I reach yet more deeply, calling from the depths of my soul to the goddess of the night sky and deep black water, and I sing, and I sing with all my body, and within my body I hold the excruciating and shimmering moments where the dark sky and the waters meet, a line that can only be perceived from afar, for within its essence it does not exist in matter, and only fleetingly in time and space, ever dissolving, evanescing as another emerges, sparkling. And yet within that place of evanescence and emergence exists all the darkness of the night and the water, reaching up into the infinite eternal height of the skies and into eternal depths of the earth below, and I sing. And as the song floods through me, my goddess fills me utterly, and through me the circle is washed with the darkness of life.

Opening my eyes, the druid moves towards me and I see his soul naked, throbbing with breath and blood. He sinks to the earth at my feet and calls out a prayer of welcome, and his words echo through the silence of the meadow and through all time. He stands, and slowly walking towards me, coming closer, he closes his eyes, drawing his gods into his soul as he moves, murmuring his prayers with the voices of his ancestors, voices that rumble like ancient lazy thunder from a storm far far away.

And when he is before me, he opens his eyes. Firelight dances wild and bright in them and, in his gaze, that fire touches my darkness. There is a moment of cataclysmic resistance. He stumbles, taking a step backwards, and I almost break. But through me, my goddess whispers, *Come!* And the voices of our ancestors move through him once again, as he murmurs, slowly and with such strength, My Lady, at your bidding. And I close my eyes as his light moves into my soul, bringing with it every balefire and hearth fire, every banefire and grain fire, every blade of the forge, every slow drip of molten ore, every cut and every yell that has been the craving of man to survive. And when I open my eyes, that craving is love. And I open my soul and the druid, with his flaming eyes, touches my mouth with his lips, and in that moment I accept the light, the tribe, the people, into the night, into the dark waters, into the womb of creation.

Does it matter that nobody knows what is done? The seer and the druid walk together across the circle, and kiss. The wakeful may feel the wild storms of conflict and the union shimmering somewhere in the air, but this is all that is seen. A kiss.

Tearing ourselves apart, he steps away, and bows low, and his words spoken to me in trust are murmured again, this time into sound, *"My Lady, at your bidding."*

And my soul leaps in shock as, on the cue of those words, the whole gathering erupts into a clamour of cheering, clapping and stamping, drums, whoops and jigs. The first deed is done and they yell, bashing sticks together and hollering for more.

I know I must move, but suddenly I am not sure how. I have done this rite so many times: is it my tiredness or is it Eos that makes it now so difficult? Two priestesses appear on either side of me and, finding my feet, we move to where the druid stands by the great stone. Torches are lit from the fire, and I breathe deeply. Caldreg looks into my eyes, and the smile of his soul lends me a little strength, *My Lady,* he whispers, *as ever, you are ...* There is no word for what he says, for instead of language, for the briefest instant, again he opens his soul, provoking my goddess to rise within me.

The fluster of young girls moves towards the stone, gathering in a huddle, trying to be quiet, hand in hand, but in truth filled with fear. To be so close to the wild power and sorcery of the island's seers is enough to send most of them into tides of trembling. Again I see Sianed's daughter. A maiden of the island, she holds nobody's hand, for the village girls keep a little distance from her, but still she is too nervous to look at me, biting her bottom lip with excitement.

Caldreg calls out a prayer and blesses the knife, as a young man from his people pulls the goat across the circle. When he's close, the creature is taken from him, the druid's young apprentices dragging him by the horns, much to his bleating indignation. Beside me, Gwenlli cannot help but murmur to the creature in the marsh tongue, *"You are honoured, brother, so honoured."* The goat butts away his captors and turns to her; in the brief moment we have together, our eyes meet and I whisper a prayer of welcome from the darkness. It is a moment of perfect stillness. Then, pulling his head back around, Caldreg slits his throat in one sharp movement, calling out his thanksgiving. The creature goes limp, blood pouring into bowl, as I watch its spirit turn again to Gwenlli, looking up at me. And again Gwenlli murmurs, You are honoured, dear brother, so honoured.

I bend down and offer my hand, and slowly it moves towards me. I close my eyes as it enters the darkness of my soul, disappearing through me, as one of the apprentices hauls its body up onto the stone. The other lifts the bowl and moves with his teacher to the group of girls. They quiver, wide eyed in the firelight, as Caldreg dips his fingers into the bowl and, one by one, marks each girl's breast with the blood, giving a blessing to each one for the fire-blessed night of passion they each hope will come.

On the other side of the fire, the young men have gathered. I make my way towards them, bidding them come closer. Gwenlli is at my side. She is little older then some of these boys, but this year she holds herself tall and independent as a priestess in training, standing upon the status of being my aid. I smile at her determination, but a part of me, longing for Eos, wishes I were as young as she, and that he were amongst this flock of boys.

In the firelight I sigh and look into their faces. Some are familiar to me, brothers and sons of my own community, some I have seen on the marshes and waterways, fishing or travelling from island to island. Each recoils from my gaze, except one. He is proud, strong and good looking, no more than sixteen summers old, and unaware that it is pride that might inspire my choosing.

I nod to Gwenlli, who steps into the group and takes his hand.

"What's your name?" she whispers, bringing him forward to the great stone.

"Morfran," he says nervously, still holding his head high, but looking into her face to see if really she is human or a marsh sprite that will enchant his soul away to lifetime of unimaginable pleasure, pleasure that is too often held excruciating just out of reach.

She and I exchange a smile.

"Are you ready for this?" I hear her say in the common tongue.

"Of course I am," he mumbles, looking around the gathering who are again cheering and clapping.

"Don't piss," she whispers.

I look into her face. My quiet Gwenlli has more mischief in her than I knew.

He stares at her, terrified.

There is quiet around the circle as Caldreg's apprentices hold the boy's hands firmly against the stone. My hood hiding my face, my back to the fire, he will see nothing of my expression nor my humanity. He stares into the darkness of my face, doing all he can to hide his fear, determined to say nothing. Sianed passes me the blade and I draw it into my soul, blessing it with the darkness of the goddess who breathes within me. When I look up into his face, I know that I must not let her take control, *guide me, my Lady, but know this is my blade. Let him feel your presence, for what is done is done in your name. Let him feel you, but let him feel me too ...*

I lean forward and, silently drawing him into the darkness, I kiss his mouth.

Then lifting the blade, I let the tip touch the muscled flesh beneath his shoulder.

Giving him a long breathless moment staring into the darkness of my face, I make the invocation and tear the blade across his skin. His squeal is immediately drowned out by the cries of the gathering, as drums roll into rhythms and hollering applause fills the air. I turn from him, closing my eyes to find my own breath, then face him once again. He is limp with shock, tears running down his face, but he is standing and determined. And again I smile as Gwenlli whispers, "Well done, Morf."

Sianed is drawing the other youngsters near to the stone, and each one, a little paler than before, steps towards me. Running my fingers across the boy's wound, I mark each one with his blood.

"Would you take me to him, dear child?"

She smiles tenderly, "Of course, my Lady."

The meadow is again filled with the noise of music and dancing, children running, people shouting and laughing, meadhorns raised and emptied, women shouting from cooking fires. In the centre, by the great stone, someone is skinning the goat to roast. Yet above us is the silence of a star-scattered sky. The full moon is shining. And through the clamour, I see Eos, sitting alone on a tree stump at the bottom of the slopes of

Bryn Fyrtwyddon, as still and silent as the whitethorn beside him. His head is in his hands.

I call to his soul, *Eosaidh?*

Looking up, he sees me, Gwenlli at my side, and he stares into my soul.

As we approach, I touch Gwenlli's hand, "Let us be, child. I will be alright."

She bows and steps away.

I turn to the old tinner and wonder what to say.

"May I sit with you, Eos?"

He looks up into my face and, reaching out a hand, he says softly, "Dear Vivi ..."

Chapter Ten
Sensuous Fruit of Love
(Eosaidh)

I t is the morning of the whitethorn moon. Vivian has been busy for the past week preparing for the festival of the beginning of summer, and we have not spoken since we parted at the Red Spring. I have seen her in passing often as we have gone about our tasks, exchanging glances from far off, feeling heart's longing across a meadow or through a stand of trees. I pause for a few moments to rest from the swinging of the axe I have finally managed to repair, and survey the results of my labour, a high pile of wood that will find its way into tonight's bonfire. The morning sky is a soft blue, the first puffy white clouds of summer drift by. The thorn high on Wirrheal is at full bloom as if a white summer cloud were somehow reflected in the fresh green grass of the hillside. For a moment, I see in my heart the bright white linen bundle as it slowly sinks into the waters of the sacred spring, containing the precious blue shards of the cup of life.

Vivian has told me little of the fire festival. I think she expects me not to understand the sacredness of the Fires of Bel, the celebration of fertility that marks the beginning of summer in the marshes. She distrusts the laws of Adonai, which are so different from the laws of her Mother. And why should she not? *Thou shalt have no other gods but me* does not leave much room for her. Truth be told, it leaves little room for most human souls in the world. I think she fears Adonai. Not his power to destroy, but his power to change. And for the people of the marshes, change and destruction may perhaps be the same thing. I do not know about Adonai, but I wish she would not fear me. For I am not, perhaps, the most typical subject of that warrior god from the Sinai desert. I have been too long among the Dumnoni, Parisii and Avernii of Gaul, the Macedonians and the Achaians, the Phoenicians, the Ephesians and the Egyptians and, always, the Romans. I know in my heart that Adonai exists. But even the tradition of my people recognizes Adonai and Ba'al to be the same word. I have seen too many people searching for God to believe that any one of them has found him as he really is.

But there is the rub. For Adonai is 'he'. Until Vivi, I would not have believed an old Iuddic tinsmith from Cornualle could seek the Mother. The lad did, I think. Perhaps that's why Vivi cared for him enough to give him the cup. The lad knew because his mother knew. And yet more, because of the Magdalene, who some called 'the beloved disciple'. And of all my race, perhaps the one who knows fullest is young Sarah whom I have not seen since Massalia, who is now nearly a woman herself.

What is it about this isle that teaches the mind to wander so in paths of mystery? Fianna will come looking for me if I do not get the handcart and move this wood to the festival site!

At mid-afternoon, after stowing tools and bathing in the shallow waters, I make my way back toward the meadow. I pass the spot where once I had built a small prayer hut to remind me of the Temple in Jerusalem. After the committal of the cup at the Red Spring I took it down. Perhaps because I knew it would please Vivian, perhaps because I have learned that the Holy cannot be contained within a hut. I smile as, once again, I realize even my own scriptures have owned this truth.

I pass through the bluebell wood where yesterday I held Vivian while she cried for her son. Sadness still lingers under the boughs, though the scent of the flowers tempers that heavy emotion with a sense of hope.

I emerge from the wood into the meadow that leads down to the marshes. Instantly my heart is lifted by the sight! Where have all these people come from? In the centre of the field is the great pile of wood I have helped supply, ready to be set ablaze. For a moment I feel the stiffness in my muscles and wonder that the central focus of this ancient celebration has been provided by my own axe. Nearby is the great stone, a hoary old whitethorn hovering over it as if to protect a fallen loved one. And all around, there are people! Hundreds, dressed in all the colours of the rainbow. And children! They are everywhere! They wheel and weave about one another, making preparations, like a great troupe of musicians tuning their instruments for a performance. Vivian stands quietly by the stone, her hand on the old thorn. She is lost in her thoughts, an island of stillness in the human sea.

The crowd slowly becomes quiet, forming a ring about the stone. I step back to the edge of the field to watch, for some reason not wishing to be seen. Vivian and a young man step into the circle, and I feel a pang of jealousy, wishing that I would be her partner in this sacred rite. No, he is not so very young. Indeed it is the druid, Caldreg, who is an elder. It is Vivi's agelessness that makes him seem youthful, or perhaps the ache in my bones. I have seen this Druid on the island a time or two, but we have not met. Then a truly young man, painted in woad, comes forth from the crowd carrying a burning torch. With a shout he thrusts it into the woodpile, which is instantly ablaze. I feel the heat in my own body, though I am not near enough to feel the flames. Drums around the circle begin their slow throb.

Following the gaze of the crowd, I turn to look at the top of Wirrheal where other flames arise in answer, sending the message of the Fire Festival across the countryside. Soon all of Britain will echo the celebration of this meadow. Vivian

and Caldreg sing in concert and antiphon as the people bring
offerings to the stone in honour of all their gods. They are
the same offerings my people once brought in the wilderness:
barley and honey; milk and fruit. But also the iron of the hills,
whitethorn, salt, and many things I cannot recognize from
here. In all the world human beings honour their gods with
the same gifts. Why cannot they so honour one another?

Out of the general turmoil two circles emerge, one of the
young girls, the other of the boys, dancing around the fire,
stepping to the centre to drink from the mead horn and
be blessed by Vivian or Caldreg. Around me, out here on
the fringes, Fianna's little charges have been dancing, too;
practising for the year they will circle the fire. For a time I
turn my attention to the little ones playing at the edge of the
gathering.

When I look back, the circles are disbanding, bringing a
lull to the ceremony. Vivian has disappeared somewhere. Men
gather around Caldreg as if in a meeting, while cooking fires
begin to appear around the meadow. It is time for the evening
meal. Fianna comes over to where the little ones are playing
around me. "Go, little ones," she laughs, clapping at them.
"Your families are waiting for you, go and find the feasting!"
They all run off skipping through the grass. My eyes search the
crowd, but Vivian is nowhere to be seen. Fianna steps to my
side.

"It is a ritual, and her duty as the Lady, Eosaidh," she says,
as if to reassure me that Vivian is not taken with the Druid.
I struggle with my own thoughts: *He is an Elder of his people,
Eos! Yes, but he is nearly a generation younger than you!* I smile
and mutter something silly, looking down at my feet and
nervously picking up a garland dropped by one of the little
girls. "You needn't be shy," Fianna smiles. "That a bond has
grown between you is plain enough for all to see!" She looks
up at the stars emerging in the growing dark. With a sweep of
her hand she acknowledges the field of revellers and the great

fire. "On a night like this, Eosaidh," she says, "It is not proper to be shy!" We both laugh out loud, but still I nervously finger the garland.

"Fianna," I venture.

"Yes?"

"She had no child that lived, other than her son?"

Fianna is instantly serious, knowing the deepness of my caring. Her eyes drop to the ground, and she takes a moment to answer. "Not one," she says.

"How many did she lose, Fia?"

"Manann was her fifth."

Then we are silent, and I feel the nearness of Vivian come and go.

One drum marks a slow, steady beat. The people leave their meadow-hearths and gather around the great fire in the centre. There, Vivian stands weaving a spell of song, and Caldreg approaches as if drawn, fearful, yet fascinated by her presence. The burning passion of his soul dances about the shadowy darkness of her mystery. It is as if the sun and moon circle each other. As the drum continues its beat they step to one another, and kiss. It is only a kiss, yet it feels like the birthing of the world. Again I feel the stab of jealousy, in my heart, in my loins. The whole crowd breaks into riotous song and dance. The young girls move to the centre as Caldreg holds high a great knife that flashes in the firelight. Someone drags a goat into the circle. It cries out and kicks in all directions, frightened by the fire and the noise. Grabbing the goat by the horns, Caldreg twists its head around and in one motion slits its throat upon the stone.

I am no stranger to the sacrificing of goats. They are in more danger in the Temple in Jerusalem than on this meadow in Affalon. But I wonder if this is the only time in the cycle when any creature loses its life to a blade upon this island. In both places the sacrifice bears the meaning of life. But in Jerusalem it is the covering of human sin. Here, as Caldreg dips his hand in the blood and marks the breast of each young girl, it represents the fertility of the tribe, and prepares the girls for the wonder of discovery that lies before them. What is it like to be a young girl of the tribes, I wonder? To feel the hand of the Druid, and the warmth of blood, caressing the flesh of my breast? What awakening of sexuality does that touch bring? What thrill of difference do I feel as I step back into the circle? Can it be, in the honouring of the gods, that it is not the gift that matters at all, but only the heart of the giver? *I have come that they might have life,* the lad once said, *and have it abundantly.* The blood of bulls and goats is not meant for the forgiveness of sins.

Then a young man steps forward in front of Vivian, Gwenlli holding him by the hand and speaking softly to him. He is stripped to the waist. Vivian takes the great knife and holds it to her breast, and for a moment, I fear the worst. She leans forward to kiss him. The crowd is silent, waiting, watching. It is as if she were making love to him before the whole gathering, a powerful young woman without fear or inhibition. But when her hand moves it is only to draw the point of the blade across his chest. Again the whole meadow breaks into shouting and drumming, as Vivian draws her fingers across the bloody wound and marks each of the young men present.

But I am no longer a young man. No longer can I interest a woman who bears the sexual power of the Lady of Affalon. No longer do I walk in the realm of fecundity and fertility. It has been too long. I turn from the circle and walk up the slope toward the foot of Wirrheal, to sit, fittingly, on an old stump in the moonlight. The meadow is filled with music and dancing, but here it is quieter. I have turned from the celebration to stare at the great whitethorn that first welcomed me to the island. Its crown of white blossoms scatters the moonlight across the slopes of the hill. How much time passes I cannot tell.

In my head I hear her call to me, *Eosaidh.* I turn and see her, with Gwenlli at her side. As they approach, she says something softly in the old tongue. Gwen bows, and turns away, going back to the celebration. Vivian takes the last steps toward me alone.

"May I sit with you, Eos?"

I look up into her face. Reaching out my hand to take hers I say softly, "Dear Vivi ..." and she comes to sit beside me. Still holding her hand, I put my other arm around her shoulders as if to shield her from the evening chill. But the evening is amazingly warm. She rests her head against me and I breathe in her closeness. For a while we are silent, listening to the drums in the meadow.

"I wondered if, hoped that, you would come to me," I say softly.

"Once I could not have," she answers. "But, after all these years, the fires and the choosing will go on well without me. This, being here, is my choice."

She turns her face to me and I can see the reflection of the full moon in her eyes. Can I even see the images of stars, or am I that hopelessly in love with this magical woman? I can feel the warmth of her breath on my face. Her lips part to speak, *Eosaidh,* and I am kissing her softly. A night wind through the thorn blows a shower of white petals around us. "I am frightened by love, Vivi," I say. "It has been such a long time."

"As am I, dear one," she answers. A tear falls down her cheek, but her body is calm.

Across the meadow the dancing circles twist and weave together. Slowly at first, then with more enthusiasm, couples begin to disentangle themselves from the group and drift away toward the trees.

I brush her hair with my hand. "There will be many young folk in the woods tonight," I say. Then, sighing, "But I fear I am too old to spend the night on the ground." She laughs, and it warms my heart.

"Eosaidh, dear Eosaidh," she whispers.

"Come," I say, rising and helping her to her feet. "I have

mead in my roundhouse, and some barley bread. And it will be quieter there than in the woods tonight."

Like two grandparents leaving a family party, we walk quietly through a patch of woods to the base of Wirrheal, part the door covering, and enter my small hut. An oil lamp hanging from a roof pole gives a little light. I go about lighting a small fire for warmth. Vivian draws her cloak about her, and sits on a low stool, watching me closely the whole time. I sneak glances at her from the corners of my eyes. The fire started, I slice some barley bread on the small table, pour two cups of mead, and hand one to her. Sitting on a corner of my cot, I look at her closely for the first time since we entered.

"You look so young tonight, Vivi," I say quietly.

She smiles. "It is not real, Eos. Yet nor is it glamoury. It is the magic of the rite. But it does not make this body feel young, nor does it return skills long unused and nearly forgotten." She looks down into her cup.

I set my cup on the table, and move to kneel before her. "I have not lain with a woman since last I set foot on this island," I say. Her eyes widen for a moment, and then soften, as she places her hand over mine on her knee.

She looks down at me softly. "Twenty-five cycles have passed since we were together last. I was too old to bear children even then." She lifts a hand and touches my face, smoothing the lines of my skin. "Eos, what are we doing?"

"Vivian," I breathe, "I have always honoured you with my mind. These last three months I have come to honour you with my heart. When it is time for us, if it is time, I shall honour you also with my whole being."

"Now is the time, Eosaidh."

She is silent. For the first time, I find I can look deeply into her, and understand. She is calling for the strength and courage that she needs, and I realize she fears and cherishes this moment as much as I. As if in answer to her call, the space around us, within us, fills with a dark fluid energy, like the waters of the marshes. Not cold, but warm, and wet, and life giving. My people, like the druids, have always looked to the sun for warmth. For Vivi it is the dark dampness of the marsh that is life. I am immersed in it now, as I am immersed in her. It washes through me with a thrill that brings pleasure from within.

She draws my head towards her as she leans forward, our lips almost touching, but for an age of the earth we do not touch, and the power of the closeness is a flood of deep waters, as slowly we open to each other, soul touching soul in the extraordinary power of intimacy, before flesh touches flesh. In that closeness she holds my eyes in her gaze and the intensity is excruciating. With each movement of our eyes, each blink of an eyelid, each soft caress of breath upon tender skin, the sensuality is breathtaking. To touch would be to break the spell, or to invite annihilation.

When our lips do touch, it is nearly the latter, for she holds the power of my soul in the depths of her being. She calls forth to my spirit, as if I were pouring my life breath into her, sliding into her soul cup, a cup as black as a cauldron. Then, as the touch grows, the softness of our breath and our lips is given substance by the hunger of taste. She draws me closer, my arms pulling her to me, drawing her from the stool to the straw mat where I kneel. In our kiss we become one, like currents of the great ocean meeting, and swirling together, and blending into a single sea. And it goes on and on, as the ages of the world move past outside us, and we breathe from each other, and merge into a single being with two souls, touching from the inside out, even as our hands begin to search for the soft sensuality of the other's flesh.

As the first moment calms, we are lying together on the mat, the wall of the roundhouse rising above us as though it were the shaft of a living well through which we have passed into the waters of the deep earth. We hold each other's faces in the palms of our hands, lying side by side in the silence of the night. The next kiss begins even more gently, but when she opens to me a great hunger awakens and we seek to taste the depths of the other. In my loins I feel a stirring I have not felt in years, and that I had not thought ever to feel again. My hand slides down the length of her body, feeling her nearness, resting on her hip that is pressed so close to mine. "Vivi," I breathe, my eyes lost in hers, "Come to me." She nods, and kisses me softly on the cheek.

I help her to rise. It is not easy for either of us. We both struggle with the sorrow and the humour of age. But when we stand our embrace renews, bodies wrapped around one another, hands caressing. Our bodies melt against each other, becoming one. Suddenly a searing pain flashes through my limbs and I cry out! Vivian looks into my face, alarmed. "It is all right, Vivi," I say to her. "I am all right. It is only," tears begin to flow down my cheeks, "It is only that I have felt what it feels like to be you." I knew she bore the psychic pain of fear for her people. I did not know the awful physical pain that tears her body, the result of agelessness among the marshes. Answering tears come to her face. She kisses me gently as I fall into her being. It is as though I live through her, feel her pain, see our loving through her eyes:

With each movement, the pain in my body breaks over me, yet with each breaking wave I find myself more open to him. There seems no reason to stop, no path left on the shore with which to retrace my steps, my soul now too close to the fires of his, and as his hand moves over my body, finding the hard bones and soft flesh, I feel him gathering me up and drawing me closer still, urging me in his whispers to come to his soul's fire.

And with my fingers weak with wonder, I pull at the knots of his robe. He smiles with such tender care, putting his hand upon mine, and unties the knot, taking the robe from his shoulders and, at my silent bidding, after a moment of hesitation, he pulls his tunic over his head.

Vivi, he murmurs, though no longer in sound.

I know, I whisper and I breathe in the strength and the vulnerability that we share, letting my fingers move over the softness of his old skin, the thick tangle of white upon his chest, the marks of his age, browned by so many harsh summers. I look into his eyes, and unclasp the old bronze broach of my outer robe. Gently, he pushes it from my shoulders with hands that seem big enough to hold my entire body. Then he lifts my flaxen shift over my head. For a moment he searches my face with a fear, feeling the fragility of my body, and I am afraid. Perhaps I pull away for he whispers, "No ..."

"Eos, I am old and my body is .."

"Vivi, I am sorry, I was shocked, you are so thin. But we both are old, and your body bears the beauty of the ages."

I close my eyes, but his hands are upon my face and his lips touch mine with a thousand kisses like drops of rain, and as our eyes meet, he murmurs so softly, "I love you, Vivian." And the words are like rainfall reaching into the depths of my soul. I reach to unlace his leggings, and then there is nothing between us. I have never said those words as Lady of Affalon. *"Eosaidh, Dear Eosaidh, I love you."*

Knowing now how fragile she is, and her pain, I bend, reaching behind her shoulders and knees, and lift her in my arms. Then I kneel, gently settling her on the cot. For a moment I stand and drink in the sight of her. In the low firelight she smiles and holds her arms out to me. Gently, to keep from jostling her body, I lie beside her. We draw our arms around each other becoming one flesh, fingers exploring, lips caressing, spirits joining in celebration. She moves her hips to bring us closer. I gaze into her eyes, her lips on mine, as I dissolve into the depths of her being. Together we cry out in joy, spinning into the darkness of oblivion.

I awake to the sound of a soft rain, though the sun is already high in the eastern sky. I am alone, but the soft scent of Vivi lingers about me.

On the table is a branch of whitethorn. Scattered about its blossoms are a handful of dried apple petals from last month's blooming. In the centre, a small dried fruit, which I must look closer to identify. Where had she gotten this? From Armenia in the east, perhaps traded through Gaul, a golden apricot, the sensuous fruit of love.

Chapter Eleven
The Dragon's Song
(Vivian)

When we reach the top of the hill, my legs are shaking. Every half dozen paces I have stopped and called to the spirits of the earth to give me strength, to allow me a certainty that might settle my limbs, and I have felt their song beneath and around me. Yet, though the earth has moved beneath me as ever it does, the hill flowing like a slow current allowing me simply to lift my legs one by one for progress to be made, even the lifting of my legs has now exhausted me. I wonder how many moons have passed since last I stood on the top of Bryn Ddraig.

Eos is unsure what to do. He takes my hand to help me but I push him away and he murmurs in the tongue of his people, some indignation about the curse of my independence. But there is gentleness upon his face, an acceptance and respect, as I sink to the grass with relief at having made it.

"I wish you had -" he begins again.

But I wave my hand and shush him, and point out over the landscape to the north and east, the high summer sun warm on my back, albeit now sliding toward the sea. "Look," I say, covering my legs with my robe, ensuring there is no more talk of my shaking, "you can see the fields of barley now turning to gold."

Still standing, beside me, he breathes deeply and sighs, "Oh Vivi, how I have grown to love this land. Look," he extends his arm, bare and nut brown from this rich summer's sun, "that must be Herinn Water, and are those the cattle of the Durentes? You said they had wealth but that is quite a herd! I didn't realize you could see so far from here."

He looks around, further to the west, and for a moment his eyes settle on Bryn Llyffaint in the distance, and I know he is remembering, but he is silent.

I smile, "Sit with me, Eos. You can see as much from down here."

He laughs, but crouches beside me, setting a kiss upon my cheek, "Now you want me close to you! Impossible woman!" In his tunic and sandals, his legs are as brown as his arms, and I run my hand over the grey fur of his thighs where the cloth rises. He sits down upon the grass and I am comforted again by the warm strength of his presence.

"The sunlight on the waters," I murmur, watching the brilliance of the light upon the lakes and rivers of the landscape, shining with such giving, reflecting a thousand hues as if upon an old and polished plate of bronze. Snakes of light shimmer from boatways through the marshes, and I breathe in the rich green of the meadows and forested islands, the colours finding their depth again as the sun slips nearer to the sea.

"Look, Vivi," he says. I turn, and follow the sweep of his arm across the horizon. The sun flashes off the slow summer currents of the Bryw waterway through the marsh, lighting the slopes of the far hills. "The Polden Hills feel close enough to touch. What is the local name?"

"Bryniau'r Pwllborfa. The ridge of hills that runs towards the south east of Ynys y Niwl we call Bryniau'r Pennard."

He says the words softly, then his eyes are reaching beyond. "Can you see the hill fort of Caer Iwdon from here?" I smile and shake my head, but his mind is already travelling beyond. "South of there are the plains of the Belgae, and then the great waters. Two days sailing brings you to the coast of Gaul, and the Sequana, the wide river that takes you south to the village of the Parisii. From there it is overland to the next river south, the Rohodanus, through a land far larger than Britain, to the busy port of Massalia. From there you board a ship to journey across the great sea at the middle of the earth, the Mare Meditarraneus. It is a journey of many weeks, on that vast water, with many stops, before you come to the land of Iudea, the home of my people. I have travelled it often. It is a wide, wide world." For a few moments we gaze out into the distance at the ends of the earth.

Softly I say, feeling the mystery beneath my feet, "It is also a very deep world, Eos." His sudden intake of breath tells me he sees what I already have seen and hoped he would not. I close my eyes, feeling his heart sinking. In my soul I can see the view he is taking in, the image still clear: vast clouds of smoke rising into the clear deep blue skies, the barley fields of clans a few days ride to the south, burning down to the dry mud.

They cause no harm to those who give in, to those who give all they are and all they have, feeding the legions, slaughtering sheep and goats, the sacred cattle, the men feasting on butchery that leaves villages in poverty. Yet those who don't submit are killed, or raped and mutilated and left to die. I hear again the words spoken at the council, that some clans are burning their crops to deny the Romans the grain. Others speak of the armies burning barley and oats upon orders from their leaders, fields set to flame in the lust of bloodshed.

"They are no closer," he whispers.

"I can feel them, Eos. I can feel it getting closer."

"They won't come this way yet, my love." He takes my hand and I watch the pain that weighs down his heart, "It will take them a while to wreak their destruction through the west, to sate their greed in Cornualle's mines. These battles here are no more than skirmishes, soldiers holding ground that has already been won, needing to be fed and fornicated." He sighs, "Bored young men a long way from home."

He turns back to let his eyes meander across the apparent peace before us. A flat boat is moving through the open waters towards Llyn Hydd, silent and easy: a shepherd boy with a dog heading to an island where his flock are grazing. Strangely, for a moment, I see him through Eos' eyes, and realize the figure is no more than a silhouette at this distance, yet I feel the youngster's song somewhere in my bones.

Eos stretches out his legs and again I push my fingers through the grey curls of his brown thigh and he smiles, enjoying the touch, reaching an arm around my waist, comfortable and comforted by our closeness as am I. Yet I look into his eyes to seek out the worry that I feel in his soul.

"I was out at Pentreflyn the other day, the village on the lake, talking with some of the men," he says, drawing in his soul to hide his concern. "Travellers in the marshes tell them of a Roman encampment on Hod Hill. The slings of the Durotriges were no match for the legions. The hill fort was overrun and taken. They are planning to stay awhile." He gestures again towards the distant smoke behind us. "They are provisioning the fort. The vanguard of Vespasian's forces have reached Bodmin Moor. They've taken the tin mines there."

"I am sorry, Eos." I bring his hand to my lips, feeling his fear. "Are your family close to that moor?"

"It is another few day's ride. Perhaps the druids will yet take a stand against them."

But his words provoke anguish in the depths of my soul.

I shake my head, "No, Eos. I fear it is not a hope we can depend upon."

Our eyes meet. For a moment the flood of love almost overwhelms the anxiety of my desolation, the two tides meeting and rising, filling my vision with confusion, with joy and with fearful rage. I look away, towards the cattle of the Durentes, recalling the uproar at the council gathering, and he puts his hand over mine, knowing what is passing through my mind.

"Myrledd did wrong," he says softly.

"But there will be other druids who do the same, selling their people and their land for some unsealed vow of protection.

I watched them, and even though I knew every face, every priest in the gathering, I saw in their eyes a death-glow of fear. Myrledd was an ambitious man, as was his father before him, but to betray his gods as he has done! He has lost his ancestors' blessing. The land will turn against him. Then what will an allegiance to Roma do for him."

"They are giving up integrity for safety, my love," he answers. "That sort of bargain is Rome's stock in trade. Yet your words of the council are ominous. If Roman negotiators are already moving through the marshes, there will soon be legions in the Mendydd."

I feel my soul shudder and whisper to my gods for strength.

But on creaking legs, he stands, breathing deeply, with a courage born of his long life's travelling. "The day is too beautiful to speak further of Vespasian," he declares and takes the few steps back to the very summit of the tor. As he gazes out over the landscape, I wonder how much of this brutality he has seen before, Iuddic blood on Roman blades, violence I have only seen in the waters of my visions. I find my soul reaching out to the settlements of the south, seeking understanding.

"Vivi,' he says gently, "it is so beautiful up here, with the world all around. Yet I hardly ever see any of the women of your community here."

His ploy to ease my soul from the anxiety brings a smile of tender affection to my face.

"The druids have ancient rights to come here twice in the sun's cycle, when the tides of light turn at midsummer and midwinter."

"I thought I saw a gathering and was surprised to see it was druids on your island."

"Yes, its a right my grandmothers have allowed to continue, and so do I."

I raise myself slowly, and sigh, walking to his side, for his eyes have taken his song upon the evening breeze down into the valley, to the springs, to the old red well where small shards of blue glass lie deep in the earth.

"This high place is a man's place. I am surprised our ancestors didn't bury some pompous old chieftain in a great round earth tomb right here on the top."

He puts his arm around my shoulders.

"I rather like it as it is," he smiles, "like a soft bare breast. And there," he points to the patch of earth upon which no grass ever grows, where the druids have set a cairn of stones to the ancestors, "that is the nipple."

"Perhaps," I smile. "Perhaps that is why such high places are sacred to men and young children."

He laughs, "But not to you?"

"The power of the tor is within it, Eos." And I search his soul for a moment to see if I should follow my heart, but what I find is his courage and his trust in me, and a deep response within myself to honour both. "Come, let me show you something."

I take his hand and draw him to the dry earth around the cairn. The children have been up here again since the druids' rite, rearranging the stones in order to stand securely on the top, and I hear Caldreg's voice in my memory, indignant and proud. But the wide strong warmth of Eos' hand is in mine and, as the moments pass, nothing else seems important.

"Look around," I whisper, "and imagine you are an important druid of the council, and your lands stretch out over some considerable island, or even extend to the mainland." He smiles, playing the game. "Are your feet on the ground?"

He squeezed my hand, "Of course, Vivi."

And I sing to the dragon.

It doesn't take long. He squeezes my hand tighter, murmuring, "Vivi?" as he is taken up on the swirling heat of its breath, his spirit rising, as he cries out, "Lady, what are you doing to me?" And I whisper the blessing, sprinkling herbs upon the grass, bowing to the creature who slips again into the dry mud, and Eos is reeling, stumbling to find his balance on the ground before me. "Vivi, what did you do?"

I smile, reaching up to touch the snaggles of his beard, whispering, "That's what the druids do, but don't tell them I told you."

"I feel hopelessly dizzy!"

"If you breathe in the right way, you can fly on the dragon's breath."

"I think I believe you!" he says, trying to plant his feet more firmly on the solid earth.

"Sadly, I think some of them are flying to close to the sun. The beeswax they use to hold their feathers is going to melt, as the saphers say."

He holds onto me more tightly to still the swirling of his head, but in his arms there is passion. I look up into his eyes, seeing how the dragon's fire has vitalized his soul, and he kisses me tenderly. A mistake: I laugh as his world begins to spin again. "I have no need of dragons or herbs, my Lady," he declares, his eyes sparkling. "Your lips are quite adequate to the task! And though I have no feathers, you do a fine job of melting my heart."

I push his chest with my hands, "You are soft, tinner. Come, let me show you something else."

Reaching for my staff, I stumble. He hurries to pick it up and, handing it to me, says softly, "We needn't go further if you are tired. It's late, Vivi. I could carry you back down." But I dismiss his concern.

"Don't be silly. I've something to show you."

In truth I cannot walk down the steep side of the tor and for a moment consider the long road, down the gentler incline and around the side, but instead, on the slope, I sit down and gently slide myself down the soft grass.

Eos shakes his head, smiling broadly.

"Come!" I say.

"Yes, my Lady," he laughs again and sits himself upon the grass where, holding his staff above his head with both hands, he gives himself up to the slope, sliding down after me. With his greater weight, he slides quickly and, as we drop down a steep incline between the grassy terraces, we come close to colliding. "Eos!" I cry out, but sliding into me he holds me and we roll together onto the flat, laughing out loud. And when all but our breathing becomes silent, he looks at me, smiling, brushing the hair from my eyes.

"Vivi, I don't know about you, but I am too old for this!"

I place a finger on his lips, "I said you were soft, tinner. Come, we are almost there." And I point to the small outcropping a few yards below us.

As we slide towards it, his eyes still shining, I see him taking in all that he sees: the old whitethorn who bends over the ground, offering protection, she who we know as Wyddonwrach Wen. And under the tree, the large round stone that our tales call Maen Wyddraig, the dragon's egg. He gets to his feet and walks towards it, crouching to lay his hand upon its smooth pale surface. He looks up to where I sit, above him on the slope. The sun's setting is hidden now by the hill, but its light shimmers off the waters, deepening still further the colours of the land, the lush green of the islands and the golden fields of barleycorn. Yet here, in the shadow of the hill by the old whitethorn, the temple of our world is soft and cool and grey.

My eyes fall upon the stone. How often have I done this with girls of our community, those who already have the power of sight and sensitivity? It is a task taught by others now, but there were many cycles of the sun when it was my responsibility, sitting in stillness, listening to the music of the spirits, teaching the song of my grandmothers by guiding each one to hear the earth herself. To be here with Eos takes me back twenty summers to a time when my life was ... What was it? Easy? The patterns of change did seem to shift within some clearer frame of order. How long that order had been in place, I do not know. It was certainly the order known by my mother, and hers before her. It is hard not to wish that this flood of killing men had invaded during someone else's span of living.

Eos is watching my face, quietly, wondering at my thoughts.

I slide myself down til I am beneath the thickly leafed branches of the old whitethorn, hung as she is with lichens and murmuring in the evening breeze. I touch her song, whispering, *blessings to you, sister,* and for a moment we share breath. Then I find my feet and, with my back to the hillside, I draw Eos towards me, wondering if he will feel the power and, if he does, how it will change him. He puts his arms around me and we are close enough for me to feel his heart beating in the warmth of his chest. He looks into my eyes, though what he is seeking is the path to come.

"You must be with me, Eos," I whisper. "Don't let go."

I'll never let go, Vivi, he says softly in silence. *I will never let go.*

I close my eyes, letting his words sink into my soul, and we are falling through the thin layers of grass and mud, slipping into the current of the ancient song, each note too low to be heard but with the soul of the seer.

But almost immediately I am struggling, for he is too heavy, weighed down by a burden of hope that I simply cannot carry; I call to his soul for release, for permission, for I have no choice but to tear it from his belly. He cries out but suddenly the weight is gone, and we can move. I hold him tight and feel his soul clinging to mine, his mind filled with wonder and fear, with exhilaration and emptiness, with the darkness that glows with perfect life, and we slip through the currents like otters in the black waters of Llyntywyll, tumbling and diving, holding onto each other, as I take him down, further, into the earth, breathless with its power. But when he sees what is below him, he tries to speak, *Vivi, what - ?* and the blunt edges of his thoughts jam a rudder into the flow and we are thrown, our bodies crashing into mud walls and crosscurrents, and he clings to me more tightly, fearful with not understanding, as I call out the song again - and an ancient grandmother reaches up towards me, her hand shining in the dark, drawing us down further and back into the current. But now I dare not take him in: the cauldron, revered through all time, is listening to my every move. Have I dishonoured by bringing this man into her presence? She glows, the heart of an ancient fire, molten bronze in the utter darkness, waking every flame of life in each atom of my body. And I hold him with all my soul, knowing this is as far as I can go. For a moment, we drift, floating in darkness above the fire-pool of the goddess.

For the first time in my life, I want to share all that I am. And I am horrified to discover that it is not possible. I feel him weakening in my arms, his fingers loosening their grip upon my soul. Through the darkness, in another time and space, I feel his heart pounding, his body gasping for breath. And gently, quickly, I move up, breaking through the land and into the evening twilight on the slope of the tor. He moves away from me, breathing deeply.

I look into his face, sweat wet on his brow, his eyes searching for understanding as he gazes into the earth at his feet.

I step towards him, "Eos, forgive me."

But he does not hear me. He steps back again, leaning against the old whitethorn, exhausted and dazed. The spirit feels his presence and softly moves around him, for which I am grateful. I hold myself at a distance and wait. His heart slowly calms, and he searches for words, not yet able to look at me.

"I thought," his words are barely audible. He breathes in deeply and tries again. "I thought my identity was being wrenched from me." He steps away from the tree, who unfolds, releasing her embrace. She listens as I do, as he moves to sit upon the stone, still gazing at the earth. "Then I realized I was actually merging with you. Still whole, still independent, somehow even more me for the connection." He looks up into my face, seeking affirmation, and I listen. "It seemed we were hurtling down a dark flume, its waters crashing around us on all sides into the earthen walls. When I looked without, the hurtling water and the crashing walls were frightening beyond words," a shudder courses through his body, "but when I looked within, I seemed to look into you, and all was safe, and silent. All the while you held me close, and the earth tore me away."

He rises and turns towards the hillside, his eyes searching the bare ground, tufts of grass, an old rabbit hole. The sacred door, Danfyd Ddrw, is beyond his vision. He stares at the earth, willing to see the entrance, willing to look down the passage through which we had journeyed, but he sees only the side of a hill.

"I was submerged in the torrent of water. My mind screamed out to me that it would perish in the flood, but you kept telling me I would live. The place where we were - was it a cave? - was alive. I could hear the music of life in the waters and I felt, I felt ..." His words falter. I feel what is to come, what rises in his mind, and I step towards him, placing a hand softly upon his arm.

"Yes, dear one," I murmur, wondering how hard it must be to live within the rigid high walls of a man's soul. He turns to me, with tears in his eyes. *Tell me,* I whisper.

"I thought I felt my mother, and I was lost in a memory of images without words." A tear falls, and he turns again and sits on the stone. I smooth another from his face. "I heard the rush and swirl of the waters all about me and, as if off in the distance, in a steady undertone, the thrum, thrum, thrum of her heartbeat."

My heart fills with his tears and I move closer, standing before him, my arms around his shoulders, drawing him close to me, and I sing, softly, feeling his human soul's tenderness, the old marsh song of comforting seeping into the twilight. Yet, as his soul begins to still, a deep shudder rises from the centre of his being, trembling through every part of his body, and he cries out in pain and fear. I hold him as he shakes, whispering a prayer through my song.

"Suddenly, just as I thought I heard her answer me, I was wrenched from her presence. I lost you. I was alone, and flying back in the opposite direction, my bruised body crashing against the body of the earth. I was sure I was going to die - then a cold rush of air, and then the empty void of total loneliness. And I collapsed against the old thorn," he looks up at the tree, bewildered and exhausted, "and the world was back."

His words linger in the quiet of this place, the air growing darker and thicker with the slow falling of summer's dusk. The wind song is gone. I lean down to place a kiss upon his head and, holding him gently, whisper a spell of calming, feeling the whitethorn beside us adding her blessing of age-old serenity. And slowly he finds peace, this boy child stepping again into the body of the man.

He looks up into my face. "I have no way of understanding how this can be, Vivi," he says softly. "Help me."

"I have no way of guiding you to understand, Eos."

He gazes at the ground in desolation, "Then -"

"No, dear soul. That does not mean you are lost." I move to sit beside him, pushing him along, as much to feel close to him as to find enough space for my old bones. "It is simply how nature is. You cannot know what it is to be a woman, Eos. There is nothing I can say that would adequately explain to you the currents of my soul. Nor could any woman."

He turns to me, "Is that what I am seeking?"

"It is what you are asking. In the womb of the earth, the temple cave of this tor, I carried you into the heart of darkness. That is my essence, Eos. It is not blessed with the light that reveals understanding, so how can it be understood? It can only be felt. By the gift of my craft, I could allow you to feel it. To feel her, the heart of my island, the womb of life from which my people are born. But you cannot understand. Just as I can never understand the thrill of standing on the high hilltop and believing that I own the world, or rising up on the dragon's breath pretending I can fly." The beginning of a smile flickers over his face and he lifts his arm to put it around me, drawing me close.

"I've never asked to understand the mysteries of a woman."

"That is not true, Eos."

He sighs, "You're right. Perhaps I have never expected to, but still I seek." He is silent for a moment and then adds, almost wistfully, "Perhaps I have never understood the mystery of being a man."

I gaze out over the marshes, the landscape fading into darkness. The only sign of life is the flickering light of a fire in the east, glittering in the night: shepherds camped on the island shore across Llyn Hydd. Above us, in the soft indigo sky, the summer stars are waking to watch over the land.

Chapter Twelve
Morla's Tale

(Eosaidh)

Below us, the lower slope of Wirrheal is yellow with hypericum. We are sitting in the sunlight, watching Fianna shepherd the young ones while they gather the healing wort. "Only the freshest plants, little ones," she cries out. "They make the best oil!" Ever since the solstice, a moon's cycle ago, I have been wondering about Vivi's unease over the presence of the druids on the tor. Even now it haunts the joyful project I have been working on for the past hour. Proudly I place upon her brow a newly woven circlet of summer daisies, and ask, "Why don't you just forbid them to come?"

She looks at me for a moment, shading her dark eyes from the sun, trying to find my train of thought. "How could I? Their presence is a part of the song of the island."

"But, Vivi, you are the singer of the song. Why keep those notes that trouble you?"

She frowns. "I don't have to like all that nature presents me. Take the . . . what do you call it?" She gestures to the wild shrubs with their bright yellow flowers.

"I know it by hypericum, the Greek name."

"We call it sun wort. I can't abide it. In the heart of winter, when the herbwise make brews for the ailing, to me it's like an undisciplined and arrogant child, shining out with no heed for the beauty of the quiet darkness."

Who in Rome or Iudea would have thought my life's great work would one day be trying to understand this mysterious woman? No, not understand. She has taught me that much, at least. I wonder if she loves or abides the daisy crown she wears so beautifully. I would wish her to love it, but one does not wish anything upon Vivian! One waits and discovers, and one accepts.

"And for you the druids are like sun wort, hard to abide, but necessary? My ancestors had such a relationship with the sun, in a land where it could bring life, or kill." I search her eyes, which now I see are clearly pained by the bright light. When will I learn that Vivi is not bound by my assumptions? That I love the warm sunshine on Wirrheal blinds me to her response. I ask, "Is it a part of you to prefer the darkness to the light?"

She changes hands to shade her eyes, continuing to look deeply into mine. Though the sun is shining, there is a still, soft darkness over her face. "It is not a part of me, Eos," she says. "It is me. For it is darkness that glows in the heart of me. I come from the darkness: it is my source and my home. I was born from the dark and ancient fire of this land." Her eyes hold a wondering look, even as I wonder at the notion of dark fire. She continues, a quiet strength in her voice, encouraging me to understand.

"In the tales my grandmother told, the druids were not this way, but a great many cycles have passed since that time. There are still some wise men amongst them," she sighs, "but most now reach for the light. I feel it is the influence of saphers, of priests and seers travelling from the east bringing stories of gods and heroes, of sources of power, of patterns written in the atoms that hum songs of other lands. Once, so my grandmother taught, the druids did seek out the mysteries ..."

She pauses, and takes the daisy chain from her head, for it is slipping through the fine silk of her hair. She holds it softly in her weathered hands, then brings it to her nose, breathing deeply, and touching the petals to her lips, closing her eyes for a moment as if seeking a connection.

"Then something changed and they began to seek knowledge above all else. And now they seek power. Such is the curse of those who follow the light."

The curse of those who follow the light. This is something crucial, something that defines a remaining divide between our two views of the world. I need to explore this, but not here. Not in this bright light that is so painful to her.

I stand and stretch. The sun is near noon and it is warm in this Wirrheal meadow. Offering Vivi my hand, I say, "Come, my love." She looks into my eyes and smiles, but it is a sad smile, wondering whether I ever will make the connections she hopes for me to make. I help her to rise, and we walk down the hill, Vivian turning the daisy circlet lazily in one hand, lost in thought.

As we approach the children they swarm about us with baskets full of sun wort. Vivian smiles at them, but a roll of her eyes toward me is to remind me of her aversion to the herb "I am sorry, my Lady," Fianna says, "But it is near to lunchtime, and they are excited."

"My Lady," cries young Olwen, making an attempt at a curtsey, "Look at my beautiful yellow flowers!" Vivian reaches out a hand to accept one. "How lovely," she smiles, "Perhaps the sun wort will bring some ease to my aching bones that give me such trouble even in high summer." She places the sprig of sun wort in her hair behind her ear, and Olwen beams with pride. Fianna sees that we are headed out to Dolgwyl Waun, and offers a small basket. "You will need something edible also, my Lady," she says. Again Vivi smiles, and I take the basket of bread and summer fruit. As we move away, we hear Olwen shouting proudly to her little companions, "She took my flower! Did you see? She took my flower and put it in her hair!"

As we head out across the meadow Vivi catches me grinning at her.

"Well, what could I do?" And this time she smiles at me. She takes the flower from behind her ear and weaves it into the daisies. "It does no harm to the sacred darkness to bring joy to the face of a little girl." And I fall in love all over again with this woman I will never understand.

We are not far across Dolgwyl Waun when Vivian realizes where we are going. "To Bol Forla?" she asks, "I didn't know you knew of it."

"I did not know its name. It is a peaceful place," I say, "and there is shade there. I saw it from Wirrheal on the day I first returned to the island. I have heard the marsh folk find it a sacred place. Sometimes I have found great solace there. I hope I have not been mistaken in feeling welcome."

"It is one reason people come to the island." She turns to me and touches my face with her fingertips, creating a moment of quiet intensity in that strange way that she does, and she murmurs softly, "I am glad the spirits there have made you welcome."

"Bol Forla?" I ask, "Who is Forla? It sounds a sad name."

"Her name was Morla. In the old tongue the sounds change like currents in the marshes." As we walk across the meadow, hand in hand, she tells me the story.

"It is an old tale, as old as the marshes," she sighs. "Morla was the wife of a tribal chieftain. She was young and beautiful, but she dishonoured him by falling deeply in love with an outcast of the marshes. He was a young man said to be possessed by a water spirit and, banished from his village, he lived wild in the marsh. He was known as the . . ." She pauses, saying the name quietly in one of the marsh languages, then smiles, "There is no exact translation in the common tongue: it is a poker made of red reed. The people call him Crika, which is a shortening of the old marsh words." A heron rises up through the trees and, in the stillness, we watch its flight. She squeezes my hand as if to acknowledge the beauty of the landscape which we are sharing, and we continue to walk, slowly, across the meadow.

"Morla became pregnant by her lover, and for many moons she convinced the chieftain it was his child. But in the last tides she could not hide the marsh flush on her belly. The chief was so horrified that she should have lain with an outcast that he banished her from his roundhouse and, heavily pregnant, she went in search of Crika. But he was nowhere to be found. She became weaker and weaker, and her grief overwhelmed her, so she cried to the sacred spirits of the marsh to take her soul, and that of her child, that she might find peace."

The hill - in truth, a small rise, not really a hill - is for most of the year a tiny island in its own right. It is only during these few months of summer when the marsh waters recede sufficiently that it is possible to reach the sacred place on foot. We pause at the ritual stone, normally at the water's edge, and Vivian bends down to touch it with her fingers, murmuring a prayer, before we continue over the soft ground, still hand in hand.

"It is a long time since I've told the tale," she says, as if reliving it herself. "Morla waded into the waters, calling her prayer, and the waters took her soul, allowing her the peace she needed to die. And in that peace, her body was washed up on this rise. It is here that Crika found her and, his heart breaking with love, the young man cried out to the goddess of the water."

Vivian pauses in the story to gaze out over the marsh to the open water. For a moment I sense the water goddess in Vivi, see her darkness in her eyes, feel her love for her, and the sorrowing loneliness of Morla. Is it truly so lonely, being a woman?

We reach the foot of the rise that is Bol Forla, rounded and soft, like the belly of a woman not far into carrying her child. It is clear on the top, save for tall grasses and dog roses, but the waters around it, fed by the River Bryw, support a stand of willows that encircle all. Vivian stops again, this time to pick up the fallen petals of a dog rose, quietly acknowledging the beauty of the shrub, its long thorny branches in a mass of brambles beneath a willow, then touching the flowers softly with her fingertips. We turn to walk sunwise along the willow circle, the shallow waters of the marsh on our left. She is silent for some moments, as we walk side by side.

"And the goddess," I venture, "did she indeed hear the anguish of this man?"

"Yes, the goddess heard his cries and sent spirits of the marshes to whisper Morla's song in the trees, guiding her back. Crika, remembering her song, kissed her, giving her breath to find life again. And as she awoke, her body began to pulse with the power of birth, and with the marsh spirits around her, singing the songs of the goddess, she gave birth to a daughter. Now the marsh folk speak of the daughter as a wild dark child, half sprite and half human, and so do they bring all such children, born with too much marsh power, to Ynys y Niwl for us to bring up," she smiles, sadly, "and those whose parents are taken by the waters. But here, Morla's daughter is described in all her beauty, as a child crafted by love. And this place has ever been a sacred place, wrapped about with the tale. Women come here for their unborn children to be blessed, for the goddess to ease the birthing, and heal the damage wrought in the tide of giving birth. And some, who have courage, come here when their hearts are broken for they have fallen in love with men," she hesitates, "with men they should not love."

I stop short, dropping the lunch basket and my staff, so quickly that Vivian continues several yards before she realizes I am not beside her. She turns to see me standing, alone, a stricken look on my face.

"Oh, dear Eos," she says, holding a hand out to me. I step forward to take her hand in mine.

"I am not such a man," I say. She is silent, but her eyes do not leave mine as she allows my arms to encircle her waist and draw her close. Her hands press against my chest for a moment, then she moves even closer. There is an invitation in her eyes, drawing me to bend and cover her lips with mine. The breeze playing through the willows is a caressing music as our kiss deepens and grows in passion, the musk of her scent filling my mind. Her lips against my neck, humming a marsh tune under her breath, my hands move with gentleness over her back, and shoulders, and hips, feeling the wonder of her nearness. My words at the tor come back to me, *I am too old for this!* Perhaps for sliding down hillsides, but surely not for this. Vivi has given me again the passion of youth, but with the understanding of age. The thought of age brings back to me the sense of her fragile frame beneath her summer robes. She looks up at me again, and I think I see the same frustration in her eyes that I feel: that it is age, rather than youth, bringing us together. But if she thinks this, she does not say it. Her eyes soften, taking my heart with them. It is only here that matters. Only now.

"The island blesses us," she says. She kisses me again, and whispers, "Come."

We follow the willows around to the north side, out of sight of the rest of the island, and sit on a large root of an ancient tree, which overhangs the water. A school of little fish swim in the eddies around the roots, one occasionally darting to the surface to catch insects unawares. It has been ages since I have gone fishing. I ought to try my hand at it again. Vivi kicks her feet in the water, and the splash brings me back from fishing in the reeds.

"My people have a similar tale," I tell her. "The woman's name is Hagar. She and her son live, but she never connects with her lover again, who was also the husband who rejected her. Is such a burden ever and everywhere the lot of women?"

"Yes."

A simple answer that carries much meaning. It is all she wishes to utter on the subject, but I urge her to say more. She sighs reluctantly, but goes on.

"A woman's soul is broader and deeper than that of a man. Its current is slower, for there is no race to be won for her. It gathers more into its song and naturally discards less along the way, allowing her to embrace more fully and feel more deeply. When a woman loves, the one she loves is not her direction, not her goal. The one she loves becomes her breath, her light, her mud: the very source of life."

"Then how can a woman ever love a man," I ask, "who is always moving on, always seeking beyond the next mountain?

"It is not about how," she replies, "it is simply that she does. Even if the man she loves is ever slipping away, leaving her in pain, a woman needs to love. For it is through love that she touches and is touched by her gods, without which her soul fades, unnourished, and she dies."

I look back at the fish swimming about our feet in the cool water. Can I have come this far in life to understand tin mining and fish better than men and women? "A man needs also to love," I say. "But for most men, I think it is because love helps them keep the illusion of youth, and drives from their hearts and minds the fear of death." I turn to her and kiss her softly. "Are we doomed to be ever unfathomable to one another?"

She smiles, looking into my eyes, "Eos, if you are forever reaching to understand me, then yes, we are 'doomed'. And yet," she sighs, "when I forget I cannot hold all that you are, I am equally misguided. There is an ancient and sacred place where we can meet, and the gods have shown us that place, Eos. We can ask no more."

Vivi hands me the circlet of summer blooms, as lover and as priestess.

"Make an offering, Eos," she says softly.

I take the white and gold flowers, hold them up for her kiss, and kiss them myself, then hold them close to my breast. *Blessed Mother*, I say, awkwardly, in my mind, *hold this woman near to your heart, and keep peace in her land.* I pause for a moment, and almost in afterthought I add, *Blessed are you, Adonai, for you bring healing to your people.* And I toss the flowers into a small dark eddy of water where the willow roots reach into the marsh.

Vivian reaches out a hand to touch my face. She kisses my forehead, then my cheek, then, softly, my lips. "Thank you," she says. "The ancient waters are moved by your words." She gets up and walks a few steps into the centre of the grove of willows, then turns to me, searching my face with black eyes. *"But Adonai?"*

I am silent for a long time, gazing into the waters, watching the flowers turn in the slow current. She is silent with me, walking a bit further off and leaning against an old willow. I look up and watch her, stronger now in the shade, her back straight but her shoulders bearing the weight of centuries, her head bowed, singing softly a song of the marsh. For a second time this day she presents me with a crucial issue between us. This time, *But, Adonai?*

Finally I rise and go to her, stopping a few feet away, leaning on my staff. She does not turn. Not out of rejection. She is allowing me the space to face what I must.

"Vivi," I venture at last, "I was born in Cornualle, in what my people call the Diaspora, the Dispersion. Only in my adult life did I come to know the land of Iudea. But I am a Iudde, and Adonai has been woven into the fabric of my being by the generations. When I turn to him in prayer, it is not out of conscious effort, it is who I am. All my life, and for all the lives of my ancestors, Adonai has been Father."

Still she does not look at me, though now I wish she would. Instead, her eyes seem fixed in the dark depths of the water beyond the willows, where all I see is the water's surface, shining with the golden reflection of the sun. Light and darkness, and the waters of the marsh.

"The song of our own ancestors always calls within us, Eos," she says, "hoping that we'll respond. When we can, when all we wish for is to be a part of that great and ancient song, we are blessed. When we can't, when another song lifts our hearts, our soul can be filled with clamour." As the midday sunlight gleams off the water's surface in a thousand flashes of light, playing across my face, blinding my eyes, I know the meaning of her words, for my soul is filled with turmoil, and desires the deep peace that she seems to know.

Still silent, we walk on a few more yards. Before us an ancient wooden walkway ventures out into the marsh. The single planks of ash and oak lie precariously over the support pegs and crossed poles of alder, visible now that the summer water levels are lower, revealing the extent of its disrepair. Many of the poles are out of line, some missing altogether, and about twenty yards out it disappears completely, the remains dropping down among the reeds, immersed in the dark currents.

"I wonder at the way the marsh people do not keep such things in good repair," I say, testing carefully with one foot the old planks that lead out from the shore. "They seem to allow with such ease the process of decay."

"They do, Eos, but it is birth they allow as well as death and decay. Today there is a newer walkway at the end of Bryn Fyrtwyddon, serving a newer need." We both remove our sandals, stepping out onto the old walkway. Vivian continues, "We think in cycles, Eos, with the changes in tides, the wandering of the water's currents. Things just come and go. We don't need to hold onto things. A walkway ceases being used and falls to ruin. Another will be built when and where it is needed. One day it, too, falls to decay, and another is built somewhere else."

We walk a little way out, and sit, dropping our feet again into the cooling marsh waters. Branches of a willow hang sheltering overhead, offering a little shade. Several swans glide out in the marsh. A buzzard soars in the blue sky. Vivi opens the small basket and hands me a piece of barley bread. Together we eat in silence, watching, feeling the marsh waters swirl around our bare legs. My mind goes back to the sun on Wirheal, and I wish to know more about what she means by the curse of the light.

"In all the stories, light is a blessing to my people," I say. "And darkness a danger. The darkness of night, the depths of a cave, are places for bandits or jackals. But in the daylight, from the hilltops of Iudea, one can see for miles. The sun is ever present there. It does not retreat in the winter as it does here. Indeed, it is in the winter the sun is friendly. In the summertime, it kills. Perhaps it is this harshness that gives Adonai his harsh edge, even though he is the giver of life. In each region there is a town called Beth Shemesh, House of the Sun. For before my people knew Adonai, the sun was their god." The sunlight through the willow plays a marvelous trick, as I am sitting in bright sunshine, and Vivi in shadow. "Even today in our sacred songs we sing of the sun. In the heavens he has pitched a tent for the sun, which is like a bridegroom coming forth from his pavilion, like a champion rejoicing to run his course!"

I pause for a few moments, but Vivi waits for me. The shade here by the water is so beautiful and refreshing. "Yet in the desert, in the summer sun, there is nothing more welcome than a small bit of shade."

Vivian leans down to the water with a piece of soft barley bread, and a fish rises from its cover in the reeds to nibble on the gift in the willow shade. She murmurs, "I cannot imagine a land that is not blessed by tides of nature. How can the land or the people rest if there is no winter? How can they learn how to die?"

"For my people," I reply, "the tides are those of history. We are not strangers to death. But for us it is the end of the journey, not part of a cycle. Some accept it with grace when it comes. Some fight it off until the end. But when it does come, it is the end of light, and the beginning of darkness. This is why I do not understand your words, the curse of those who follow the light. Light has always meant blessing to me."

"And darkness an ending? A place without blessings? Oh, Dear, Eos," she says, touching my cheek and leaving her hand there. "The problem is that men cannot seem to avoid the path that leads from seeking the light, to pursuing knowledge, to amassing power, to committing violence."

I am silent as her words sink in. Light, knowledge, power, violence. Then I ask, "But, Vivi, must it always be that way? You seek knowledge, too, do you not?"

"There is a great difference between seeking it out, hunting it, like a doe in the forest, and allowing the patterns to emerge by watching the currents as they flow. We know about the herbs of the meadows and marsh, but not because we have resorted to hunting them down or taking them apart. We watch the spirits, we listen to our grandmothers. So does knowing come to us, not always in the light, but as often in darkness, in twilight, at dawn." So it would be, I realize, for those who live by the cycles of the world.

"Eos," she says, "The heart of darkness is a place within. I do not always need the shade of willows. Come with me, dear one, to the top of Bol Forla."

She takes my hand, and we step into the clearing. The warmth of the summer sun envelops us like a mother's breath with a child. Overhead, high white clouds float in the blue sky. Insects buzz all around us. A startled marsh hen takes flight. I want to ask Vivi the names of all the wildflowers, but this is a moment meant only for each other. The rich awareness of her presence crowds out all else from my mind.

At the top of the hill there is a spreading whitethorn, past blooming, but not yet bearing the thousands of berries that will be her autumn crown. We have left sandals, and picnic basket, and staffs back at the walkway. Each barefoot step raises the heady scent of moss and loam. Vivi steps toward me and lifts my summer tunic over my head, dropping it to one side. She looks at me as I stand before her. I wish I were not so old, that my back were straighter, my body leaner. She steps back and removes her clothing, her eyes always fastened on mine. "Lie with me, dear one," she says.

At first I am concerned for her frailty. "We have brought no blanket, my love."

She sits on the ground and says, "Moss and mud on occasion make a fitting bed for marsh lovers." And she lies back, her white skin and black hair blending and contrasting with the olive green mosses and rich, dark earth of Morla's hill.

I step toward her and kneel at her side, my heart beating wildly, blood racing in my veins, driving my body to a response of passion I cannot believe. As I lean over her, the jubilant lust of youth overtakes me. For a moment I wish Vivi, too, were young, for I need to thrust strong and deep into her, know the animal rutting of abandonment to insatiable desire, and feel the wild response of her hips in reply. I feel my muscles tense for the plunge.

Then, out of the sunlight, beyond Vivi's shoulder there stands an old woman, ancient of days and gray of head, but kindly in appearance. Her look is gentle, but it has a power that stops me short and binds me to her voice.

It is a precious gift my granddaughter offers you, Eosaidh of Cornualle. Do not dishonour such a gift.

Thank you, Lady, I say in my heart, I give you my word, I will honour her. And with a nod of her head, the vision departs.

Rather than descending upon her like the hunting of a doe, I lie by Vivi's side, and turn her gently towards me. We cradle each other in our arms, feeling sun-warmed flesh, and tasting the sweetness of our love. It is not the satisfying of hunger that drives us, but the celebrating of life. The afternoon sun begins its journey toward the embrace of the sea. Shadows lengthen, and the spirits laugh with us, as, with the gentlest of caresses, we bring to each other a joy we had never hoped to see again in this world.

Chapter Thirteen
The Current

(Vivian)

I look up, my spirit rising through the water, breaking the surface and inhaling, just as Gwenlli's feet arrive at the door of my sanctuary. I hear her breathing, seeking out calm and courage, and I whisper to the ancestors to let her come in.

She moves the first of the hides, allowing the thinnest arrow of light to slip into the darkness. I close my eyes against its sharpness and breathe to still my heart, wondering what calamity would provoke the intrusion upon my rite. Yet I have spent long enough in its embrace to wait quietly for Gwenlli to come to my side.

What is it, dear child?

She bows in the darkness and puts her hand gently upon mine.

"My Lady, accept my presence. Morfrenna is here."

Here? I open my eyes.

"She says she must speak to you, my Lady."

I breathe deeply, gathering my spirit back into my body, until I find my tongue and am able to speak aloud to the child. "She is here?"

"Down by the red willow on the shore, my Lady. She was afraid to come further, but was desperate to find to you. She drew her boat close and made the call."

"I heard it," I whisper, "in my dreaming."

"She is waiting, my Lady. She has been crying."

I struggle, for a moment unable to find my legs, but the girl holds me with strength and care. Bent over beneath the low arching frame of the hut, she guides me to the door and pulls back the hides. The light scorches my soul and I recoil, murmuring in pain, but Gwenlli holds me still, giving me my staff, and settles a cloak around my shoulders allowing its hood to veil my eyes. There is a chill in the air that unnerves me, and as we make our way down to the shore, I see the sun light is golden on the water. It is evening. I have been in the darkness since nightfall yesterday.

Morfrenna rubs her nose on her sleeve, sniffing back tears, as she looks up and sees us drawing near. She bows in respect and bites her lip, and I call to her softly, seeing her fear, "It is harsh to draw an old seer from her visions, child, but I honour that your reasons demand such an act. Tell me what has brought you to my isle."

"My Lady, it's Eosaidh -"

My heart falls through my body, *No!* But Gwenlli quickly takes my hand in hers, saying, "He is not harmed, my Lady." She glances at Morfrenna, who urges her to tell the tale. "It is just that ... there is someone come to the island in search of him."

The shock lifts slowly and what takes its place is a blend of fear and rage.

Gwenlli steps away. She waits, as does Morfrenna, her boyish face wet with tears.

And I murmur, "Take me to him."

Instead of the marsh ways that would take us to the northside of the island and our community, Morfrenna takes the flat bottomed boat around to the west, bringing us into Bae Fyrtwydd, beside Dolgwyl Waun, where the slopes of the Bryn Fyrtwyddon rise before us. When she can, she jams her paddle into the mud, steadying the boat, and Gwenlli helps me to my feet. We step over the edge into the cold shallow water.

Walking along the lower slopes, the grass thick and long beneath our bare feet, I can feel how empty the island is.

The mist is gathering, but the skies are still clear, for the first time in many days. Every able hand, man, woman and child, is gone to the corn fields, from Pentreflyn and the other settlements around the lakes and through the marsh, and from my own community, too, a dozen women taking with them not only the strength of their bodies, but spells and caring.

And I wonder yet again how many druids now have broken their bond, that the gods are now forsaking their people.

Having drawn the boat onto the shore, Morfrenna runs to catch us up.

"Who is left on the island?" I ask her.

"Sianed has been calling the mist with a circle of the older women," she says, out of breath, "and Fia's with the younger children who didn't cross to the fields."

"You didn't go today?"

"My Lady," she shakes her head, "the waters have risen further over the past few days, flooding some of the summer grazing. I had to move the sheep to the higher ground of Bryn yr Afalau. A couple of ewes were looking lame."

I notice Gwenlli glance at her to tell her to be quiet and the girl looks down, catching her breath, striding beside us though we walk too slowly for her pace.

The fire outside Eos' roundhouse is lit, a flicker of flames beneath his rusty kettle, and I reach out my soul to see if I am mistaken, to check whether Eos is there, but everything I am tells me that my precious Iudde is with the others, sweating in the fields, bringing in what is left of the harvest before night falls and the rains come again.

The figure of a man comes out of his dwelling.

"It's him," Morfrenna snarls under her breath.

He sits himself on a log, facing the fire.

And I whisper a mist spell, its song repeated by the girls as we draw close, silent beneath its veil.

We are right beside him before I speak, breaking the spell.

"Who are you?" My words ride towards him on a current of rage.

He yelps, his drinking cup clattering over the firewood, and he turns, reaching for his blade. But before his fingers can close about the shaft, Morfrenna's short staff cracks upon his hand, and he is down, the heel of my own yew wood poised above his throat. I murmur to my goddess in the old marsh tongue, "Wake him to this dishonour!" and we step away.

His eyes are wild with shock and suspicion as he clasps at his hand in considerable pain. His thick black hair is cut short like a Roman and he wears the tunic of a traveller from over the southern sea, but as I reach into his soul I find no malevolence towards Eos. Sun-browned and strong, he is younger than Eos, his skin even darker. And on the ground before us, he dares not move. Though his eyes search my face in the gathering dusk and fire light, not a thought forms in his mind, his fear crafting enough strength but allowing nothing else.

Through all the gossip he has heard, he believes we are sorcerers.

Morfrenna murmurs in the old tongue, "His boots are Roman."

Catching the one word, Roman, he burbles in a language we do not speak, prodding his chest with his fingers and shaking his head.

Gwenlli breathes deeply and says softly, staring at the stranger, "He says he is not Roman."

I motion for him to get up, and he pushes himself back a little before getting to his feet. His eyes don't leave mine. So I form a thought and whisper it into his soul: *Be careful, outlander, for the spirits of this land will feed upon your soul.*

He looks away, his body rising in defence as he stares at the grass, and again he speaks, fast and harsh in his own foreign tongue. What the words mean does not matter, for what he is saying is evident, and it does not ease the sinking feeling within my soul. I call to my ancestors to support my focus, and breathe my goddess through the darkening air.

"Be quiet!" I say sharply in the common tongue. If he has spent any time in the Brythannic lands, he will know those words. He stops talking and looks at me, his head to one side, his eyes narrowed with distrust. And again I send a thought into his soul: *Listen to me, outlander. Did Eosaidh invite you to this place?*

He answers by taking another few steps back, picking up his cup and pointing at the ground beneath his feet, and with a few determined words in the common tongue, "I - stay - here - Eosaidh."

I lift my hand to stop him speaking, blowing a spell from my fingers to still his tongue. He rubs his mouth and glares at me. The darkness is rising too strongly within me, the deep rage of the goddess flooding through me, and I begin to whisper the mist spell, the girls joining the song, as we step away, the final thought let loose upon her current towards him: *You are not welcome here.*

Gwenlli pours from the great black kettle into the drinking bowls, taking out the largest leaves before placing one by my side and handing the other to Sianed. She looks into Gwenlli's face and says softly, "Thank you," bringing the bowl to her lips to sip the warm tea. Gwenlli bows and moves to leave the roundhouse. Our eyes meet before she disappears and she confirms my need with a nod, *My Lady.*

Sianed turns to me and for a moment there is nothing said.

Within the silence I watch to see if her thoughts will form and she waits, offering me the space to allow my own. It is a humbling moment for me. For although this is our way, without judgement, simply to hear, to observe, I am aware that I have done something that no Lady of this island has done before me. I have allowed a man to stay. And by doing so, I am crafting a tale never told before. I look down at the bowl of tea, but can find no strength to lift it.

"Sianed," I say softly, and look into her eyes. *If I speak aloud I will find words that are not purest in truth, words that express my strength and my position within this place.*

With the merest movement, she bows her head, closing her eyes in understanding, then meets my gaze once more. *All you speak is truth, for even in these words you are true. I am listening, my Lady.*

I breathe, feeling the summer's darkness around us, aware of our ancestors and the strength of this sacred community, yet also conscious of the loneliness. In my mind I see my mother's face, a quality of colour in her deep marsh-green eyes in the moon tides before she died, and I realize that strangely hollow colour was loneliness. I glance around the roundhouse, half expecting to see her, but there is nobody there, no spirits to guide me.

Into my memory slips a vision: myself as a young child, sitting on the summer grass in the tuition of old Margren, unable to find the answer to some problem she had laid on my lap. Her voice courses through the cycles to echo in my soul, *Thinking won't help you. Open your soul, child.*

I look up at Sianed, who watches me, patiently.

Did I do wrong to let him stay?

She knows it is not a question.

He came upon a current, my Lady.

Like a fallen branch washed into a marsh way, does he not break the reeds and widen the path for others to follow?

For a long while we are both silent. Thoughts move through me like isolated clouds in the indigo of the summer night sky. The harsh winds of the sand god I have seen so often in my visions. The fear and loathing in the eyes of the stranger, my staff at his throat. Lying in the thick grass, the sound of bees in the meadow flowers, and the strength of Eos' arms around me. The desperate desolation of the people waiting outside the council gathering, crying for help, escaping battles in the south, their children ragged with hunger, wide-eyed with the memories of bloody death. Then Fianna and the children with the first bread of the new harvest, the laughter and the sunshine. And the taste of his kiss.

Again I look into the bowl of tea, feeling my heart breaking.

My Lady, Sianed says softly without sound. *He has brought nourishment ... to us all. The children played with him, he taught them crafts we did not have in our community, they loved him. My Lady, in truth, he has taught us all. Your bond with him has taught us, each woman here learning of love simply by watching how you are with him.*

Her eyes are gentle with the words.

Sianed, I ...

The thought is too wide to find form.

Holding my gaze, she says, "My Lady, he has given you life."

The deliberate action of speaking those words aloud, letting them lift and linger in the smoke of the roundhouse, wakes me to their truth and their importance. She continues, her thoughts now moving from her soul to mine.

For that we are all grateful. For that, we each accepted him. For that, we have loved him.

"Oh Sianed," I whisper.

We honour your courage, my Lady.

I breathe deeply, feeling through the flood of loneliness the threads that connect me to my community, the strength that it brings me only intensifying the responsibility.

This current upon which he came is one I do not know how to ride, priestess. I have journeyed as far as I am able, seeking guidance through the stories of our ancestors. Yet I can find no time like this. This story is a new story, Sianed. I do not know how to ride it.

We don't expect you to know, my Lady.

Footsteps outside distract us. She smiles with the sadness and solemnity of our conversation and bows before rising to her feet and going to the door. I hear Gwenlli's voice, and Morfrenna, then Sianed turns to me with a tenderness in her eyes. I breathe and nod. She pulls back the hides. Eos bends low to enter, our eyes meet but for a moment, then guided by Sianed he moves around the fire to sit upon the fresh hay mats and hides. Gwenlli comes to my side asking if I need anything. I kiss her forehead, whispering, "No, child." She looks up, a little surprised. Perhaps it is an intimacy I seldom express. She bows and leaves, glancing at Sianed, who crouches by the fire, as she goes.

I close my eyes.

My Lady? Sianed murmurs.

I look at her, so aware of Eos' closeness and the weight of his emotion.

She speaks in the marsh tongue. "I too will leave you, but, please, my Lady ... perhaps the gods brought him upon this current to allow you the strength you need ... for all of us."

I gaze at her, letting the thought find its place within my soul.

She rises, bows, and leaves, careful to close the door behind her.

And slowly, all too aware of my heart pounding, I turn to Eos.

But he does not meet my gaze.

Dusk was already falling when we left his fire, so it would not have been long before he returned from the fields. Morfrenna, waiting at the forest edge by his dwelling, would have watched the way in which he greeted the stranger, then stepped forward to tell him that I was waiting. Here before me, his hair and clothing filled with barley chaff, the sweat and scent of his labour still upon him, I watch him as he tries to lay his thoughts into order, the distance cast between us like a noxious fire.

"Vivi," he says quietly. He looks up into my face, but my expression does not offer him courage and he looks down again into the fire's glow. "His name is Trophimus and he is come from Arelate in Gaul. He left Iudea with me all those years ago, after the lad died. We fled the Romans together. He brings news of them now. For weeks he's been evading Vespasian's patrols south of the marshes. It has been Trophimus who has been bringing news of their movements to Pentreflyn."

And again he looks up at me, his eyes pleading for my understanding. He knows how deeply I have feared the coming of such a problem and, that this is a beginning, fills him with as much anguish as it does me. He is about to move towards me but my face must still show too much dark rage, for, thinking better of it, he resumes his seat by the fire. He looks down once more, waiting for my words.

And I close my eyes, for the pain is almost beyond what I can bear. If this man has been brought to me to give me strength to face the violence to come, it is a strength I have yet to understand, for never have I felt so weakened by another human being. *Is this how you teach, my Lady,* I whisper into the night, *by breaking me apart, that I might find a new frame of bones with which to walk?* But again, there is no answer, no spirit to guide me.

"Vivi? My love,?"

What can I say to him?

"Vivi, he is an old friend."

But no words rise through me. When I turn my soul to the stranger at his dwelling, I am filled with rage. When I turn to this man I love, it is a desperate sorrow that floods my soul. And yet both flow from or to the bewildered horror I feel when I recall the sacrilegious dishonour of those who have sold their people to the eagle of Roma.

Again his words break the thick quiet of the air.

"Surely we are closer than this, you and I? Vivi, please?"

And I open my eyes.

He slams his fist upon the ground, "No, Vivian," and he shakes his head, crying out, "Don't look at me like that, Vivi! I have not betrayed you."

"Then he must go, Eosaidh."

"He is an old friend, Vivi. And he is no danger. At least not for the moment. He is badly frightened, and he has a broken wrist."

My eyes upon him mix a question into the anger, and he answers.

"Apparently one of your women is skilled with a short staff."

"Morfrenna," I breathe. "She was protecting me. He reached for his blade."

"He was frightened, Vivi. He fears this is an island of sorcerers."

"And is that not enough in itself for me send him from its shores? He must go!"

"He is hunted, my Lady. The Roman scouts are now seeking him out and they will find him in the village and crucify him as an example, to terrify your people."

"Then they will also seek him here."

"He is defenceless. Morfrenna has seen to it that he cannot even use his blade. You owe him your protection, at least until he heals."

"I owe nothing to one who brings hatred to my island."

"So where is he to go? !"

"Let him follow the trail to his ancestors."

He is silent, staring at me, then quietly he says, "You mean, let him die."

My eyes don't leave his, though my heart is bleeding. From all I have learned about the traditions of his people, I know that to die is for him to face an ending, a final journey with no expectation of rebirth or reunion. Yet I know too that Eos understands my words do not curse his companion with such an ending, only that I wish him the courage to leave my land and make his journey knowing he will live again.

"He is one man, Eosaidh. His presence heightens the threat to my people."

I do not know what I have said, but its effect is more crushing to Eos than I could have anticipated. He falls back against the wall of the roundhouse, lifting his hands to his head, half covering his eyes as if seeing some baneful vision. As I watch him, I question what I have just said. What else can I do? My heart longs for peace, but the need to protect my people drives me from any other course.

He looks up at me, his hands slipping away from his eyes.

"Vivi, I was on the great council when they debated the fate of the lad. In the middle of the night, when tempers flared and fear reigned in their hearts, the high priest ended their arguing with these words: *It is better for one man to die than that all the people should perish.* He meant to sacrifice the lad to the Romans in order to save his people. But now the lad is gone, and Rome still rules in Jerusalem."

"Oh Eos," I murmur, seeing his pain rise from its root. "How cruel is this day that has brought us to fighting."

"Vivi -" he whispers.

"You must know that this is ever what breaks my hope into worthlessness: that I too will give all I am ... and still they will come."

"Vivi," he rises, moving around the fire until, crouching before me, he takes my hands in his. "We cannot fight each other, my love. You must know that I am as filled with loathing and dread as you. We can do this together."

He leans forward to kiss me, but I lower my head and his lips touch my hair instead, the pain in my heart still awash through my soul. I tighten my clasp on his hands and feel him finding succour in our sudden return to closeness.

"Vivi," he says softly, "my love, in this hour we may truly learn about love, and perhaps honour as well. But we must do it together."

I close my eyes, "I am so tired, Eos."

How much more do I need to learn, my Lady, before you let me die?

A few times in the darkness, the fire a warm orange glow, I woke to find Gwenlli pulling hides back over me, whispering gently, "Sleep, my Lady, sleep." It was comforting to feel her curl up again beside me as I slid back into fitful dreams.

But now my waking leaves me unable to find a path into sleep. It is still and softly dark in the roundhouse, and Gwenlli herself is sleeping soundly. And for a while I listen to the night. An owl calls from the forest and its partner replies, the shuffle of a badger moving along its old track behind the dwelling, the mice taking their share of grain from a bag by the door. And, noiselessly, a spider crafts its web from the curve of the ceiling above me.

Sitting up, I gather my cloak around my shoulders, feeling the chill of the hours before dawn, and make my way out, onto the dew-wet grass, to breathe the scent of this ragged world. The first glimmers of light are creeping into the eastern skies, and I make a prayer of thanks and hope for another day of dry sunshine to allow for harvest.

Breathing deeply, I look up to the south west, to the hills that rise behind this ancient settlement, slopes that gather together beneath the trees into the curves of Bryn Ddraig and its high tor. In the sweet stillness, barely lit, it is hard to believe that beyond this sacred island there is such bitter war.

And then I see him. His grey-white beard just visible, he sits on the old stone wall at the edge of the clearing, watching me. Is he so deep in my heart that I can no longer tell the difference when he is close or far? In the silence, I walk towards him. And when our eyes meet the bond between us tightens around my heart. Without words, we fall into each others' arms, our souls coming together, two streams in the darkness of the night, listening to each others' breathing, breathing each others' breath, knowing that amidst the chaos of change, in this moment we have found precious certainty.

"Have you been here all night?" I murmur.

"I knew I would not sleep."

"Yet you held me, until sleep took me."

"I couldn't leave while you were weeping."

I look into his face, *I cannot lose you now, Eos.*

He gazes into my soul. "You are all I have, Vivi. You are all I have."

Chapter Fourteen
The Curse
(Eosaidh)

Please, my Lady. You must eat." It is Gwenlli calling from the fire before the roundhouse. We both look up, and she raises a bowl with something steaming in it. "Please come and eat, Lady," she repeats, "and let me help you refresh yourself."

Vivi's eyes turn back to mine, and she holds me more closely. The last thing either of us wishes to do at this moment is to let go.

"It would be a good idea, my love," I say. "And I must go and look in on Trophimus, if indeed he is still here. He will be beside himself by now, having spent the night alone."

Together we walk over to Gwenlli, who hands Vivian a bowl of barley porridge She takes it reluctantly, knowing the immense strength she must maintain for the day ahead. I kiss her gently. "I will return as soon as I can, Vivi, with what news he brings." I start to move away, but she holds me for another kiss. I laugh with joy.

"Some things may be beyond my control right now, tinner," she says, "but I can hold this moment a little longer with a kiss."

Gwenlli clears her throat with a mixture of authority and delight, and with a sigh, Vivian looks into the bowl, lifting the spoon, murmuring complaints in the marsh tongue that cause Gwen to chuckle. We exchange a smile, set with courage, and I set out across the island, for my first real reunion with Trophimus.

The trackway past the tor takes me to the Red Spring, and I pause for a few moments at the wellhead, where the healing waters bubble out from the earth and begin their journey to the marsh. Somewhere below, the shards of blue glass hold the memory of the lad's life blood.

Adonai, if you can hear me from your throne in Jerusalem, honour the memory of the lad, who loved this land so well. He spoke so often of how mercy is more precious than judgment. Show us mercy now, Adonai, that we may be merciful one to another.

But there is only silence. In these days Adonai no longer seems to speak out loud. Only the sound of the wellhead, and the stream, and the ravens in the yew branches above. Can these be the words of Adonai? Vivi hears them, I think, as the voice of the Goddess. Is it possible for the Goddess and Adonai to speak one language? I imagine the lad might have believed so, but I cannot see how. They are as different as night and day, darkness and light. But I cannot believe Vivi and I are as different as that. I will not believe it. What good are gods who will not honour the love their children hold for one another?

Looking into the waters of the well that now forever holds the cup, I let my mind drift, unable any longer to frame logical arguments for divine wisdom. It is dark in the morning shadows of the towering yews. One shaft of sunlight pierces the gloom, diving into the well waters. Far away, at the bottom of the shaft, there is a glint of blue. With that sign as a kernel of hope, I rise and head down the hill.

Trophimus is waiting for me when I arrive at the hut, a fire started out front, and a newly caught hare spitted and turning over the flames. I utter an oath under my breath, casting a glance to heaven to see if Adonai is watching over this comedy at all.

"Trophimus! Glad to see you survived the night!" I bellow in Greek, striding over to the fire.

"Eos, I . . ." he starts to greet me, then is struck dumb, for without further comment, I lift the poor hare, spit and all, from the fire, and lay him on the ground a few yards away. I stop and look at the half roasted carcass for a moment, and say a reflexive prayer for the creature's safe journey to the otherworld. I admit I have surprised myself as much as I have puzzled Trophimus.

I turn to him, his jaw dropped open, and say, "You can bury him later, after we've talked." Then, thinking better of it, I spread some loose soil over the remains. I have enough trouble without the scent of roasted meat wafting over the island!

Offering a hand in greeting, I explain. "Good friend, there is no eating of flesh here," and I show him where to find the barley bread and fruit.

"Let me see that wrist," I say. He winces as I take his hand in mine. The right wrist is swollen larger than his forearm, sporting a magnificent blend of purple, blue and black. "Does that hurt?" I ask, holding his wrist between my thumb and forefinger.

"Ouch! Yes, damn it!" he shouts, jerking his arm away so quickly it only increases his pain. "That young sorceress wields a nasty staff."

"Sit down, friend," I say, pointing to the rock so often used by Vivi. I wonder for a moment whether he will be able to sense that. No, I think not. "Let's get some things straight. If you're going to eat here, you'll have to forget about meat. If you're going to stay here for any time, you'll have to forget about sorcerers."

He grunts and sits down.

With a slab from the woodpile and some cloth from the hut I make the best splint I can. The wrist will heal or not, as it will, but immobilizing it will at least ease the pain in the process.

"Trophimus, my friend, it's been a long, long time. How are you?" The next two hours are spent in the boisterous reunion of old friends, while we share the barley bread, a jug of goat's milk, and some of my remaining store of hazel nuts.

The Magdalene and Sarah are well, living in Aix upriver from Massalia, with Miximin and Sidonius. Martial is in Limoges. Eutropius and Cleon have passed to the next world. Lazarus, the lad's good friend, is overseer of the ecclesia in Massalia. That is strange. Overseer? Ecclesia? I do not understand what he is saying, and make a mental note to ask about it further, as he moves quickly into news of the Romans.

"Vespasian has taken the Second Augusta Legion as far as Bodmin Moor," he says. This I knew from the lakemen, who knew, as it turns out, from Trophimus. "He deems the rest of Cornualle not worth the effort." I sigh with relief, thinking of my family at Carn Euny. Perhaps they would be spared the worst. "The lead and silver of the Mendydd are a greater prize," he continues, scowling at the barley bread he chews, and casting a glance in the direction of the buried hare. "He expects little resistance there and is sending only token forces. Some are now camped at the western end of Polden Ridge, with boats waiting to take them across the water. Others are gathering on the highlands to the northeast. They will come at the mines from both directions, meet in the middle, and take it all." He looks out at the marsh, from which a gentle morning mist is slowly dissipating. "Adonai be blessed for these mists and marshes," he says. "A man could hide from the Romans here for ever."

Not for ever, Trophimus, I think. And perhaps you should be thanking someone other than Adonai.

Out of respect for my friend's wrist, I take the hare to the edge of the woods, dig a hole, and bury it. Trophimus wanders down to the water, kneeling to splash some on his face. When I am through I join him there, and we walk together along the edge of the marsh, the north face of Wirrheal on our left.

"You did not come all this way to warn me about the Romans, Trophimus."

"Well, to be honest I truly expected to be here before them," he says, "and my news would have been more helpful. But no, there is another reason. Claudius is exercising his imperial muscles in Rome as well as here. He is making louder and louder noises about his displeasure with the Iuddic community in Rome. We expect he will move to expel them at any time, and we fear that will effect the ecclesia as well, and those of us who follow the Way in Gaul, at Massalia and Arelate. The Empire may soon become a dangerous place for us, Eosaidh."

The strange words again. "Trophimus, you confuse me. What do you mean by 'ecclesia'? That means a congregation of people, no? And what is the 'Way'?

We arrive at Dolgwyl Waun, the festival meadow. A herd of deer, lingering at their own breakfast, look up at us and slowly move away to the west end. *O Trophimus, I chuckle to myself, what you might think of the celebrations I have seen here!* He drinks in the pastoral scene like a man whose eyes have not seen peace for a long time.

"I forget that you have been living here on the edge of the world for twelve years," he says. "Much has been happening among followers of Iesu around the Mare Medterraneus."

"Followers? The lad had only a few followers. Most of them are doubtless dead and those who remain, like you and I, are scattered."

"You really don't know, do you?" He replies. "Eosaidh, he is more than just your nephew, now. He is the Christus, the Chosen One of Adonai, the one come to save us from sin. All across the Empire thousands are flocking to him. In Antioch they have even given us a name. 'Christians,' they are calling us, Little Christs, to mock us. But we are beginning to wear the name proudly. It is a new movement, Eosaidh, and we call it the Way."

A late summer thundercloud covers the sun, and darkness spreads across Dolgwyl Waun. The deer have disappeared into the woods. There is a long, deep silence before I speak.

"Vivian is right, Trophimus. You cannot stay here."

It is the hardest thing I have ever done, and it strains our old friendship to near breaking. But in the end Trophimus says he understands, and agrees to my terms. He will stay with me in my hut while his wrist heals, but he will have no contact with the community. When he is able to handle a paddle and a blade again, he will return to Pentreflyn where he has made friends. He will still be safe from the Romans there, and he can send news of their movements to us here. He is genuinely dismayed at my refusal to turn the lad into some kind of god.

"Dear friend," he says, a gentle hand on my shoulders. "You were so close to him. You cared so deeply for those of us who followed him. What has happened to you here at the end of the world?" He pauses, then takes the risk he should not: "Have these witches cast a spell on you?" His accomplishment is to enable me to feel the rage Vivi feels, to help me understand her even more.

"Stay to this end of the island,' I say coldly. "Go no further inland than my hut, and meet me there at sundown." I turn on my heels and leave him speechless in the middle of Dolgwyl Waun, where the circle of maidens once danced and twirled in celebration of life.

When I return to Vivian it is mid-afternoon. Gwenlli sits at the door of her hut, mending a tunic. She looks up and smiles at me. "She is finally resting, Eosaidh," she says. "But she asked that you go in to her when you returned."

I step into the cool darkness and see her form on the hay and hides, wrapped in a light wool shawl. For long moments I stand watching her, listening to her breathing. She is a woman of contrasts, of mud and faerie, of weakness and power, of age and agelessness. And she is no sorceress. Or if she is, then there is another meaning to the word that the world must learn, for there is a blessedness in her spirit. And I am deeply and truly in love with her. I kneel beside her, and reach out to touch her shoulder. "Vivi, my love," I breathe gently. It takes her a moment to respond, but she sighs, stretches her body like a cat, turns and smiles at me.

"My dear Eos." She pulls herself up, and I can see her wince with the pain of limbs that have stiffened in sleep. She pauses, closes her eyes, murmurs a prayer, then whispers, "Help me up?" I help her to sit, and offer a drinking bowl of water from which she takes a sip. Then looking into my eyes, she says, "So tell me of your friend." But before I can speak, she smiles, "In Pentreflyn they call him Llygethin. Does he know that?"

I join her laughter. "Well the 'swarthy' part is true enough!" Then my face turns serious. "The 'shrew' part I would have debated, until today." I fill her in on my conversation with Trophimus, watching her face cloud as I tell her of this movement called the Way. "But he has agreed he will not remain," I conclude. "Apparently they are willing enough at Pentreflyn to let him stay there. He can help them and us keep track of Vespasian. Vivi, he is an old friend, but I am angered at him and fearful of the news he brings."

She touches my face with a hand, smoothing the tangles of my beard with the softness and certainty of her love. "My dearest Eos." And in her voice there is empathy and sorrow, enough to help me to feel she understands the confusion in my soul.

"When I came here I was fleeing from the Romans, even as Trophimus is now. But I have been here for nearly six cycles of the moon. And it has been more than ten years since I left my companions at Massalia. Vivi, it is more than Romans I have left behind. I no longer know my old friends, and now they have more in common with strangers than with me." I place the palm of my hand on her cheek and try to offer a smile. "But what I have left behind, my Love, does not compare to what I have found."

"Are we living in a dream, Eos? Sometimes when we are together I feel every spirit of the land carries our love in its song; it rides upon the wings of the skylarks, and I feel so young and filled with life. It shimmers in the moonlight on the water, and I feel there is nothing more important in all the many worlds, and that is such a precious gift of perfect serenity. Yet ..."

My hand continues to trace the lines of her face, the gentle wrinkles about her eyes, the lines of smiles and frowns about her mouth, the smoothness of her cheek. She stops for a moment to feel my touch. I lean to kiss her forehead, and then her lips. She returns my kiss with tenderness, taking my hand in hers as she continues.

"Yet I know too that our love is in the leaves of the trees, that play in the wind though they are now heavy with the cycle's passing, and in a moontide they will be flushed with russet and gold, waiting for the moment to let go, to breathe out into the dance, that most beautiful dance, that takes them to the waiting forest floor."

She fears what has come upon us, and I have no doubt she understands the meaning of it more than I. She sees the turning cycles in our love, an autumn that approaches so soon after springtime. I cannot accept this vision, cannot share in it, at least not yet. For the first time I see the strands of silver in her long, black hair. A betrayal of age, or of worry, I cannot tell. She brings my hand to her lips, then studies the lines and weathered roughness of my skin, and sighs, "It seems strange that I have not seen the leaves fall with you, not in this life."

I nuzzle my cheek against hers. "We shall grow old together, my love," I say. "We shall watch the leaves turn and fall."

"Oh Eos, my dear tinner!" There is a teardrop in the corner of her eye. "I fear there are cycles that turn sooner than that."

I kiss the tear away, but her trouble is deeper than a tear. "Vivi, dearest. What is it, Vivi?"

Before she can answer, Morfrenna's face appears in the doorway. "Pardon, my Lady, but the news is urgent!"

She looks up, and the moment is over. "Come, daughter."

Clearly agitated, Morfrenna steps towards her and whispers something in her ear. Vivian grows suddenly cold. She turns to me with the look of ice and fire in her eyes. Suddenly we are apart.

"You must return to your roundhouse at once, Eosaidh of Cornualle," she says. "A boat with four men has been seen at Bae Fyrtwydd." It is a wrenching end to a moment of closeness.

She allows my kiss on her cheek in spite of her anger.

I turn quickly, and leave her.

As I emerge from the woods above my hut I see them. A boat is pulled up on the shore, and Trophimus is speaking with four strangers, from one of the Gaulish tribes, by the look of them. He turns to me as I approach. A late afternoon mist is emerging from the marsh, beginning to ring the clearing.

"Everything has changed, Eosaidh," he says. "I had expected to find these Brothers already here, but they were delayed by the Romans even more than I." He turns to them to indicate each in turn: "Casticus, Sedullus, Valetiacus, and Orgetorix, of the Ecclesia of Lazarus in Massalia." I greet each by the hand, but cannot help noticing they look upon me with worried eyes. "They have been weeks on the road," Trophimus says, and they have brought us this."

He hands me a parchment scroll. The cry of a red kite swooping over Wirrheal splits the air as I unroll it, my eyes searching each of the five men. It is freshly written, in the long hand of the local common tongue. I read it out loud, my voice becoming increasing tense, my body shaking:

To Philippus, Apostle of Gaul, and to the Ecclesia of the Household of Lazarus in Massalia,

Greeting.

In recognition of the danger to your community that arises from the threat made by Claudius Caesar against the Iuddic peoples and the People of the Way in Massalia, and in recognition of our brotherhood with those Gauls among you who have become part of your community, I do hereby grant to one Trophimus and his companions, together with

Eosaidh of Cornualle, the ownership of twelve hides of land on Ynys y Niwl, to establish themselves in community thereupon, for the worship of Iesu mab De, the new god of the people of the east.

Added in Greek, in Trophimus' hand,

Attested this 14th day of Aprilis, in the second year of the Emperor Claudius.

And in a bold hand at the bottom,

Arviragus derwyddon,
King of the Britons

"We are not going anywhere," Trophimus says. "We own this very field. We are staying."

In shock, I drop the scroll to the ground. Trophimus hastily retrieves it, and returns it to its leather case.

"But this is not possible!" I say. "Who is this druid, Arviragus?"

"He is cousin to Caradoc," answers Sedullus, "Who himself faced Claudius' elephants on the plains before Lughdunum."

"Caradoc was defeated," I reply.

"Yes, but he now plans with the Silures to stand against Vespasian here in the west. His cousin, Arviragus, has taken civil command of all this area."

I stare at this newcomer with a mixture of rage and disbelief. "Whatever this cousin of Caradoc claims to be, he has no authority on Ynys y Niwl, and certainly no right to give it away. What did you say your name was?"

"Sedullus," he answers, "Diakonos of the Eclessia of Iesu Christos!"

"Liar!" I shout. "You claim to be the servant of the one man in all this wide world who would never be served! I was with him, were you? *I have come not to be served,* he said, *but to serve others.* And he gave his life for that. Do not betray him by claiming to be his servant!"

Fuming with anger, every muscle in my body tensed to attack, I storm up the hill to my hut, throw aside the door hides, and enter the welcome darkness. I bring my hands to my head, let out a scream of anger, and the room spins about me. In my mind I see the lad again, standing with me on the Mendydd hilltop, as he pointed across the waters to the tor rising in the distance. *Tomorrow, Uncle Eos,* he said, *let's take the boat out to that island. I want to see that strange hill that reaches to the heavens.* Oh, lad! I miss you now more than ever! How would you handle this? What would you say to a boatload of men from Gaul who proclaim you Chosen of God, and in the name of some druid cousin of a warrior claim ownership on this holy isle?

Trophimus steps into the hut and finds me pacing the floor. "Dear friend," he says gently, "do not turn from us. In these past thirteen years those of us who follow your 'lad' have come to understand him not only as Adonai's Chosen, but as his Divine Son, who brings light to the world. We have come to bring the light of life to this dark land."

No! I cannot be hearing this!

I storm out of the hut with Trophimus at my heals. The others are huddled around the fire pit in the gathering chill of the evening. Clearly this is not going as they had expected. The mists have fully engulfed the clearing before the hut so I can barely see the marsh before me, or the trees behind me. In the center, the fire pit glows with a pale light.

Strange how the mists can come so quickly. My mind is reeling.

"Vivi!" I cry out, "Vivi, where are you? I need you!"

The Gauls turn to look at me, but almost immediately their attention is taken from my desperate cry to the strangeness of the mist. Trophimus begins to explain the great value of such a place, which is hidden so well within such regular dense mist, when an eerie chanting stops his words. We are quiet, listening. Sedullus jumps up, saying, "There is someone here,

I saw a shade in the mist." And I have a feeling in my belly which turns my blood cold while at the same time fills me with exhilaration: we are being encircled.

The screech of a raven draws my eyes upwards, but the mist is now as thick above us as it is all around.

Then lightning splits the air, a crash of thunder followed by another crack of light, and in the sudden storm the mist flashes and swirls like a whirlwind, and before us it rises up into the air and vanishes. And there stands Vivian, Lady of Affalon, holding her yew staff aloft, her voice raised in the song of the storm, showing not the slightest sign of frailty. The four Gauls fall to the ground, Trophimus cowers in the hood of his robe. Even I take a few steps backward.

Then comes the fire, as if set ablaze by lightning , flaring up in the fire pit in a great column of intense heat and light, and I realize she is now singing to the spirit of the fire. But the heat is extraordinary, and the smell of burning is venomous, what did the women put on the fire? As it blazes higher, each of us tries to move away from it, but suddenly it is out of the pit and chasing itself around the circle they have cast, so that all six of us are imprisoned within a circle of flames. My heart is racing but I reach for her, hearing her words now, recognizing the marsh word as she calls to the sun, her voice like a blade of light cutting into the darkness, and the sinking sun glares upon me, reflecting off the water blinding me, fire and sun and smoke, and the acrid smell of this baneful herb, the fire growing in such heat, I am coughing, choking, disoriented, as I watch the other men fall to the ground.

I am losing a sense of what is happening.

A voice of power and anger surrounds us, coming from everywhere, and nowhere. In my swoon I cannot tell if it is Vivian, it seems too large for her. *Do you seek the light? Do you wish for light? I have given you light! You wanted light, and now you are cursed with light until it burns your nostrils and you are sick with it! It is light you wanted, and it is light you have!*

Trophimus and the others are in shock, eyes wide and glazed over while the poison of the fumes does its work, stinging eyes and nose, and mouth. I feel a horrid retching in my stomach, and vomit out the little I have eaten today. By the sounds I hear through the roar of the flames, the others are doing the same. That I know this is the practical magic of Vivian, and have seen the circle of oil-soaked hemp rope before, recognize the sight of the greasy, almost solid flames, and the effect of the burning herbs, does not diminish how well it works on me. I can only guess at the horror in the hearts of the others. As the flames begin to die down, the smoke rises with greater vengeance, burning, suffocating, intoxicating with a mindless drunkenness.

Then the fire is gone, even the fire in my cooking pit, the fire of my hearth, is no longer burning. The punishing smoke is slowly lifting, drifting away above the treetops. The sun is beneath the trees, and dusk is near. Vivian, too, is gone. It is silent.

Slowly, painfully, I rise up to sit and look around. The others still lie where they have fallen. Among them I hear moans of fear and distress, but they also begin to stir.

Then I see a girl, right before me. My head still spins from the burning herb, dizzy, reeling, unclear. She stands firm on the earth, but drifts in the uncertainty of my blurred vision. I cannot recognize her. She looks like Vivi, but fifteen years old. Born the year the lad himself was killed. She has the palest white skin and long black hair. Her marsh green eyes penetrate to the soul. Nobody else is in sight.

"Eosaidh of Cornualle," she says, her voice the voice of a young girl, so beautiful, so precious, so soft and innocent. I hear each word she says as if she speaks directly to my heart. She speaks in the common tongue, to me alone, knowing that only I within this circle will understand.

"What will grow of the seedlings planted this day by your people upon this ancient sacred land, has already grown, and is already wilting, and dying, for these seedlings of another land will never drink of the ancient sacred waters of this land. These waters will never quench your thirst."

"Vivian?" I whisper, "Is it you?"

But she continues. "This land has sung the songs of my people throughout all time. Your song has no music here, for the creatures of this land do not sing with you. Yours is but one passing shout, raised in the anger of fear."

She then utters words in an old marsh tongue I do not understand, but when she speaks again it is in the common language, translating for me.

"It is the breath of my people you breathe. It chokes you. It always will."

And when she has finished speaking, quietly, she ceases to be before us. It is not that she leaves. She is simply no longer there.

She looked deeply into my eyes as she spoke.

It must have been Vivian. Or a daughter of hers, but I know of no daughter. Right now I know nothing. My mind is bleary with the drug. In rage and fear the others demand that I tell them her words, and a part of me is surprised that they too have seen the child. And I translate for them, finding each word has been carved into my soul. Once I have told them, not one of them responds. They simply sink to the ground.

The mist is coming down again as darkness begins to fall. Silence too falls again except when we are retching, or choking, bent double, lying on the ground.

How long did this last? Long, apparently, for the drug is strong. The last bronze glow of the sun has disappeared in the west, darkness has surrounded us, we have no fire. My head is pounding with the poison. My mouth is so dry, I am so thirsty - a part of the curse, I know. Vaguely I see one of the Gauls at the water's edge, drinking, but the water comes straight back up. I realize the herbs must be emetic, and will not allow any of us to drink or eat for some time to come.

Oh Vivi, my love! Why have you forsaken me?

Then the rains come. Too weak to rise, to travel the distance to the hut, we all of us instinctively crawl towards the fire pit, though there is no fire. It is dark, and cold, and we are soon soaked through, our light clothing no shelter from the storm. The pain in my head grows worse, and a deep wracking cough rises up from within my chest. Lying there in the rain as consciousness ebbs, I feel the ground rise up under me, spinning me into the unknown, beyond any consciousness, into the dark.

Chapter Fifteen
The Choosing
(Vivian)

My Lady."

Her voice is gentle. It touches my heart and, as I turn to her, looking into her face with its youthful glow, its wakeful sincerity, I feel a depth of affection I was not aware had grown within me. It is Eos, I realize: just as he has taught me again how to love, how to open my heart and care deeply for another human being, so has my heart opened to this young woman, now seventeen summer's old.

She looks into my face and I sigh, "I cannot stop weeping, Gwenlli."

She nods, tender acknowledgement.

"They have found him, my Lady. Morfren and Fia are bringing him now."

I turn back to the black water of the pool as she takes a few steps away, and with a deep breath I slip again into the spirit, breathing the water into my soul, feeling its life glowing within me, calling my prayer of thanks. And as I rise, Gwenlli is beside me again, taking my arm, handing me my staff.

After a night of torrential rain, the settlement is humming. For these past few days, with everyone away at the harvest, it has been so quiet, so empty here. After a sleepless night during which the confrontation seemed to fill my soul, it is strangely surprising to feel the community still alive. Walking into the clearing, I can feel the tension, the waiting, and a few faces turn to me expressing their apprehension. Yet even so, the women are busy with their normal tasks. Bronwen herds her scattering group of little children, a flurry of laughter provoking faces to turn and watch, to breathe in the blessings of innocence. The hens move around our feet, unawares.

Sianed is waiting for me in the roundhouse, attending to the fire.

She looks up and nods, *My Lady.*

"When they arrive, shall we bring him in here?" Gwenlli asks softly.

It is Sianed who answers, "Yes, child."

She nods, seeing I am comfortable, and leaves us.

Sianed sits close and for a moment we are silent, hands touching hands, the old prayers moving through us, the roots of our people securing our bond. When I open my eyes, she is gazing into my soul.

I stand by what I said, my Lady. He came to us on a current that we cannot alter.

But, priestess, what he now brings ... The words have no form within me.

You went to the Pool. What did you see, my Lady?

I look down into the fire, then back into her eyes, for to find words for the vision is beyond my strength of will. *Find it within me, priestess,* and opening my soul to her further, I allow the vision to fill me.

She gasps, suddenly breathless with rage.

She sits back on the hides, covering her eyes, then looks at me, saying into sound, "Who betrayed us? Which one of them betrayed us?"

"One of the council must have been involved, and my soul speaks of Myrledd, but it was not him whom I saw in the vision. I don't recognize the face of the druid. He claims and wields considerable power - I am sure we would know his name. But it is a power of men, not of gods."

But the men who have come: they are Iuddic, like Eosaidh?

Yes, they are of the same people.

But Eosaidh is hunted by Roma. These men have allied with the enemy of their people?

I nod, *But I don't believe Eosaidh knows that. What he does know and does not like is that they are crafting the course of a new stream within his people's tradition.*

She sighs, gazing into the darkness to find understanding.

"Teach me, my Lady."

"When Eos was here last, do you remember?"

"I was a girl," she murmurs, "younger than Bronwen. But I recall clearly he brought with him a very beautiful young man," and she laughs softly at her memories, gazing through her sadness. "We all fell in love with him."

I too smile sadly, "He grew up, that young lad, to be a powerful seer, a teacher, a priest to his people, to the Iudde, not in Brythannic lands but on the other side of the world, in the old lands of the Iudde, where Roma has been in power for many generations."

"You have not spoken of this, my Lady."

"At the time, it was important." Our eyes meet, *You were too young to know.*

Did he craft this new stream, that young seer?

I gaze into the fire, shaking my head barely perceptibly. "He was killed by a Roman chief, fifteen cycles ago."

"My Lady, I don't understand how the death of a seer, across the other side of the world, has the power to influence the currents of our people."

"No, Sianed, neither do I." My heart sinks, "But, it seems, two things have happened to make it possible. First, some of his followers have declared the lad to be a god."

She frowns, disbelieving. "I have heard saphers speak of such things."

"Yes, it is a disease of the sun, I believe."

She stands, gathering wood from the back of the roundhouse, and placing another log onto the fire. "Wasn't there a chieftain of the Rigatones who declared himself a god?"

I half smile, "He was alive when my grandmother was Lady of this isle. His people killed him before he could live the day through. They crafted a tribal gathering house of stone, and set his head upside down into the wall that he might ever look over the discussions of his people, seeing their bickering, pissing and feasting, knowing that no man could ever be a god."

"It seems a strange notion," she shakes her head. And for a while we are silent, currents of time moving through us, the fire dancing in the half light of the dwelling. Then again, she shakes her head, "No, I cannot understand it. What would be the purpose?"

"Perhaps," I murmur, "it is a way of creating a perfect person."

"A living man is still flawed and mortal. If he were to claim he were a god, he would need absolute power and distance to retain the glamour, allowing nobody close, holding each soul in fear. But if he were dead ..."

"If he were dead," I sigh, "and you told the tale of his life to those who never knew him, it wouldn't matter how truthful you were. You could deceive very many. For people are ever willing to honour a hero."

Our eyes meet.

And a dead hero who is said to have power over the living gives the teller that power over those who hear the tale.

Yes, priestess.

Again we sit in silence.

"You said two things had happened, my Lady, two things that brought the Iuddic seer's death to our lands. What is the other?"

There is noise outside, women's voices, footsteps running.

"The other is Eos."

Gwenlli lifts the inner door hide, "My Lady, can we bring him in?"

I close my eyes, my heart suddenly pounding, but again Sianed answers for me.

How they lifted him, I do not know, for he is barely able to walk. Between Fianna and Morfrenna, his weight is brought over the mats and lowered onto the hay and hides. He coughs repeatedly, his mouth chapped and open, his body wheezing for breath. His face is deathly pale and the fire of a fever glistens on his skin, clinging in his robes already drenched by the night's pouring rain.

Morfrenna wants to tell the tale, but Gwenlli whispers that she must go. Fianna follows, and Sianed looks into my eyes. "Let us make no decisions, my Lady. Not while he is sickening." She gets to her feet, and whispers a prayer to the goddess of the land, a blessing of healing. "We shall hold the mist fast until he improves."

Thank you, priestess.

As she leaves, Seren arrives, the old woman looking into my soul.

I wish to be alone with him, Seren.

Too bad, Lady. He needs my healing first.

I concede and sit back to watch, holding back the flood of emotion, as the herbwise settles on the floor beside him and, with Gwenlli's help, carefully empties spoonfuls of a thick white brew into his mouth. Delirious with the fever and the poisons in his blood, he pushes them away and Gwenlli murmurs a song of comforting, and great tears well up in his eyes and slide down his cheeks. And a part of me wishes I could kill him, tearing him to pieces in my rage, yet longs too to kill myself, that we might journey home together, released into endless peace.

Pulling another hide over his trembling body, Gwenlli murmurs to Seren, then reaches for more wood to put on the fire. It is a warm day, though damp still with the night's rain, but the herbwise will build his fever now, needing his own soul fire to fight it. When I close my eyes to be beside him, to touch his song, the world spins and blurs, and the vague images of men fighting fill the dwelling, and my heart breaks to know such visions are moving through his soul. And when the flames rise, bringing light, he cries out, shielding his eyes, and Gwenlli looks into mine.

When at last the herbwise is done, she staggers to her feet and says simply, *Let him rest.* She bows in her abrupt way and leaves, murmuring to Gwenlli, "I'll be back when the sun is high."

"Yes, priestess," Gwenlli replies, saying to me when we are alone, "Would you have me leave you now, my Lady?"

I nod, unable to bring a word into sound, and as she walks through the door, my heart breaks like a crashing wave, the entirety of my life flooding out from the depths of my soul in a grief that is more than my body can bear.

The day passes, Seren and Gwenlli coming and going. Seren feeds him the white brew, Gwenlli refreshing the strips of cloth that I am laying on his forehead, encouraging me to drink water, to rest, watching my exhaustion grow, watching Eos' body begin to settle.

By sunset, he is no longer shaking, the fever receding, and upon Seren's instruction I am guiding him to sip spoonfuls of water, and slowly his soul gathers back into his body. I am lying beside him, my head upon his shoulder, when he whispers to me, "Vivi?"

I sit up, "My love, Eos," smoothing his beard, my fingertips stroking the tears from beneath his eyes, "Oh my love." And such joy fills me to feel him return. I kiss away the tears that now flow from his eyes, his body shaking as he weeps with relief and confusion.

"I couldn't find you, Vivi," he whispers.

"I know, my love," I sob softly, " I am so sorry."

"I thought I had lost you."

As night draws in he seems to get stronger, and so comes the rain again, pouring down on the island, bringing a covering of enforced stillness. He sleeps deeply for long periods, allowing me to rest curled beside him on the hides. During one such time, Morefrenna slips in and we share the tea she has brought with her as she gives me news of the strangers.

"By the time we found Eos he was alone in the rain, lying in the mud before the cold fire pit. The others had already found their way inside his hut. Perhaps because they are younger and stronger, they fought off the bane more easily than Eosaidh." She looks down at where he lies beside me, and smiles with a sadness, barely able to understand.

They are stronger with years, my love, I whisper to his soul, *not weakened by the pain of a broken heart.*

She looks up, sniffing away the emotion that touches her, emotion she can not yet feel in her young soul. "I looked in on them again just a while ago, my Lady. They are weak and sick, their bodies aching for water, and very likely confused and angry, but they are still there, and they are sleeping."

When I can no longer sleep, I sit beside him and softly sing, ancient songs sung to me by my ancestors, songs of the moon and of the waters, my soul moving upon the currents of the songs with my eyes closed, lifting him with me, telling him in the old tongue of my life and my people, of my land, as he sleeps.

It is in the depth of the night, as I sing to him gently, that he wakes. As a song comes to its end, I open my eyes and see he is gazing into my face, in the faint and flickering light of the fire.

"Don't stop," he whispers.

In the darkness we are held, blessed by my goddess, and again I sing, softly lulling him back into rest, finding another moment of strength in the prayer.

At dawn, Gwenlli creeps in.

"Have you slept, my Lady?"

A little, I murmur, lifting my head from his chest.

She refreshes the fire, sending a flurry of smoke into the roundhouse and he coughs, waking, and I kiss his lips, no longer concerned that someone see this expression of love. And he smiles, for the first time in so very long.

Then for a while we are overwhelmed, for Seren enters to check on him, gruff and impatient, and Gwenlli lifts me to my legs, insisting I walk and accept her help of refreshment. Outside in the clearing, in the damp softness of another early morning of late summer, a cauldron is steaming over the central fire and women are emerging from dwellings, stretching, quietly murmuring greetings, breathing the sweet air.

Allowed to return inside, albeit with a bowl of porridge, I see Seren is leaving Eos' side. She looks into my eyes, *Don't tire him out!* And at the door, she turns, adding aloud, "He might eat some of that porridge, for you surely won't."

Don't pester me, herbwise! I snarl.

She mutters in the old tongue and I turn to Eos, smiling, exhausted and reprimanded, and he smiles back with tenderness. He is sitting up against the hay pillows and stretches his arms towards me, "Come here, my love."

"Shall we try and eat this mush," I say softly.

"Vivi," he breathes deeply, "how are they?"

"The strangers?"

He speaks slowly, thoughtfully, his voice husky from the sickness. "Trophimus was an old friend, Vivi. We shared many joys and dangers together, a long time ago. But it seems we have grown apart over these last years. I no longer understand him."

"Eat, my love." He accepts the spoonful of porridge I offer, swallowing with difficulty.

"Your kiss is more nourishing."

"Another spoonful," I whisper.

"As for the others, they are Gauls from Massalia. Gentiles. I have never met them. Apparently this new movement they call the Way embraces Iudde and Gentile alike. But, Vivi, I feel some responsibility for them. How are they?"

"And what is a Gentile?"

He starts to explain, but his returning strength and our nearness entice him to playfulness. He kisses me, "You are, dearest!" But my face must reveal my concern. Gently, I whisper, and he sighs, conceding. "Gentiles are people of other nations. Those who are not Iuddic, not us. If it is true, if the Way does embrace Iudde and Gentile, it would certainly be a strange development."

"Are they travellers, then?" I ask.

"Travellers?"

"They have clearly given up reverence for the gods of their own people, and they choose to revere the god of another land, while not even in that god's land. It seems to me that also would be a strange development."

He is thoughtful, considering carefully what I have said, accepting another spoonful of porridge. My soul is also deep in thought, my fingers unsteady, and I spill a drop onto his lip. He smiles, wiping his mouth with a hand, and our eyes meet for a moment, recalling for us both the depth of our bond.

"When you put it that way," he says quietly, "it does seem strange. I'll ask them about it when Seren lets me up."

We fall silent for a while, sharing the porridge.

The thought of him returning to them fills me with dread.

"Vivian?" His brow is furrowed with worry as he asks again, "Please tell me. How are they?"

"They are not as bad as you." I watch him struggle to find words, his frown deepening the ridges across his forehead, and I speak again to ease his soul, laying my hand upon his. "They are stronger than you."

"Vivian, you do know that more than anything else, I want to be with you."

"I know, Eos. But you face a crisis of honour. As do I."

His expression changes.

"I worked with the Romans for a long time. Honour to them is a way of enforcing loyalty to the emperor, and is not a pretty term. You must mean something else by the word, my love. What is it?"

I laugh softly and shake my head, "Eos, this is why there are so many laws in the empire of Roma, so many laws amongst the Iudde. And this is why they call us 'incultus' out here on the very edge of the world! We know what that word means: not just wild, but unable to live with decency. They call us barbarians. We do have few laws here, very few, that is true. The druids, forsaken by the ancestors and reaching for this complicated adorned lifestyle of the Romans across the water, oh the druids are inventing laws at every council. But the people ignore them. We need no laws. For we live by honour."

"But you said it was law that bound you to smash the soul cup," he says.

"Because in the common tongue that is the closest word. I could think of no other that you would understand. I was bound to release the cup."

"By what, by whom?"

"By my ancestors, by the spirits of the islands, by the gods, by nature."

He coughs, clearing his throat, his breath starting to wheeze again.

"We should stop talking, Eos. You must rest."

But he shakes his head, "No, Vivi. This is too important. We don't have time to ..." And for a moment he closes his eyes, and I feel anger in his soul. When he looks into my eyes, though, there is urgency and love. "Is it like a covenant? Abraham, the ancestor of my people, made a covenant with Adonai, that he would obey Adonai's teachings, and Adonai would grant him homelands and a great posterity." He looks at me with brightening eyes, hoping to find common ground. "This covenant with Adonai is the cornerstone of the spirituality of the Iudde."

But I sigh, wishing it were easier to find a connection with this man I love so deeply.

"No, my love. Covenants are made between men who are only speaking with their mouths, or hands, or bellies, needing something. When we see clearly, when we see truly, there is no need to make a covenant. We simply make a relationship."

"But see what clearly?"

It is my turn to frown, for with each question I realize how little he knows me, how little he must really understand my people. "Life, Eos," I say softly, breathing in the strength of the earth to hold back the weeping that is rising within my soul.

He feels my grief, and takes my hand, whispering in his broken voice, "I am trying to understand, my love. Please explain: what do you mean by life? When you see a man before you, what do you see clearly?"

"His soul, his ancestors, his children, his land."

He looks into my face and for a while there are no words.

Then he says quietly, "You see all that touches him."

"And all he has touched."

"But this, too, is the meaning of life for my people. Soul, ancestors, children, land. Vivi, this is exactly the same thing I understand as a Iudde!" He sits straight up, waving aside my concern as his coughing begins again. "My people see this codified and guaranteed in a covenant relationship with Adonai." He drinks from the water bowl as his thoughts pour into the words he is eager to say aloud. "But the lad, the lad often taught that there was a meaning to life deeper than the laws of the covenant, deeper than the codified agreement. No one understood him." His eyes fairly gleam as he looks into mine. "So honour," he says, "is living the relationship simply because you do, without need for the motivation of a covenant?"

In my heart I untangle the words he has spoken, removing the name of this god Adonai and finding an understanding that holds the song of my land.

"Yes," I say, " with no covenant. It is all in the relationships that we live, my love. If we are aware of the relationships that exist, the threads of the spiders' webs that connect us all, soul to soul, blood flowing into blood through birth, breath flowing into breath through story and song, then we can live with honour."

But I feel his heart sinking, and watch again his forehead furrow. He turns to me and says slowly, "Then you must have seen in the souls of the men whom you cursed their ancestors, their children, the whole 'web' of their lives."

"Of course." I place the porridge bowl on the ground.

"You knew exactly what you were doing."

I look into his face and see clouds begin to cover the brightness that had flashed so briefly. For a few moments he sought to understood me, but now, with that understanding, we seem again as far apart as ever we have been. A wave of desolation moves over his soul and he lies back on the hay, staring up at the roof as if from the bottom of a deep mine shaft, the wheezing in his chest rumbling into fits of coughing.

"If, if we are connected in one web of life, Vivi - and I can understand that, I can remember the lad saying he wished all of us could be one, even as he felt at one with Adonai. But, if we are all connected in one web, then how can you cast a curse upon someone in the web without it touching yourself? The curse you aimed at Trophimus and the Gauls has hurt me more than them, and cast a cloud of fear and sorrow over the relationship that is yours and mine."

Oh my love, I murmur. "I cannot change the course of a river, Eos. All the curse does is wake a soul to the current and his own ability to ride it or not. The curse only intensifies what is already there."

But he cannot hear my words.

"You cursed me, Vivian. You cursed us. Don't you see that?"

"Eos," I say, shaking my head, closing my eyes, "my love, the curse held you while you stood amongst them, for they can't ride its current, and while you stand with them their weight brings you down. When you step away, that weight is lifted from your soul. When you came back to me, the curse fell away from you. You are getting better now."

He stares at me, his soul crying out, *Why do you make me choose?*

And with a hand I reach across the divide now gaping between us, my fingers aching to touch his skin, my soul whispering, *Why do you still feel there is a choice to make?* But another fit of coughing breaks over his body. He pulls away from me, rising to sit, holding onto his sides. The pain in his chest is wearing him down and I call out, "Seren!"

He sighs harshly and growls, "Don't bother her."

But tears rise in my eyes, "Please, Eos."

Gwenlli is first through the door, murmuring, "She is coming." The herbwise is close behind. Shuffling in, she looks into my eyes, *I told you to let him rest.*

I turn away, unable to cope with her accusation on top of his pain.

When at last his coughing subsides, Seren instructs him to drink her brew. He holds the bowl with shaking hands and swallows what he can, flinching at the taste of what are no doubt bitter herbs. She sighs at his expression, saying, *Your anger won't let the song into your blood, fellow.*

I turn to her, *He can't hear you.*

She glares at me, saying aloud and in the common tongue, "Perhaps he hears more than you think, Lady."

And something snaps. I hurl my soul at her face and scream with the power of thunder, "GO!"

Gwenlli stares at me as the herbwise disappears through the door. My rage has brought silence to the settlement, a brittle moment of apprehension, of waiting. I breathe, then look up at Gwenlli and acknowledge my mistake, *I am sorry, child.*

Her fear turns to tenderness, and she shakes her head, her soul murmuring, *Everyone knows how hard this is,* and she bows, "What might I do for you, my Lady?"

But there is nothing she can do.

When she has left, Eos opens his eyes.

"What did she mean?" he says, hoarse from coughing.

I breathe deeply, not wanting to show him my weeping.

"She is worried that your anger will slow your healing." I brush tears from my face and look down into his. "But she felt that you already knew that to be true."

"Vivian, I am sorry. I don't know why this is happening."

"It is hard," I say weakly, "to know what to do."

Exhausted, he closes his eyes, and murmurs, "Vivi, I fear that honour is something for the gods, and too much for mortals. It is love that is important for us."

Love. To feel such love and yet so much distance between us is unbearable. I gaze into his face, his body straining for breath, and I feel acutely the anguish that overwhelmed him when, down in the meadow, he faced the storm of the curse. I realize he still believes that I have rejected him.

I lean over and kiss his mouth, a tear falling from my face onto his. But he is no longer with me, and in his dreams I hear him speaking, *If you love only those who love you, what good is that?* His eyes move under their lids, awake in another place and time, and I catch a glimpse of his nephew, the seer, his deep brown eyes, his tender strength. *Love your enemies, pray for those who cause you harm*: the words touch my mind.

And as he falls again into a fitful sleep, I wonder at those words, spoken without sound in the otherworld of dreams.

How much of the day passes, I do not clearly know. I drift into sleep myself, curled up beside him. The sounds of the community move through my awareness, the chattering of the hens, the glas chits and robins, soft voices talking, the crackling of the fire, children's feet running, the bleating of the goats. Rain comes down upon the roundhouse thatch, dancing in the puddles, then the spirit of the land rises again, breathing up into the skies. The cry of a kite, circling high above the island, now and then wakes me into anxiety.

At some point I get to my feet and drift out into the damp air of the day. Morfrenna is watching the strangers at the base of Bryn Fyrtwyddon, the mist is holding us secluded, there is news of fighting in Pentreflyn, a skirmish with Romans, a druid council has been called. I share tea with Sianed and speak of calling a gathering here on Ynys y Niwl, and we craft a list of those druids and seers whom we believe we can trust.

And when we hear him coughing, she touches my arm and smiles, *Seren says he will be strong soon enough.*

But, priestess, he wishes to return to the others.

She looks down, *Perhaps he is seeing in circles made small by his sickness.*

Made small by love, priestess. Your truth can hurt no more than the pain I feel already.

But it is love, Lady, that is confused by loyalties.

She pours more tea from the old kettle.

I sigh deeply, *Sianed, I have been thinking. I realize I have made a mistake.*

She looks into my eyes, *No, my Lady. Nobody sees that you have.*

"Last night," I continue, speaking softly in the marsh language that we share, finding the need to give the clarity of edges to the words that I say. "Last night, we called to the gods of this land, to our ancestors, to all whom we live with here in the marshes, that they might rise with us and make it known to these strangers that their presence is not welcome."

"And it is not." She frowns, affirming her belief. "My Lady, we are bound to offer hospitality to those who bring to us need, yet only to those who do so with honour themselves. These strangers bring no such honour."

"And in that is my mistake, priestess. We made it clear that the spirits of this place do not welcome them. Yet these people do not listen to the spirits. They have abandoned the gods of their own land, the gods of their people. They do not care if they are welcomed or not, for they live walking on the surface of the water, where the light is reflected. I fear that what we have done will only aggravate their determination to stay."

"But they cannot fight the spirits!" she says, drawing so beautifully and so clearly on the certainty of our people's songs.

And the weight of this moment falls through me.

Yet before it lands in the depths of my soul, our focus is drawn to a clamour moving through the orchard mist towards us. A young girl of no more than ten summers runs ahead, scattering the hens, her tearful cries of, "Mama" , breaking the stillness of the air as a woman runs from the storehouse and takes her up in her arms. Behind her, two more young girls are running, and then Fianna emerges through the mist and trees. Morfrenna follows, in her arms another child, sobbing with tears.

Sianed runs towards them, embracing Fianna who, in the arms of such strength, herself breaks into tears. And I watch, sitting on the old stone wall, as the grief rises into a howling of rage and sorrow, the intensity of emotion allowing its song, and I close my eyes, feeling the earth and the rain holding the cries as they have held those of our grandmothers.

And when the tide of grief recedes, the air shimmering with the story expressed in wordless sound, the rain falling quietly, Gwenlli comes to my side.

"My Lady, you must come into shelter."

But I shake my head, "I must speak to him. He must know of this. Fetch Fianna."

He is, of course, wide awake, for the women's cries have drawn him from any place of rest. Alone in the roundhouse, he is sitting up, waiting, and I see a thousand thoughts have been in bloody conflict, raging across the plains of his soul.

Our eyes meet as I enter but there are no words spoken. I sit on the hides beside him and we drift through the moments that pass, horribly aware of the cavern that lies between us. When Fianna draws back the door and steps inside, I see his face soften almost imperceptibly and a tear wells in the corner of his eye.

"Tell him what has happened, priestess," I murmur in the marsh tongue.

Her face is still wet and reddened with her own tears, and she kneels beside us, looking into his face.

"Eosaidh, I am afraid."

They are such powerful words, spoken by this woman who has faced the death of her parents to the marsh, who nursed her own husband as he died from battle wounds, who has guided women in the cries of birthing and calmed the souls of children traumatized by loss and brutality. Eos knows it, and to hear them further breaks his heart. The tear falls from his eye, slipping down his cheek to find its hiding in the grey of his beard.

"Fia," he whispers, his voice shaking. He almost reaches to take her hands but has not the certainty or courage. He is so lost and so alone.

Tell him, Fianna, I murmur.

She speaks through her sobs. "We were down on the shore, Eosaidh - Olwen, Tegan, Saillie, Elen and I - across the bay from Dolgwyl Waun. You know? - where the children love to play in the hollow willow?" She looks down, "The forest separated us from your dwelling, but they must have heard us. Suddenly they surrounded us," she turns to me, "each one with a heavy staff, cut so roughly from the trees I could see the spirits bleeding."

If I look at Eos, it would be as if I were blaming him, so I close my eyes and let her words fall into the air.

"I couldn't understand what they said, only one seemed to speak the common tongue and then only a few words and in a thick accent. He said, 'Woman,' and waved his staff at the children, 'You teach?' I explained that we were learning about the water grasses, and showed him the different reeds and rushes the girls had collected. But he threw them to the ground, and said, 'I teach,' and the five of them came closer around us, and the girls became so afraid. I asked what he wanted to teach, and they laughed and talked loudly in their own tongue, then he said, 'I teach you of Christus, the Living God.'"

Hearing Eos sob, I open my eyes and see he holds his head in his hands.

"I started to tell him, Eosaidh, of the goddess of the water, of our goddess of the earth, of our mother goddess, but he shouted that there is only one god, Adonai, and his son Iesu, and," she looks at me, "that the mother is a demon. He yelled that I was a sorceress, and grabbed Tegan, and the other men pulled the girls from me, shouting that they would save them from the dark curse of the whore goddess, and the girls were crying in fear, and they slapped them to be quiet."

And again Eos sobs, and I feel my heart pounding.

"And he raised his staff at me and yelled, 'Witch!', and I shouted as loudly as I could, 'NO!', and Morfrenna came running out of the woods, like the spirit of a gale, screaming curses and they let go their hold on the girls, and I called up the mist."

She turns to me, "My Lady, we ran as fast as we could, Morfrenna carrying Tegan who has bruises down her legs. Did I do right, my Lady?"

I put my hand on hers and say softly, "Yes, Fianna. Thank you for telling the tale."

As she gets up to leave, Eos says, "Fia?"

She looks around, her face drained with exhaustion.

"I'm sorry, Fia," he says, his voice still shaking, "Tell them I'm sorry."

She nods, sniffing back tears, but I stop her.

"No, Fianna. Don't tell the girls he is sorry. Eosaidh is not to blame."

"No, my Lady," she whispers.

Alone in the roundhouse, we gaze at each other, depleted by tears shed and those still too deep to fall. And for a long while we say nothing. There is just the glow of the fire and the spirit of the earth around us in the half light of the roundhouse, my soul too tired for any thought to form. The wind is moving in the trees outside.

"You must go," I say quietly.

"Yes," he whispers.

He pushes the hides away and reaches for his boots, pulling them on slowly and tying them with hands too weary to be capable.

"I don't know about responsibility, you said you ..." I murmur.

"I said I feel some responsibility for them."

He staggers to his feet, obviously faint, and heads to the door, pulling back the hides and making his way out into the evening rain. For a moment, I wonder if I will ever see him again. I feel numb with a confusion that I sense he is interpreting as quiet cold rage, yet that further adds to the numbness.

When he is gone I stand up, but find myself unsure what to do.

A moment later, Seren is at the door, snarling in the marsh tongue, "Do you want him to die, Lady? Do you want him to bloody die? I have not spent two days bringing him from her dark hearth back to yours so you can send the pitiful dog out into the rain to die!"

I stare at her.

A moment later, Eos is once again before me, his face pale and taut with the fear of uncertainty.

She spits one last sentence, "If you don't want him anymore, Lady, at least give him til morning."

And then she is gone. I hear her saying to someone outside, "Leave them alone."

And we are alone. Like children. Children who have loved and been abandoned by love. Children who have been shamed by their own need for that love. Children whose trust has been so harshly broken.

Somehow, without words, he sits back down on the hay and hides.

"Vivi?"

Half blind with confusion, I struggle to untie his boot straps and pull off his battered old Roman boots. And as he lies back, faint and coughing, with no capacity to think beyond the moments through which I am moving, I slip onto the hides beside him, seeking warmth in the emptiness. And with his arms around me, I am once more melting into his soul.

And with not a word spoken, as we kiss, from the depths of this well of pain the tears begin to flow.

Chapter Sixteen
For All These Years
(Eosaidh)

A bright sun burns in a deep blue sky, the borders of the marsh lined with hairgrass taking on its autumn hue, mixed here and there with lady's tresses and sea-lavender. Redshank and shelducks revel in the unexpected sun. A black-tailed godwit wades in the shallows, its long bill searching for a morning meal among the reeds. Down the shoreline to the right, the mists begin. They arch around behind me, blocking the way to Glyn y Ffynhonnau, cutting off Wirrheal from the tor and the rest of the island, cutting me off from Vivian, whom I see now only in restless dreams.

It was a full cycle of the moon ago I left her roundhouse. The mists closed in behind me as I walked, alone, out of Vivian's community, out of her life. *You have to go*, she had said, and I knew she was right, though it broke both our hearts. Seren loaded me down with a supply of healing herbs. But I heard her say in my mind, *These will not heal you, unless you learn to live*. I may still be alive, but the herbs have not brought healing. The cough stays, sometimes so bad that I sit up all night without sleep. I am grateful for a sunny day such as this one with its soothing warmth. But the days grow increasing shorter, colder, and damper. I can feel the cough settle deeper in my lungs, and have begun to wonder whether I shall see another spring.

Trophimus has built his own hut a few yards from mine. And in a circle after that are the huts of Casticus, Sedullus, Orgetorix, and, on the other side of my hut, that of Valetiacus.

In the centre our cooking fire burns. Up the hill, where I had torn down the prayer hut last spring, a new one stands, large enough for us all to enter, recite psalms and prayers together, and share the blessing of bread and wine. A small flat bottomed boat for fishing is pulled up on the shore. But we dare not take it far out. The Romans are everywhere. They burned Pentreflyn a while ago after its inhabitants fled. It is only the mists of the priestesses that have saved this isle from Vespasian's patrols.

I sit by the fire trimming a spit for the pikefish Sedullus brought in this morning. I no longer eat flesh, but the others demand fish at least, when they cannot find game on Crib Pwlborfa. I am lost in the dreamspaces of memory when Trophimus sits beside me. For a time he is silent, respecting my longing. Finally he speaks.

"You are a great help to us, Eos," he says, "You are teaching us much, about how to live in this wild place, and about Iesu."

"I wish I could have taught you so much more," I reply. "It has cost me more than I can bear." Trophimus is silent. He knows, at least, what I feel, though I doubt that he understands. And the silence is strained, not like the gentle silence through which I would drift with Vivi, among the apples, or under the willows.

"It is a strange mist," he ventures. "The winds change direction, clouds come and go, but that damned mist never moves. I don't like it."

I finish carving the spit and toss it beside the fire pit, sliding my blade back into my belt. "It is for your protection," I say. "You have no idea how close you came to death for the sake of a mind that has become closed." He is silent. My breath betrays a quiet rattling deep in my lungs that will not go away.

It is time for noon prayer. Sedullus stands at the doorway of the chapel ringing the small brass bell he has brought from Massalia. Why do these men think prayer always requires noise? Trophimus and I rise and head up the hill. Near the woods, Orgetorix puts down his axe. He has inherited the firewood chore. I am the last to enter the door of the chapel, and another question nags me. Why do they insist on going inside, cutting themselves off from the world, to pray? It is because of the Temple in Jerusalem, I know. But I have come to prefer the overarching boughs of the ancient trees.

I look across the little valley toward the wall of mist. My eyes are having problems lately, and I am not sure what I see. A little girl, one of Fianna's charges, I think, not more than eight or ten summers. There she stands by the old oak where y Ffynnon Goch emerges from the woods. I have seen her there several times during the past month. Never coming near, only standing and watching. She is small, with the lithe posture of youth, and long willowy hair. If she sees that I am aware of her, she steps back into the mist and disappears, as she does now. Who is she? She reminds me that Vivi is there, inside, beyond the mists, and that I cannot find her. A cold hand grips my heart. The crushing weight of loneliness descends upon me again, and the cough returns. Vivi! Vivi, my love! My heart races across the field, headlong into the mists. Desperately I try to find my way through, crashing through undergrowth, tripping over rocks. And when at last I emerge, I am standing before the chapel, and Sedullus is ringing his bell, waiting for me.

When tears blur my eyes I know I must tear myself away from this vision and go inside. The others are already seated on straw mats, around the circumference of the small roundhouse. Who gave them the right to come here, and demand of me that I be their rabbi? Who put the perverse idea into my mind to accept? I begin the recitation of a psalm for noonday prayer.

> "I lift up my eyes to the hills;
> From where is my help to come?
> My help comes from Adonai,
> The maker of heaven and earth.

Adonai himself watches over you;
He is your shade at your right hand,
So that the sun shall not strike you by day,
Nor the moon at night.."

The others continue on droning the psalm, a mantra, like the chanting of the druids. But my mind reels. The sun does not strike people in these lands as it does in the deserts of Iudea. And the moon is a loving companion. Suddenly the hut has become stifling. I cannot see the sun or the moon under this roof! I stand, gathering up the Greek scroll I had kept in the old hut, a collection of the sayings of the lad that I brought with me from Jerusalem. Standing for a moment, I look around the inside of the chapel, and make up my mind. This is enough.

"Come!" I say. As I stride through the door I call back to Sedullus, "And bring the bread and the wine!"

A natural mist has drifted up from the marshes, and I cannot see the sun out here either. No matter. It is the world! I head down the hill toward our circle of huts and the fire pit. By the sounds behind me, I know the others have not collected themselves to follow until I am halfway done the slope. I am waiting for them by the fire, the flames dancing and hissing in a gray drizzle. They arrive confused, looking at me as if I have finally gone mad.

"Sit," I say. Because it is still chapel time, they automatically sit in a circle, around the fire. It had not occurred to them to bring mats, so they sit in the damp grass, looking a bit like sheep out in the weather. I tuck the precious scroll in the folds of my cloak to keep it safe, and lean on my staff.

"If you are going to live on this island, you are going to become acquainted with it," I begin. "Use the chapel for private devotion if you wish. From now on, prayer and teaching will be here in the open, around the fire of our hearth."

"But, Eosaidh, the rain!" says Casticus. He pulls his cloak tight around his neck.

"He makes his rain fall on the just and the unjust, Casticus," I reply. "Which are you? In any case, you get the rain. When the sun shines, you will get that, too."

I do not need to open the scroll in the quickening rain to quote the words I know so well:

"The lad said, Judge not, and you shall not be judged. Condemn not, and you shall not be condemned. Forgive, and you will be forgiven. Give, and it will be given to you: good measure, pressed down, shaken together, and running over will be put into your bosom. For with the same measure that you use, it will be measured back to you. Valetiacus, what does this mean?"

"Rabbi, as scripture says, it means we should treat others as we would wish to be treated ourselves."

"Very good, Valetiacus. And which of you wishes to be called witch and sorceress? Which of you wishes to be told the God you have given your heart to is no god, but a demon?"

Silence. The rain comes down harder. I look around the circle,

"Sedullus? Trophimus? No?"

The fire sputters, near to going out. Still the men are silent.

"Sedullus, bring the bread and wine."

He places the bowl of soggy bread on the small worktable by the fire pit, along with a skin of wine. I point to the skin, saying, "The lad once said you cannot put new wine into old wineskins. For the new wine is still fermenting and expanding, and the old skins have lost their resiliency. They will burst with the challenge. There is new wine here! Learn what that means!"

Lifting up the bread, I say, "This is the Bread of Presence. Let the lad be present among us that we may draw his teaching to our hearts." Lifting up the wine skin, I say, "Remember his life's blood given to show you love. There is no greater love than to lay down one's life for one's friends." We pass the skin and the rain soaked bread, sharing them together.

Outside the circle, beside my hut where none of the others can see, is the lad, as he looked when he last walked these shores. He smiles at me, and lifts his hand in blessing, and fades into the air.

The rain is coming down in torrents, and still the men sit.

"Go on," I say, "get in out of the rain!" And I stamp off toward my own hut.

There is a small fire inside my hut. I put a pot of water on it to boil, and drop in the last of Seren's healing leaves. *Old fool,* I say to myself. *Eosaidh, you will be the death of yourself yet! But I hope they all learned something from that!* A chuckle starts the coughing again, and I watch the pot impatiently, breathing in the vapours as they rise in the cool, damp air. Soon I am sipping the soothing liquid, hunched cross-legged on my cot, a wool fleece around my shoulders. My mind drifts back to the joyful days of summer, and to Vivi.

When I awake, fallen over on the cot, it is dark. My small fire is out, the rain is still falling. They didn't bother to call me for evening prayer, I suppose. Or looked in and saw I was sleeping and let me rest. Or thought they were better off spared of me for once. Who knows? I am too tired to tell when I drift off to sleep again. And my sleep is a heavy one, without dreams.

When I next awaken I can tell a new day has brought more sunshine even before opening my eyes. I stretch, willing some measure of response into aching limbs. When I do open my eyes, there is Caldreg, the druid, sitting before me on the edge of my cot. I blink my eyes, and he does not go away.

"Welcome back to the world, Eoasaidh!" He laughs. "I wondered when you might make the journey, and I did not want to wake you." Now it is his turn to stretch. "It is not one of the most sought after of druid tasks, watching a sleeping man for several hours!"

I swing my legs around and sit up beside him. "Caldreg, what are you doing here?"

We do not really know each other. I have heard, in the weeks I have been separated from Vivi, that he has become an important aide to her, one of the few druids she is still able to trust. I remember the jealousy I felt watching the two of them together at the whitethorn festival. But I am no longer jealous. Vivi's love lives too deeply in my heart for that.

"How is she, Caldreg?"

"She manages. She is a strong priestess. It is Seren who worries for your health. She sent us to find you."

The sudden coldness of his reply is like a hammer blow. It brings on the coughing that has become so normal a part of my mornings. This time there is a red tinge to the phlegm that I spit into the washbowl. I toss the water out the open door, pretending not to notice.

"Us?"

"Morfrenna is with me. Only a priestess can find the way through the mists. She is standing at the edge of the field, and will not come further." I turn to splash some water on my face, and remember I have tossed it out into the grass. And what I saw in it.

Clearing my throat, I say to Caldreg, "I have run out of Seren's herbs and still have need."

"She suspected as much. Partly that is why we were sent to get you." He did not add, But mostly it is that Vivi wishes to see you. They might have just brought the herbs with them. There is some other reason for this summoning.

"Collect what you need," he says. "You may be gone several days."

I leave things in the hands of Trophimus. "And remember, prayers are to be said outside, in the fire circle. Not indoors in the chapel." He nods, but I know noon prayers today will be under the cover of thatch.

When we reach Morfrenna she nods silently, turns to lead us up the path toward the springs, and we disappear into the mist. I see nothing that I recognize. She begins to sing, ancient songs in the old tongue. There is nothing to see but mist, yet I do not stumble. No rock slips under my foot. No low hanging branch slaps me in the face.

Finally the mist begins to brighten, and shapes of trees begin to appear. It is swirling and lifting, the disk of the sun appearing and disappearing, and finally emerging in its fullness. We are surrounded by apple trees, and before me with a frown on her face is Seren, the herbwise.

"Ci Bach. It is good to see you still walking," she says. I look over my shoulder, but her grip on my arm tells me she is speaking to me. I have no idea what she has just called me. "Come, let us get you to the healer's hut this time, where I can do you some good." She takes me by the arm and guides me down hill, Caldreg following.

"Vivi," I ask. "Where is she?"

"Not here, Ci Bach," Seren grunts. My heart sinks.

Caldreg answers. "She is waiting at the roundhouse, Eoasaidh."

Thank God. "Caldreg, why does Seren call me Ci Bach?"

He shrugs. "I am told ever since you last left she has taken to calling you 'Little Dog.' I don't know why. It angers the Lady."

Enough reason for Seren, I think.

Inside the healer's hut she offers me a cup of the bitter tea. I scowl at it. Its scent is the way I feel being back here: I believe it to be healing, but it is only bitterness. If I had expected friendship or forgiveness I am to be disappointed. Seren is practising the honour of her craft, but neither she, nor anyone, is happy to see me.

"Enough, Seren," Morfrenna says out of nowhere. "He must come." She and Caldreg lead me, almost like a prisoner under guard, from the healer's hut. I see Fianna at a distance, and my heart leaps to smile. But she only looks at me sadly, and turns away, taking with her the little girl I have seen on the edge of the mists. We come to the door of Vivian's roundhouse, and

Caldreg motions for me to enter. Inside, he shows me to a mat, and I sit. Vivian sits across from me, with Sianed beside her, and another priestess I do not know. Vivian introduces her as Arfel, a seer from Llyn Hydd. We sit and look at each other. I do not belong here. The coldness of ice is in Vivian's eyes, draining the warmth from the fire.

Gwenlli brings me more tea, and a piece of barley bread with honey. Her eyes meet mine briefly before turning away to sit just behind Vivian on the hides. It is in her face that I see what I long to see in Vivian's, sadness of separation, the deep grief of empty nights. But that is what I feel, not Gwenlli. And Vivian shows no sign of any such feeling.

It is Caldreg who speaks, which surprises me.

"News has come that you have a deed for use of twelve hides of land," he says evenly, the friendly tone with which he woke me in my hut now completely gone.

"There is such a deed. I have seen it."

"Under whose seal?"

"One Arviragus. I do not know him. I am told he is cousin to Caradoc, and considers himself king in this region. He is a druid, like you, Caldreg."

He ignores the challenge, and his face goes cold.

"When was it issued? Where"

"I have no idea. The Gauls who came to join Trophimus brought it. It was dated 14th Aprilis of this cycle, I believe."

I look at Vivian, but she turns from me. I look back to Caldreg and ask, "Am I on trial here? Is this an official council?"

He ignores my question. Gwenlli shifts uneasily. The seer from Llyn Hydd leans to Vivian and whispers something I cannot hear. Vivian's face remains expressionless. Caldreg continues his questioning.

"Do you accept this deed as having force of law?" Caldreg asks.

I am tired of this druid. I stand, dropping the tea and bread in a clatter to the floor. For a moment I waver, unsteady. I have been denied my staff. Perhaps it is still in the healer's hut. I remember a vow I once made never to be without it in this place again, and my anger boils over.

"Druid!" I say. The faces before me are surprised that my voice trembles in anger, not fear. "I am tired of your questioning. I am tired of your suspicions, all of you. And I am tired of being treated like a dog." I seem to feel energy returning to me, and, for the moment, my lungs are clear, and my back straightens, and I stand taller than I have in recent memory.

I step toward Caldreg, who stands to face me. "I do not care about this contract you speak of." My voice deepens and rises in volume. "Its weight is the belly feather of a marsh chit to me. I have no desire to own this isle, or any other part of Britain. The same Romans who threaten you are even now taking control of my family holdings in Cornualle and the Mendydd. I did not summon Trophimus or his comrades here, nor was it I who imprisoned you in this wall of mist."

Vivian is pale. Her eyes are black and cold. I throw my hands in the air in an expression of rage and desperation. "I am tired of all of you!" I bellow in my native Aramaic, and I turn on my heels to leave. But my lungs cannot retain their strength, and I am hit by a fit of coughing, bending double with pain. Again there is blood in what comes up from the depths of my chest. "I am so tired of it all," I say barely above a whisper, and I fall to my knees.

"Leave me alone with him." It is Vivi's voice, expressionless. Slowly they answer to her will, leaving only the two of us, Vivi seated on her hides, I on my knees by the door.

"The curse stays with you as long as you stay with them."

"Then we have a crisis of honour, my Lady."

Still without expression, she says to me, "You must explain to me why you stay with them. You have no peace in their company. Do you not recall that we let him go?"

"A person does not drift out of this world as easily as that. We let his life go, my Lady, but we did not let his memory go. That remains always a part of me." I get to my feet and turn to face her. "You sent me to them when I would have remained by your side. You cannot expect me to leave them now because they have done something that does not suit you. I have no peace in their company, but I am bound to them as you are bound to Sianed or Gwenlli. They do not know the lad as I did, but they cannot be condemned for their ignorance. Someone must teach them." I stand before her, and she rises to look into my eyes. "Lift the curse, my Lady, or I shall die by your hand."

Something moves across her eyes that I have never seen before. It is as if a curtain is temporarily drawn back to reveal a cavernous gorge of desolation within her soul, the raw earth and stone left after a great landslide, within which the songs of her ancestors cry out with a grief so great it is clearly killing her. She has forgotten to breath for a moment, and when she takes a breath finds her strength once again, and looks directly into my eyes. But she does not managed to cloak her soul as ever she had done before. How much of myself do I continue to hide from her?

There is a tremble in her voice as she says, "You force me now to make a choice, as I demanded of you before. But you have allied yourself with those who stand as enemies of my people and my land."

I step closer. "Vivi . . . ," But she raises a hand to silence me.

"You arrived in need, and I took you in, breaking the traditions of this sacred island. For you came with gentleness and respect and it would not have been honourable to turn you away. You stayed, living beside us in honour. And I gave you my heart in trust. My soul learned to dance with your song. But how much now must I sacrifice, Eosaidh, to satisfy your need?"

"Is it a sacrifice, then, to open one's heart to embrace others?"

Her eyes fill with tears, but I cannot tell whether from sorrow or rage. None escape to trail down her cheek. I am not being asked for compassion.

"Will you always misunderstand me?" she asks. And I am not being asked for an answer.

She closes her eyes and again breathes deeply, seeking strength, listening to something I cannot hear but somehow know to be the songs of her dead. Perhaps because her quiet sigh here bears on its shoulders the haunting sound of their distant wailing. Again she looks into my eyes.

"It was hard to open my heart to you because of the death of my son. The Enaid Las was a sacrifice indeed, for the gods took of me more than I had offered." She is silent for a moment, hesitating, not wishing to go on. But the words must come. "It seems again to have happened, for the space in my heart and amidst my people that I gave to you is now being paid for."

There is hardly any space between us, but we do not, cannot touch.

"Vivi, paid for?"

"With life, loss, death," she shakes her head slowly. "With so much pain."

I hold out my left hand, just barely, turned upwards, open, hoping. The moment she looks at it is the time of eternity. Then, slowly, she puts her hand in mine. But she turns our hands as she does so, telling me clearly this will only work side by side. Somehow we help each other to sit on the hide-covered hay.

"Tell me, Vivi," I whisper, "of the grief you hold for your son."

Another tremble runs through her, and she looks at me in shock. "How can you ask such a question at such a time?"

"Vivi, the grief of your ancestors is large and far off. The grief you hold for your son is stone lying on your heart."

She looks away, and for a moment I think she will get up and leave. She is silent, but I can feel the tears she holds within.

"Twenty five summers have passed since his dying, Eos." For a moment she lets me take her hand again, but then she takes it back. "It is not for my son that I grieve, it is for all the world within my care." Then the tears fall, though her voice is so steady you would not know she was weeping. "My son was a powerful young man. He held the vision of my grandmothers, and that of his father, too."

"His father?"

"A myrdden, once a high druid of the Dubonii. When I knew him he was a travelling teacher, a wise spirit-walker with extraordinary power. He was a legend." She sighs, with a smile that is torn by sadness, "I did not love him, I was in awe of him, in awe of his mystery. The council were pleased with the mating." She says the word with bitterness. "Much attention was given to ensuring I had a child who survived."

"He must have been older than you."

"He was as old as the hills." Her eyes search through some other time. "And soon after, he left, and from that day appeared only in the visions of seers. My son, crafted of magic, birthed through magic, had a destiny laid out before him. I was given fourteen precious cycles of his life in which to teach him all that could be taught to a boychild. Then he was sent to apprentice with the high druid of the Dubonii. He was to be a great man, one who would guide our people from the throttle-grip of Roman coins and corruption, and now this bloody slaughter ..."

"Vivian," I answer. "It is the same slaughter that claimed the life of the lad. And the same slaughter that seeks the lives of those who are building up a new religion around his memory." The words fall coldly upon my own heart. I needn't guess what they do to hers. "The life of your son has given power to the life of the lad, whose memory now may change the world."

She is paler than ever. There is dark power of devastation in her eyes as she looks into my soul and asks, "Why do you imagine your kin to be more important than my son?"

The question hangs in the air. All the gods there are, and the mothers of every child, wait for an answer. A wren flies from one perch to another high in the roof, and cocks her head, listening. Two human hearts beat, not quite in tune, their rhythms shifting and changing, until they move in unison.

"He is not," I say.

The silence embraces us, and we sit together for long moments, not thinking, not understanding, but being in one another's pain. At last, she speaks again.

"You said that I sent you from here, when you would have remained at my side. I did not ask you to leave, Eos. You claimed responsibility for them. You chose to be with them, when you knew their presence would compromise our safety."

I have no illusion that my response was so noble or so foolish. But she is teaching me the meaning of mercy by such a proclamation. In my heart, I know I was simply unable to choose.

"Perhaps, in time, I can help them to understand. Perhaps the two communities may find a way to live in peace."

"Eos," she answers, "Do you know why Arviragus gave you the deed?"

"No, Vivi, I don't. I thought perhaps it was because he is seeking help to resist the Romans."

"Help? From you?" She shakes her head, holding back laughter. For the first time, I begin truly to doubt her love for me. Perhaps it is mostly pity, thinking I will never understand the mysteries of her isle. How can you love someone who you believe is stupid? What hope is there for us? She drops her head into her hands and murmurs,

"Oh Eos. What hope have we?"

"There is always hope where there is love, Vivi." But my heart sinks to the ground at her reply.

"No, I mean us. This community. This land and heritage."

My sigh is deep, but I keep it inside, away from Vivian. I will never become a part of "us". Soon now it will be time to return to Trophimus and the others.

"My Lady, now that Trophimus is here and Pentreflyn burnt, I have no contact with the world outside. It is a strange feeling for one who has travelled all over it. What is happening? What is this news of Arviragus?"

"Arviragus considers you irrelevant, Eosaidh. Powerless, for you have abandoned your gods and your land: to a druid, you are nothing, for you have no wealth and no hope. You are outcasts. Do you understand what that means?"

"It means we are fair game for anyone," I answer. "But, Vivian, is this what you think as well?"

"Don't play with such questions, Eosaidh!" She turns to me again, this time her expression too mixed to understand. "It is said at the council of Bryn Cadeodd, where Arviragus now holds court, that a Gaulish druid asked him a favour, to hide these men that now pollute my sacred isle. They were told how to reach the island and that you were here, sheltered by the seers. It is well known that you are here, and now you are a trinket of barter, a favour cast between druids clinging to power."

"I thought Bryn Cadeodd was taken," I said. "Vespasian passed through that region weeks ago."

"His army passed by as if he never saw the fortress. Bryn Cadeodd still stands. The power of the gods and the ancestors is still with him. He knows it is also still here on Ynys y Niwl, and that I still hold that power."

"I know the Romans far better than you think, my Lady. I have feasted with Vespasian and drunk wine with him until sunrise. I know what he will do. But I do not understand druids, nor," I add, "priestesses. What are you telling me?"

She stands, staggering to the woodpile, picking up a few logs and putting them onto the fire. I can see she is weaker.

Instead of returning to the hides beside me she sits by my feet and takes my hands, looking into my eyes. There is so much in those dark eyes of hers. A thousand people, the marshes in the twilight, the power and the rage, and through it all the darkness of that ravine of desolation. But beneath it all, underlying it all, I see what my heart so hopefully seeks. I see love.

"Arvigarus considers you outcasts," she continues, "albeit of another tribe, another land. He believed you had no power, were but a fugitive hidden in some corner of the island, given scraps by the priestesses. He sent deeds of use for the meadows because he didn't believe the Gauls would make it here alive. And if some quirk of fate allowed them safe passage, he had no doubt that I would do my worst upon them." She pauses to make sure I am following. "But there was you. He didn't account for my loving you."

"If I were not amongst them, you would have sent them away?"

"Don't ask such questions, Eos! Of course!"

"Vivian, what of compassion -"

"Don't, Eos!" She closes her eyes, breathing deeply before looking again into mine. "The point is that Arviragus expects you to be dead or within my control. But neither is true. My love for you has ..." she hesitates, searching for words.

"Vivian?"

She sighs, "Arviragus assumed my power was intact. The council see otherwise. Your presence is now considered to undermine the safety of the sacred isle. It isn't just us they are concerned about, the women, the seers; more important to the council is the dragon's power. I have been telling you so for a long time. And now the council have decided, Eos." She lowers her voice, looking deep into my eyes. "Caldreg wants you dead."

Her words hang in the air like Mendydd lead. Finally, into the silence, Vivi says, "You once said you had only ever given your heart to one woman, and that a long time ago. Who was that woman, Eos?"

I take her hands in mine, gently, allowing her to choose whether to respond. When she does, I look into the eyes I love so much and say,

"It was you, Vivi. It has always been you."

"For all these years?"

"For all these years."

Chapter Seventeen
The First Apple
(Vivian)

It is the dark of the moon.

Within the next moontide the first frosts will come, and we shall make our rites to close this cycle of the sun, to welcome and prepare for winter. By the scents in the wind, the songs of the trees, I feel it will come within the next hand or so of days. After so much rain, the skies are now clear, looming blue above the mists, bringing cold air like an old and much-sharpened blade.

With another sleepless night drawing to its release, I have been sitting down by the shore of this island, Ynys Hyddwen, watching the ageing copper sun rising over the waters. Seeing it lift above the trees so much further to the south, feeling the nights getting longer deep within my soul, a song stirs in my heart, slipping through me into sound, an ancient keening song of my grandmothers. As its notes find currents of the water upon which to play, I realize that I believed I had understood its story, but as the weakening sun slowly makes its journey into the skies I know that only now do I have an idea of its meaning.

I gaze out over the marshes, the black calm of Llyn Hydd, the islands moored in the mist, in the cold stillness of early morning. The only sound is that of the first birds waking, singing their own ancestral songs, yet within this peacefulness there is dying. The once green forest canopy has taken its autumn mantle, all the colours of fire muted by the damp mist, but there is a dying that I was not able to see til this moment. The dying of an era. I strive to listen in the stillness for the slow-sung final notes of this song, a song that my people have been singing for hundreds of generations, passed on at the hearthfire from parent to child, soul to soul to soul. It is barely possible to grasp that such a song could have an ending, but in my soul I feel no doubt.

I want to cry like a child, pulling at the robe of my grandmother, whining, "Why do I have to do this? Why can't it be someone else?" Am I to be the midwife of the dying of my people? An old crow, sleepy with the damp cold of the night, alights on the ragged blackthorn near the water's edge. She turns to me and I hear her soul's words, *Why are you questioning? There is a path to follow. That's all.*

Voices rise behind me. She turns her sleek black head to look out over the marsh, then turns back to me and caws softly, *That's all.* She spreads her strong black wings and lifts into the wind. That's all. I say the words and I lift myself from the fallen willow. Arfel and Fianna are making their way towards me, talking in hushed grave tones, Fianna's hand firmly clasping the hand of the pale young child who walks beside her. Gwenlli looks up from where she sits by the water. She quietly unties the hemp rope that holds the boat to the shore.

"My Lady," Fianna bows, murmuring, "It seems we must make our way back through y Gors Chwerw. We can keep cover if we use the marsh paths, moving around the edge of the lake, never coming out into open water. But it will take a good deal longer."

She looks tired, her soul heavy, carrying still the pain of what we have seen: another village destroyed, torn into little pieces and scattered as if by a tempestuous child. Some of the men had clearly been taken as slaves, but most of the community were dead or dying from severe wounds; Arfel believes two days have passed since the Romans came through. And through the course of another day, until the light could stay no longer, we eased the pain of the souls who were wandering as shades through the smoking rubble of what had been their home. With herbs and prayers, we eased the passing of the few who had not yet found a way to die. And as we went about our work, out of the forest crept this young boy, his face as white as blackthorn flowers.

I look up into the trees, the leaves a thousand hues of gold and russet, the willows draped in soft yellow. An oak releases another bronze leaf that falls, swaying silently through the damp still air to land upon the muddy ground already spread with summer's end.

Gwenlli touches my hand and I wake from dreaming to look at Fianna, "Take us back as you will, priestess."

Keeping hidden in the tall rushes and reeds of the marsh tracks, Arfel guides the little craft through the shallow narrow waters. At times we take tracks seldom used, and Gwenlli, leaning over the front of the boat, pulls or cuts reeds that are blocking our way, murmuring her prayers to the gods and spirits of the marsh.

A little beyond the spit of rocks on the eastern edge of Llyn Hydd, the bloated body of a man is drifting, knocking in the quiet swell of the lake's current against roots of an old willow, themselves washed bare by the waters. His face down, I cannot know who he is, but in Arfel's soul I see the clattering pain of another stone of grief falling. Fianna holds the young boy close and he gazes out into the marsh without seeing. For a while we stop, Gwenlli keeping the boat steady against the willow, and Arfel makes prayers, calling to the gods of the dead and to the man's ancestors that they may carry his soul upon the songs of the setting sun. She ties a rope about his waist, weighting his tunic with stones dug from the bank around the tree roots, and we sing his dying as he slips to the lake floor.

How often must we make this rite, and hidden amidst the reeds?

Wet and shivering with cold, Arfel curls up in her cloak while Gwenlli, now at the back of the boat, silently paddles.

She is tired by the time we are moving along the shores of Bryniau'r Pennard and, close by, the chattering and metal clinking of a group of Romans provokes us to stop once again. 'Soldiers', Eos calls them, *milites* in the Roman tongue: a notion not known amongst my people. I look up at them, through the veils of our spells and the mesh of rushes, and see clearly that such men are not warriors. Bored and alone, a long way from home, they trudge upon the land as if in a dream, for no ancestors walk with them, and no spirits greet them as they pass.

When they are gone, Gwenlli whispers, "What a great deal of unnecessary clutter they carry with them."

And again I think of Eos. The burdens these men carry he'd call 'civilization'.

Hiding the boat in the marshes on the eastern shores of Ynys y Niwl, we make our way across the mist-cloaked meadow on the slopes of Bryn Ddraig. I am tired and my pace slows the others. Gwenlli returns to my side, hoping I will tell her what I need, and I pause to breathe and steady my soul. But what my eyes alight upon does not give me strength; for a moment I feel overwhelmed.

"My Lady?" she says softly.

"Let me alone for a while, child. I shall make my way back soon. Let Sianed know we shall talk through what was said at the council when I return." I squeeze her hand, "Yes, a little time alone is what I need."

Reluctantly she leaves me, and I watch them moving off through the mist, the child in his trance of shock, each footstep heavy with grief and determination. And I turn again to the oaks that here line the shore. A stream running down from the hill cuts through the grass and, where the flow slips down the bank, there is a pool of clear water between the shore and the marsh. As I near the oaks, I reach out a hand and touch the one that for so many years was a haven to my soul. As a child, I'd climb its branches, curling up in the crook made by a fork high up, and survey the marshes and islands out to the east. As I grew older, I would sit upon the broad low branch that stretches out over the water, my back against the trunk, my feet straight out upon its length, or lie belly-down, looking out at the world, hugging its rough bark, the pool beneath me, letting my fingertips trail across the water's silky surface.

My hand runs along the bark of the low branch, broader now than it was thirty cycles ago, and the memories rise up from the deep water of my soul. It seems like yesterday, when I lay upon its length, singing to my Lady of the waters. Manann was but twelve or thirteen summers old, somewhere upon the island in study with an elder, and finding time to myself, I came down here to feel the beauty of life.

Then there he was.

He is gazing at me, not quite seeing me, wrapped as I am in the spells of my prayer-songs. How he could have found his way through the mist or the marsh tracks, I can not imagine, and for that reason he seems to me not entirely real. I lay my head upon my hands on the branch beneath me, holding the softness of the mist-spell, and I gaze back at him. A young man, ten summers or more younger than I, I can see that his beard has not long lost its softness. In the warmth of summer, sunshine bathes him where he stands, in a simple tunic and trader's sandals, his hair thick and dark, his skin a golden brown.

Who is he? I murmur to the spirits of the trees, to the waters, the earth, the squirrel, the birds, and the answering calls are of laughter and curiosity, as others turn to gaze upon this unbidden stranger to Ynys y Niwl.

He steps closer, quietly, his forehead ridged with questions, until at the edge of the tree's wide canopy he says softly, "Are you real?" Though he uses the common tongue, his words are strange with a thick accent.

I sit up on the branch, my bare feet touching the cool water, and look into his eyes, *What right do you have to be here?*

He steps away, bows slowly, then frowns again, clearly uncertain of what he is seeing. And I laugh aloud, and with me the spirits of the marsh laugh, and the breeze in the oak leaves, and I stand, walking along the branch to the trunk, and silently jump down onto the grass, watching his apprehension, this strong young man, as I walk towards him and lift my hand to let my fingertips touch his face.

"Why are you here?" I whisper.

"You are real," he says, gazing into my face.

"Almost," I murmur. He carries a woven bag and I lift it from his shoulders, he too amazed to object, and I empty it onto the grass, sitting down to discover what it contains.

I look up at him.

"Sit. Eat with me," I smile, and take a bite from his round of barley bread.

A marsh hen cries out, splashing with her wings, bringing me back to the mist from that sun-blessed day, so long ago. I sit down on the roots of the old oak, and feel the rising ache of tears thick in my throat.

Did we talk that day? Lying in the grass in the sunshine, with the hum of honey bees and dragonflies, we did speak, of marsh tales and nature's beauty, of how high the sky truly is and other magical wonders. And hungry with the strange vitality which his presence brought to me, I had bidden him not move while I ran to pick a few apples from the orchard beyond the bank of thorn, feeling alive and strong and filled with mischief. And care.

And holding his gaze with my own, I had bitten into a perfect apple to break its shining skin, then offered him a bite, and I'd watched his strong teeth sink into the flesh, and the juice had run down into the softness of his dark beard, and as he lay on the grass beside me I'd dripped the sweet juice into his open mouth and we'd kissed. And I had felt such a hunger, such a need in my soul that I had never felt before, and we'd made love with a passion that tore the clothing from our bodies, my nails digging into his skin, my fingers tangling in his hair, driven by a craving to pull from him all that held his soul hidden, to taste his essence and cry out to the gods, and he had gazed at me with wonder, now utterly naked to his very soul, vulnerable as a child, as he held me, wide-eyed, the currents of pleasure rising through his body, until his voice cried out, in a tongue I did not know, the waves breaking over him, as he filled my body with the song of his people.

And as I lay again in the grass, my eyes closed, my body muddy, my soul awake and joyful, he had leaned over me, his warm skin upon mine, and kissed my face a thousand times, whispering, "I don't know who you are, but I love you, I love you."

I walk from the tree, in the damp morning air, to that curve in the slope where we had made love, thirty cycles ago. With the toe of my old boots, I touch the grass, now wet and tired with the cold grey mist, aware of the tears that are now streaming down my cheeks. Afraid he would be found, I had sent him from the island, back to where he had left his boat, feeling in my heart that I would see him again, that we would be together again, kissing him good bye with such confidence and sweet assurance.

And five summers had passed. My mother had made her journey to the otherworlds, my son was gone away to his apprenticeship, and I was vowed as Lady of this sacred isle. And there he stood, at y Ffynnon Goch, with his kin, the young seer they call Iesu.

Suddenly in circumstances that were formal, acceptable, with responsibility hung like a cloak about my shoulders, and his cloak about his, both hiding our truth, we had talked, barely showing any sign that we had met before, yet poignantly aware of the distance that stung the air between us. The hope that had burned as an lamp in my soul, wishing for his return, had been extinguished by time, by the pain of loss and disappointment.

I had looked at him and weighed the fear I felt had kept him away.

"My nephew was interested ..." he had said, unsure what to say. "I told him it was forbidden." He had smiled, with a deference and respect that hid so much. *Forbidden,* I had nodded, knowing that in his soul it was I the word described.

The marsh hen cries out again, and I look up to see a fox moving through the tall reeds, each silent footfall softly laid upon the unstable marsh.

As I watch, I wonder which spirit had guided that young tinner through the mist and the marsh to find me in the oak tree.

"My Lady?"

Gwenlli's voice lands like the first drops of rain upon my face, and I realize I am wet through. It must have been raining for some time. With no further words, she takes my arm and we make our way slowly along the slopes of Bryn Ddraig to the forest and shelter.

"Are you well enough to talk, my Lady?"

I lift the spoon and take a mouthful of soup, looking at Sianed over the bowl.

It matters not how well I am, priestess. There is much to discuss. Speak.

She sighs, "The council accepted my representation."

"Did they think I was too weak to speak?"

"No, I don't believe so, my Lady. It was acknowledged that you were busy elsewhere. There were many who couldn't attend the gathering, especially those with many cycles behind them. Travelling is getting harder."

I put down the soup.

"Tell me what was said, priestess."

"Arviragus is still at Bryn Cadoedd. It was said that he lost his brother in the past moontide, a skirmish with the Romans, which is why he had taken office at Cadoedd himself. They say that his kin, Caradoc of the Trinovantes, was defeated by the high chief of all the Roman empire, a man called Claudius, who brought with him huge animals called 'elephantus', like boar the size of trees."

I sigh, "These must be travellers' tales. How can we tell where there is truth in all that is said! Do they expect us to believe in monsters now? They mistake distortions of inner vision for reality -"

She shakes her head, shrugging in agreement, "Some seemed sure of the tale, while others responded as you. What is known to be truth by the council is that Caradoc has been moving west, calling to the Silures to join with him and fight against the legions."

"So we are surrounded by his blood, to north and south."

"I found out that he does not know Caldreg, but he knew his father, and there are other druids, other sons of Bryn Ddraig, who are known to him."

"Does he say aloud that he wants the island?"

"I believe at the moment he simply wants it safe, my Lady. And if we were able to hold it, he would support our presence. But Caldreg has met Eosaidh, and he sees a power in him that Arviragus would not have accepted. They say these new Christians are a small group, scattered in hiding through the empire and disliked intensely by the Romans because they deny all gods but their own -"

"As do the Iudde."

"The Iudde keep to themselves, though. The Christians hold a vow to their god to turn others to worship him, and this makes Caldreg nervous for it affirms his own fear of them. It explains to him what he perceives to be the power in Eosaidh."

"He fears Eos has enchanted me?"

"With respect, my Lady, he does not see Eosaidh as controlling the power. He feels him to be possessed by a vengeful spirit or god, one that seeks to destroy all that does not make devotions to him alone."

"Eosaidh's power is born solely of his love for his kin, the seer," I say quietly. "But Caldreg sees more in his visions. As do I. They are dangerous, priestess, these travellers, the Christians, but when I seek clarity, the real danger seems long in the coming. It is not Eos that brings this danger the druid or I feel."

"Yes, my Lady, and after the sacrifice was made, the council agreed that to be true. Caldreg withdrew his demand for their blood." I sigh, hearing the confirmation in her words. "But," she continues, "he has already told Arviragus that you do not secure the island."

My heart sinks.

"Did you say otherwise?"

"I did all I could, my Lady." She breathes deeply and pushes at the fingers of one hand with the fingers of the other, "I did what the elders here always teach us never to do: I did tricks to prove our strength. I drew the mist through the council hall, I scattered spells of glamouring, I set confusion amidst them for a few moments so no language was understood."

"At their request?" I ask, horrified.

"No, my Lady, out of desperation."

And for a while we are silent.

"Did they know what this would mean for us? Do they intend to act upon us?"

"No, my Lady. The fear now rises that with so much talk about Ynys y Niwl, the Romans will become interested. They are curious as wild dogs, the Romans, and likely to sniff around anything that others are giving attention."

"Will the council aid us if they come?"

"The young men Caldreg placed at our end of the walkway to prevent Eosaidh from leaving are now ordered to remain and protect us from the Romans."

Our eyes meet.

Perhaps it is because the threads have been pulled tense for so long, perhaps we are both simply exhausted with struggling to hold hope in the midst of such defeat, but from nowhere within us comes a torrent of laughter like a sudden storm.

"Those young lads with their short blades?"

"And their ferociously fluffy beards, yes, my Lady."

And though we try to hold back, for some moments we are helpless, holding our aching empty bellies, as this laughter tumbles through us, snorting and crying with the flood of its release.

"They can't be more than fourteen summers!"

"They couldn't protect us from an angry reed duck!"

Concerned as to our sanity perhaps, Gwenlli looks into the roundhouse, but the concern and confusion upon her face only sets us to laughing again.

It is Morfrenna's face, coming in behind her too hurriedly to be respectful, that changes everything.

It cannot be much more than mid afternoon, yet in the drizzle of the rain it feels closer to twilight. My feet are heavy upon the ground. If I had not the clear sight given me by my grandmothers, and with it a certain sense of my return through the mist, I would surely believe that I were walking to my death.

As we pass the sacred springs, I recall how wearing I found the small crowd that here gathered each day to be tended to by the seers and healers of the community, spellsingers and bonesetters, the herbwise and midwives. Now there is no one, and the space left by the absence of their needing is in itself a needing, a hollow where once birches chattered in the wind.

Gwenlli is beside me, her spirit holding me upright, yet I find myself constantly looking towards her, gnawed by a doubt that she has not come with us. Sianed is behind me, and half a dozen other women, some of whom I do not know, fugitives from settlements burned around the lakes, those with pith and focus sufficient to stand their ground. Morfrenna, with the

courage of her youth and strength, strides ahead, her staff of
oak securing a dry enough path through the muddy ground
along the south side of Bryn Fyrtwyddon.

The group of men are standing on the last stretch of the
walkway, their path blocked by the long staffs of two of the
young marshmen Caldreg has given us. As we come closer,
I see there are ten men, still and silent, standing in a straight
line upon the tattered single planks, bedraggled tunics beneath
what is now the familiar sight of a soldier's armour. Before
them are three more men, two clearly of some position in the
Roman force, the other a local trader. I don't know him, but by
his woad tattoos I would guess him to be from one the tribes
not more than a day's ride south. He has a wound on his upper
arm, badly tended to as men do, and a swollen black eye. He
flinches when I look into his face, clearly afraid both of my
rumoured sorcery and to be seen as a traitor.

Had they wanted to, the Romans could have killed with
ease these young lads whose defence of the island is entirely
notional. The two of status stand, chatting in a foreign tongue,
sturdy men in heavy tunics, leggings, cloaks and boots, their
bare heads wet in the rain that they seem not to notice. Their
horses, I imagine, are left with reinforcements at the other end
of the walkway.

Morfrenna approaches and talks to Caldreg's boys who step
away, lifting their staffs but unwilling to set themselves at ease,
staying close and alert to every move that is made. The Romans,
on the other hand, show no anxiety at all.

One turns to Morfrenna and smiles politely, but then looks
straight past her and his eyes find me. When he speaks, it is to
me, with eyes that are unreserved and unyielding.

Sianed steps forward and says, "We do not speak your
tongue." She too bows her head politely as she speaks, then
turns to the trader. "Are you in need of help?" she says simply.
The hood of her cloak blows from her head in the wind, and
her wild red hair is freed to dance. The trader looks up at the

Romans, weak with fear. I wonder who frightens him more, the Romans or us.

One of the women I barely know steps forward to stand beside Sianed, murmuring something to her before addressing the trader. "My cousin is Berwyn of Caer Iwdon. They were under the protection of the Durotriges. I recognize your mark. Do you know my kin? He was killed in the fighting in the last hand of days." Noticeably trembling, he shakes his head, and the woman continues. "Your wound looks to be in need to care. Do you need help?"

The two Romans are enjoying watching the conversation, but only because they have no respect for this man whom they have broken with his fear. When he doesn't answer the woman, one slaps him on the back, saying something to encourage him to do so. He hits him so hard the man stumbles forward.

"No, Lady," he mumbles, finding his feet again on the muddy ground. I see some of his teeth have been recently broken, his jaw is bruised and swollen. "I am taken by these men to translate their words, for I spent," he coughs, clearly in pain, "I spent many cycles in Gaul and I learned the Roman tongue."

The elder of the two Romans has had enough of chatter. He steps forward, to me, ignoring Sianed and the others. Our eyes meet and I see a man of great pride, a man who has won too often to know what it is to be humbled, a man who has not known the pain or hunger of love. He bows with a genuine respect. Then, without taking his eyes from mine, calls to the trader who comes to his side like a beaten dog.

When he speaks, the trader repeats his words into the common tongue, and ever the Roman looks into my face, holding his diplomatic smile.

"I seek the high priestess of the island."

"What business do you have with her?" I reply.

"I am a pious man," he puts his hand on his chest. "I honour the gods of my people and, here," he bows, "in your land, mother priestess, I would wish to honour the gods whom your people honour."

The rain is coming down harder, and he pushes his hands across his face with an undiluted strength, confident that patience and good manners will get him all he wishes for. If it doesn't, he knows he has sufficient brawn to take the rest.

"So why do you come here?"

This frustrates him and he says more than the trader dares translate, "It is known that this is a place sacred to your people." He returns his face to the polite smile. "Mother priestess, will you not allow us to pay devotions to the gods of your land?"

A thousand questions pour through me: should I allow them to make offerings, to take them to the sacred springs that they might drink the water and feel the blessings of our gods? Would such blessings strengthen them against us or soften them towards us? And if they know of the sacred places, will they have the wit and craft to use them for their own gain?

The druids would not have the island touched by these conquerors, yet this man seems less a threat to my gods than the Iuddic Christians who have so dishonoured the island, killing the animals, ringing their bells like knives cutting through the air, insulting the honour of the priestesses. I know from saphers and druids that Romans worship their gods in the forms of men and women, for so much of their religion is based upon human nature - love and war, justice and knowledge. Yet does that mean they know or care nothing for the powers of the skies, the waters and the earth. If they had not being raping, torturing, killing the people of these old lands, in that moment as I gaze at him I wonder if it would have been easier to sit and eat with this man than with the blinkered and bigoted Gauls who came to stay with Eosaidh.

As my mind walks its circles, the Roman waits calmly for a response.

"Why would the gods of our land be pleased with your devotions?" I ask. He listens to the trader's translation while looking still into my face. Anger breaks over him, frustration cracking his patience, but only for a moment. He finds calm again, and smiles, determined, speaking slowly enough for the translator to keep to his flow.

"All we are asking for is to make offerings to your gods. We have gold for your temple, I can send fresh barley, mushrooms, apples, salt, nuts, good wine. We are happy to provide you with all you might need. Times are hard and the markets are now few and far between."

It is Sianed who answers. "You would give us wealth and food simply for allowing you to make offerings? Lord, you can make offerings to our gods right here, letting your gifts fall into the waters of the sacred river beneath the walkway. For here too the gods dwell."

Still he speaks to me. "Perhaps we wish too to consult with your *oraculum*."

"Our what?" Sianed asks.

For a moment there is a complication as the trader seeks the right word, explaining carefully through his exhausted desolation. Then the Roman shrugs, *"Vates,"* and he nods and smiles at me, and the trader turns to Sianed, saying, "He wants to consult with a seer."

I answer, tired from standing in the cold rain, the end of the day closing in around us. "You are consulting a seer, now, with the words that you here speak."

He smiles and bows. "Would you not allow me to sit in comfort and set my problem to the seer along with a handful of coins that would express my respect?"

I breathe, feeling the land hum beneath me.

"The seer is already listening," I say quietly.

He pauses, then says, "So tell me, mother priestess, what is to happen next?"

"You cannot stay on this island." The trader's rough voice presents my words.

"But I can," is his reply. He moves his head very slightly, and within a blink the other men are standing to attention behind him. Tension breaks over the women, and I feel Sianed's prayer shimmering in the earth, holding us steady. She murmurs softly in the marsh tongue, "My Lady, let us call the mists and retreat."

"There is too much fear amongst these women, Sianed. The mist will not be enough to conceal us until we reach Bryn Ddraig."

"They will follow us then, but only as far as the springs."

In the corner of my eyes I see Morfrenna, aware that her temper is about to break.

"If they follow us that far, they will find Eosaidh."

Her reply is brutal and clear, "Do we save his life and lose our own?"

The Roman listens, his smile now cold though he has no understanding of what we say. My eyes meet his eyes, but he sees only darkness behind mine, and for a few moments there is silence as I listen to every spirit, feeling the web of threads pulled and slackened, feeling the group of women holding to me, feeling the dead watching, waiting.

I reply to Sianed under my breath, "Then I pray to all the gods that he will hide himself well." And as the words slip from my mouth, I feel his presence: he is hiding on the hillside behind us, watching every move we make. *Eos?*

My heart is pounding as I look again to the Roman, "You cannot stay on the island."

He moves forward, shaking his head, the trader doing his best to translate the words, "You have not been listening, mother priestess. This way, is it? This way?"

Two long staffs crash down, blocking his path, those of Morfrenna and a woman I do not know.

He turns to me, his voice growling with anger, "You have courage, but lack the delicacy of hospitality."

"You have abused the tribes of this land. Do you expect us to show you honour when you have shown none?"

"Of you," he says, "I expect intelligence. It would be intelligent to do as I say."

Sianed begins the chant, barely audibly, but I can hear each priestess adding her soul song to the call. I look into the Roman's eyes, "We shall meet tomorrow and negotiate. Tonight you go no further."

As I turn, his voice bellows through the twilight, *"Antistes!"* It is a word I know before the trader's voice trembles its translation, "Mother priestess." The man jams his finger towards the ground, yelling that his demands must be met here and now. But the mist is rising, distorting the air, and as I continue to walk slowly from him he is confused which further enrages him. His voice again lowers as his anger rises, and he step after me. I hear the sound of his blade taken from its sheath.

As his hand grabs mine, reeling me around, time slows. In perfect detail I see that his men have enough faith in his strength not to move an inch without his command. The other man of position stands firm, arms crossed, watching, as behind him Caldreg's boys tremble with fear, unsure what to do. And I see the man as he glares at me, seething with rage, saying the word again, "Antistes" , amidst a torrent of other words. A drop of spittle settles on his bottom lip. His eyes half close as he lifts his blade towards me in a fist tightly clenched.

And I see Morfrenna suddenly right beside me, moving as fast as a fox, her staff lifted high. I look up and block its fall, holding her violence before she brings it down. But in the moment of my distraction, it is Gwenlli who moves forward. Do we have time to share a glance, a smile? In some world it seems we do, before she thrusts towards him, her own short blade seeking to hide itself within his belly. She gasps, her spirit stepping back, as her body falls upon his blade. Morfrenna's staff comes down a moment too late, deflected by own strength. He collapses, crying out in a moment's instinctive pain, and I lift my breath and scream to my goddess, the words of the curse cleaving through me, slicing through the air, filling it with a venomous confusion that each soldier breathes.

Chapter Eighteen
The Parting
of Ways
(Eosaidh)

esinete! Stop!"

Rising from where I have been hiding in the trees, I run down toward the horror at the end of the walkway. Vivi is all but lost in the power of her trance, yet she is shocked to see me revealed to the soldiers. For their part, they are stunned by her curse, reeling from its force, so that they pay no heed to my approach. Together they all make a strange scene, an explosion of battle frozen in time. I ignore the officer, who steps back as I pass. His eyes are glassy and unseeing. Mine become fixed on the motionless form of Gwenlli on the muddy ground. I kneel by her side, dropping my staff. There is too much blood, and I know the answer I seek even before my fingers feel for her pulse. I turn to Vivi with pain in my eyes, and speak my only sentence ever in the tongue of the marshes: "She has gone from us, my Lady." Vivi's expression tells me she already knows.

Holding Gwenlli's body to my breast as I kneel beside her in the mud, I look up at the officer with a cold anger in my eyes. My voice is strong and steady. In the broken Latin of his Gaulish legion I say, *"Principales,* is this the way the Second Augusta treats with the family of a citizen of Rome?" He mumbles something in response, badly addled by the curse. I ask him again,

"Principales, is this the way you are accustomed to treating the family of a Roman citizen?" His armor flashes in my eyes, his gladius, held loosely in his hand, still dripping blood, is the symbol of terror I have been fleeing from for years. I pray I have kept the tremor from my voice, the fear that I feel deeply in the core of my being.

"It is an easy thing to claim citizenship," he finally responds. "Who are you, man among priestesses in this island of swamps?"

"I am Eosaidh of Cornualle, sometime of Arimathea in Iudea, once Minister of Mines to the Roman Army. Your General will know who I am." The second officer clears his throat, nodding as the two exchange glances.

"You would not be here if Vespasian were not also nearby," I continue. Truly I have no idea why they have come, I could not hear from the tree line. The other soldiers are still, recovering from the first shock of Vivian's onslaught. They are as frightened as I am, and anything might happen in such a moment of fear. Gwenlli's blood on my arms is beginning to cool. I draw her closer as if to offer her a warmth that is not mine to give. Vivi stands motionless, glaring at the Roman officer, unwilling to release him from the curse's chains, ready to kill him with another word. Morfrenna stands feet apart, staff at the ready, poised to strike again.

"Take me to Vespasian," I say, amazed at my own foolishness. He turns to confer with his comrade in hushed tones, knowing I understand their language. I glance at Vivi, but her face is a mask of concentrated will. A moment ago the women had been protecting me, a moment ago Gwenlli gave her life for mine. Now I seem to them to be giving it away. Perhaps, but my hope is that old ties will hold. I would not take this chance, but Gwenlli's death has changed everything. Finally, the officer turns back to me. He seems relieved to be able to stand down from his confrontation with the priestesses, to deal with a man, and one who knows his language. He signals to the first pair of soldiers on the bridge, who step forward to either side of me.

"Come," is all he says. And my heart turns to ice.

Morfrenna shifts her staff, looking to Vivian for instruction. Vivi stands still, expressionless. But I can sense her feeling for understanding, searching for meaning in the eddying currents of events, waiting.

I kiss Gwenlli's brow and gently lay her down upon the ground. Standing, I turn to Vivi. "Courage, Love," I say to her. "With luck, this is an escort, not a guard, and I will return to you."

With Roman soldiers before and behind, I take a step out onto the wooden planks, hear them creak beneath my weight. The sky is a dark violet, the first bright stars appearing overhead. A marsh chit sits in a bush just by the walkway, looking, waiting for night. A gentle breeze from the northwest slides over the tor and drops down upon us. Its chill is a warning of the cold to come. The soldier in front of me has a new pair of boots. I can hear the leather creaking, his scabbard scratching along his thigh. The wood of my staff is warm and polished in my hand, smooth to the touch. Deep in my lungs I can still feel the rattle of illness, and the taste of blood in the back of my mouth. I marvel at such a moment of utter clarity.

Eosaidh! No! No! Vivi's cry tears my heart, but I cannot stop.

As I cross the walkway towards the woods of the mainland, she steps forward to the body of Gwenlli and kneels, but her eyes are upon me. I can no longer see her face, but there is terror in her voice as it speaks in my heart. The mists close between us.

Titus Flavius Vespasian sits across a small camp table from me in his command tent, hands wrapped around a silver goblet of Gaulish wine. The walk to his camp was brief, his headquarters even nearer to the island than I had suspected. I have no idea how long I waited to see him. It is now very late. A single oil lamp hangs over us, throwing shadows across our faces. He is fitter than when I last saw him, if older by more than the intervening years. I watch him with caution, not yet certain whether my gamble will succeed, or find me chained to an oar of a trireme warship off the southern coast. We are perhaps a mile inland from the marshes surrounding Ynys Niwl. It feels like a thousand.

"It was on Crete," I say in answer to his question, "When you were serving your quaestorship and I had delivered a shipload of lead for repairing the baths."

His face softens, and a light comes to his eyes. "Yes!" he says. "I remember. And the wine flowed as freely as hot water through those lead pipes the night of the banquet when the work was completed!" He offers me more wine. When I decline he sets his cup aside as well, the sign of a wise negotiator and a careful soldier. "And the favors of the young women were flowing freely as well. But as I recall you partook of little of the former, and none of the latter."

I dismiss his comment with a smile and a shrug of my shoulders. "As you would do tonight. Sometimes it is wiser to preserve one's wits than to indulge one's body." His answering smile tells me I am making a connection.

"We were very nearly friends back then," he says. "By all rights I should be in the Senate now. And you should be enjoying a luxurious retirement. I know well why I am here, but what brings you to this god-forsaken part of the world?"

He knows that also. I remind him of the events in Jerusalem, and my relationship with the lad. He scowls. For a moment I expect him to call the guards. "That's old news," he says. "Gaius Calligula had issues with the Iudde and that new sect of theirs, but Claudius has more important concerns. You are long forgotten, old friend. You have no need to hide."

"My people at land's end and in the Mendydd would disagree, facing your legion," I reply. His smile is an attempt to ease the tension, if not to reassure.

"Eosaidh, I have not gone as far as your holdings in Cornualle, you know that. I have no desire to station troops on such a narrow peninsula. You will grow rich from the trade agreement." I raise an eyebrow to express interest, but assume there is no truth in it. He looks at his cup, thinking about another swallow. "True, you've lost the Mendydd mines." It is a simple truth for him, in need of no further explanation.

"In any case, this now is my home," I tell him, "More important for my solitude than for your tactics. There are no metals here, no highways across the marshes, only an old tinner, a couple of Iuddic companions, and a community of priestesses."

"One of those priestesses disarmed an officer of mine and might have killed him."

"Flavius, she was defending her home. The woman your principales killed was trying to protect me. There will be no sallying forth from this island to endanger your legion. And any troops stationed here would be immobilized by the marshes, lost to you for battle. Better to fortify the Mendydd, for Caradoc is not far beyond, mobilizing the Silures against you." I am telling him nothing he does not already know, but I hope it may save Ynys y Niwl.

"What about the young druids who played at defending the bridge against my patrol?"

"Surely you learned enough from that not to fear them further. Besides, they've already headed out to the north leaving the island in the care of the priestesses. They were gone practically before the boots of your soldiers left the walkway. Druids are no fools, Flavius. They will challenge you, but only on their own terms, at a time of their own choosing, by joining Caradoc."

He leans back in his chair, thinking. Time slows to the crawl of impending chance. His breathing is the only sound in the tent, but I would swear he can hear my heart race. *Vivi, I hope this was not the errand of a fool!*

"I will leave you to your little island and your priestesses, Eosaidh," he says at last, "a return for those two charming ladies you left to me that night at the banquet. Though what you find of any value in these horrid swamps I cannot begin to guess." He laughs, a great, raucous laugh of a soldier who believes he has won a battle, and slaps me on the shoulder. With that he fills both cups to the brim, and raises his to me with a wry grin. "Vinum, Virgines, Imperator!" he proclaims. Who am I to refuse such a toast from Titus Flavius Vespasian?

His time available for humouring old friends at an end, Vespasian calls an aide into the tent. "See that this man is escorted back to the place where you found him," he says.

"Yes, Legatus."

"And see that he stays out of trouble until you leave him." He means, get him out of here, and don't let him see anything important on the way. Turning to me he says quietly, "It has been good to see you again, Eosaidh. You will be left to your solitude for a while. But tell your priestesses I cannot guarantee the future if the druids want to fight." The final threat is an idle one, I know. Vivian's curse will play a larger role in keeping Romans off Ynys y Niwl than will my diplomacy.

He shows me to the door, where two soldiers wait to escort me back to the walkway across the marsh. Mists have already begun to swirl across the landward approach, and the soldiers shrink back from the enveloping darkness leaving me to cross the marsh alone, to the relative safety of the island.

There is no one at the island end of the walkway. It is early morning, hours before first light. I kneel upon the battered earth, and feel the pain it holds where Gwenlli died, but there is no sign of blood. The priestesses have made certain no traces of her remain lying, dishonored, in the open. Alone, I set out through the narrow wood between Wirrheal and the marsh, heading back to camp. The darkness plays tricks upon my eyes and within my memory.

A low sloping trunk of a tree leaning out over the water transports me back half a lifetime to the water sprite I first met on the far shore of this land. She was dark, and lithe, like a pixie, and I was then a young man with strength of body as well as heart. I thought she was a spirit until her hand touched my face, and I felt the warmth of her fingers. We had eaten together on the grass, sharing the mysteries of the marshes, and the wonders of the world. When we kissed it was the explosion of sunrise over the marshes, our joining like the wild waves of the sea. And as we lay together afterwards on the soft grass, I knew she was no sprite, but a true woman, warm and alive with love. No one had ever touched me on the inside as she had that day. In the hours that followed, as we made love again, I fell in love, for the one and only time in my life.

Years later we met again. Then she was Lady of Affalon, and the lad was with me. Our eyes met in fond remembrance, but never again did our bodies join until that festival night. Fresher memories flood my mind as I stare into the marsh water, unseeing in this world, remembering each moment of love, every touch of her body, each caress of her lips. Until suddenly I realize there is a tinge of light in the east, barely illuminating the broken, scudding clouds that promise more rain later in the day. Ahead, through the trees, I can see the cooking fire at the center of the circle of huts. Trophimus and the others will be rising, wondering if I will return, fearing the worst news from the Roman camp. Vivi will have gone back through the mists, knowing that her heart will remain connected to mine, come what may. Sedullus' bell rings, calling the men to morning prayer. I sigh, and the rattle in my lungs brings coughing in the cold damp of early morning. I have no idea whether I will find my way through the mists to Vivian, but in any case I have unfinished business here with Trophimus and the Gaulish followers of the lad. I pick up my staff, stretch out my stiffening muscles, and head toward the little chapel

I stop at the door and listen, for what I hear is not the familiar synagogue cadence of psalms and prayers.

"Credo," Trophimus intones, and the others join in,
"I believe in Iesu of Nazareth,
Attested to by God by the miracles, wonders and signs
That God has done among us, through him.
According to the definite plan and foreknowledge of God,
He was handed over by his own people to be
crucified by those outside the Law.
But God raised him up, having freed him from death,
Because death could not hold him in its power.
To this we are all witnesses . . .
Therefore we proclaim that God has made this same Iesu
Both Messiah and Lord, Amen."

Abruptly I turn from the doorway and stumble far enough away not to be heard, then fall to my knees, leaning on my staff. I look up to the heavens. The bright Morning Star shines in the east just above the widening band of light.

Therefore we proclaim that Elohim has made this same Iesu
Both Meshiach and Adonai!

God's Anointed One I can understand. Many men in the tradition of my people have been accorded that title, though none as humble as a traveling Rabbi, son of a Galilean carpenter, nephew of a tinner. But Adonai! They have called him by the Name of God! Again the rattle in my lungs, and the harsh coughing. Trophimus, what have you done? What has happened across the world while I have been here on its edges? The lad called us to a life of love, to invite the reign of Adonai into our hearts. But now you call the lad, himself, Adonai, and offer worship to him! What perversion of his message is this?

I cannot stay here. The gray light of morning reveals the wall of mist now fallen across the entrance to the Valley of Springs and I stumble toward it, pulling myself along with my staff.

In the warm days of summer I walked this path a hundred times, surely I can find my way now. The coldness of the mist surrounds me as I reach the path running along the left bank of the stream and turn uphill.

At first it is all familiar: the little waterfall over a ledge of granite, the old blackthorn hedge that overhangs part of the stream, the tangle of beech roots that make the path difficult even in bright sunshine. At last I reach watersmeet, where the stream from y Ffynnon Wen comes down from the right. But, beyond, the darkness of the mist deepens, shutting out more of the sun. I lose my footing and trip over a stone I did not expect. I run into another blackthorn thicket where I had thought the path to be, its great thorns tearing at the flesh of my hands and face. I find the path again, but now it seems to be going downward. Have I reached the crest of the ridge already? With growing confidence I start out downhill, though nothing now looks familiar and I can barely see beyond the length of my arm. But the light is growing, and the mist begins to thin.

All at once I step out of a wall of mist. The morning sun is close to the zenith; I have been hours walking, not minutes. The field is filled with the light and warmth of autumn sunshine. But before me, close enough to reach out and touch, is the door of the little chapel and the echo of the words within,

> *Therefore, God has made this same Iesu*
> *Both Meshiach and Adonai.*

And my heart seems to die within my chest, and my eyes flood with tears. I sit heavily on the bare ground before the chapel, clutching at the brown earth. Down the hill someone is splitting firewood. Two others are fishing, in the small boat out in the marsh. Trophimus is sitting beside his hut, writing something on a scroll. The world around me is brilliant with the colors of autumn, but never has my soul known such utter desolation. Vivi is beyond the tor, lost to me, on the other side of the mists. I fall forward to lie face down on the earth, with bitter tears in my heart that I am unable to shed, and my world goes dark.

Eosaidh. Eoasaidh. Wake up. I am lying on a soft cot, covered with furs. Through the darkness of my sleep I can hear Vivi calling to me, but I cannot open my eyes, cannot awaken. *Eosaidh.* She shakes my shoulder. I begin to be aware of a stiffness in my joints, the awful pain at the bottom of my lungs. I can feel the world spinning, though I cannot yet see.

Again, *Eosaidh, wake up!* But her voice is deeper. Her touch less gentle. With great difficulty I manage to open my eyes. Instantly I am blinded by the noonday sun, high in the sky. I cover my eyes with my hand, turning my head to cough up more redness. When I look back, there is no cot but only the hard ground. And it is Trophimus kneeling beside me, leaning over me, shaking my shoulder in alarm.

"Thank God!" he says. "I thought you'd returned from the Romans only to leave us for the bosom of Abraham." He helps me to sit up and offers me water from a skin. "I'm sorry it's not wine," he says. "Perhaps next spring the vines will be growing." I take a little, to wet my mouth, but my stomach rebels at the thought of swallowing. It renews the metallic taste of the blood I have coughed up, making me sorry for even the small sip.

"Can you rise?" he asks. I nod, and he helps me up with the aid of my staff. Together we set off toward the huts as the world comes back into focus around me. He is going on about being glad to see me, but I hear little. *Vivi, are you lost to me for ever?*

When we reach the fire circle Trophimus props me against a log for a seat. Suddenly I am truly aware of age, and he, though well on in years, seems so young and strong by comparison. He goes off somewhere and returns with two large cups. "At least the bees have been hard at work!" he says, and hands me the mead. "Eosaidh, we must talk," he says, "You are not happy with us."

"It's not so much that, old friend, it's just that much seems to have changed in the wide world while I have been here in Affalon." The mead is bringing back some of my strength, easing the sense of burning in my lungs. "I no longer recognize my nephew in the words of his followers."

We sit silently, each with our own thoughts. An occasional late autumn marsh wasp is attracted to the mead, and hovers around us.

"He is no longer merely your nephew," he says.

"He is always my nephew, but that is not the point," I answer.

He takes a long drink of mead and looks at me squarely. "And what is the point?" he asks.

I test many words in my mind. Once I was his mentor. And now, in his eyes, he is becoming mine. I can understand his reservations. He had thought to be joining my community. But now it is a question of whether I will fit in his.

"It is how you relate to the lad," I begin. "I do not think we are even talking about the same person. I remember the builder who learned the tin trade with me. I remember the young rabbi who traveled Iudea and the Galilee, healing those who were broken-hearted, and teaching about the kingdom of God. I remember a young prophet who talked about love, and demonstrated it by his life and his death. But I do not recognize the one you call Messiah and Lord, and neither, I think, would he."

"Eosaidh, Adonai raised him from the dead, and that changed everything."

"I have heard the tales, Trophimus. He appeared to some in Jerusalem, to others in Galilee. In one tale he walked through walls. In another, he ate breakfast like an ordinary man. The world is filled with tales of dying and rising heroes, gods who go down to the underworld and return. Even here, at the end of the world, God dies at this time of year, and returns in the spring. Here, at least, people understand they are speaking of the natural world, the fallow fields, and the new planting, and the harvesting of crops. But you, you have taken a myth about God and turned it into a true story about a flesh and blood person, and you have attached it to my nephew!"

Trophimus cries out and pretends to tear at his hair. "Heaven forbid!" he cries. "Eosaidh, you have allowed the closeness of kinship to blind you to the greater truth!" He pauses, and sets down his cup. He looks at me in all earnestness, as if my life depends upon what he is about to say.

"I know the lad was your nephew, Eosaidh. But now he is the Son of God. He was not named Iesu - 'The Lord Saves' - for nothing, Eosaidh. For now he sits, in his flesh, at the right hand of God to bring reconciliation, forgiveness of our sins. Some of us are coming to believe, Eosaidh, that Iesu is indeed Adonai himself, come to us in the flesh, the one Isaias called Immanuel, God-with-Us."

He is so sincere, so certain, so moved by what he believes.

"I do not deny that life survives," I say. "Trophimus, I have seen him more than once since coming to this isle. I have spoken with him." My old friend's eyes open wide, his jaw drops in wonder.

"That resurrection is true I cannot doubt," I continue. "I know that death is not an end, but simply another way of being. But that gift is not for gods only, Trophimus. You needn't put such a price on it. In the currents that surround us, life always returns. You needn't make him a god to know that he lives."

This man who was once my companion looks at me as though there is no hope left for me. But I am no longer in need of hope. The silence between us begins small, and grows slowly until it is a vast, empty cavern.

"And what do you expect of him, Trophimus, this young prophet whom you have turned into a god?"

"The truth, my friend. He gives us the one true way to salvation, for there is no other name in heaven or on earth by which a man may be saved."

"Saved? Saved from what, man?"

Trophimus stares at me, his eyes again wide with disbelief. He opens his mouth to speak, hesitates, tries again. After several attempts to form words, he finally says, "From ourselves, Eosaidh. From our sinful selves." He pauses, wondering, I think, whether he dare speak his mind. Finally he does.

"Eosaidh of Arimathea, you have lived too long with the priestesses of these marshes and their evil beliefs. They have led you astray from the true God. I fear you are as damned to hell as they if you do not listen to me and renounce their ways!"

Down by the shore Orgetorix and Casticus pull their small boat aground. They startle a flock of small birds -- I cannot recognize them from here - who rise up in a cloud and fly away across the marsh. Then there is silence. I look Trophimus in the eye. I see neither hatred nor anger there, but the confidence of righteous assurance. My hands work the smooth wood of my staff. My jaw clenches tightly, and I grind my teeth together. With all that is in me, I strive to contain my anger. What I must say, must do, must honor the lad, not deny him.

"I remember he once said that he had many sheep in other flocks," I say in a level, measured voice, straining for calm. "I remember he once said that he did not come to judge. I remember he once said that we are not God's servants, but God's friends. I remember him caring for the Canaanite, and the Samaritan, and the Phoenician. I remember him holding sinners in his arms. I remember him dying rather than give up on love."

I rise slowly, leaning on my staff. In my mind I see shards of blue glass at the bottom of y Ffynnon Goch and Vivi's young son, and the blue sky over Bol Forla, rich with the scent of love.

"I hope you are confident of recognizing him, my friend," I say, "For at the moment I do not think he would recognize you. Please excuse me, I have a few things to pack." And I head off to my own hut, wondering what to take with me, and what to leave behind.

And now it is the end of the apple harvest, several days after my confrontation with Trophimus. Across the island, lost now to me, the women are gathering in the last of the fruit before winter. Already there has been frost in the reeds, and the first layering of ice along the banks. It is evening, and I am sitting at the entrance to my lean-to, a fire going before me to provide some warmth. I am wrapped in layers of wool and hide, but the cold seeps into my bones anyway. I cannot breathe without wheezing. The rattle in my lungs grows worse. I no longer know whether I am cursed, but certainly I am ill. I no longer live with the ones who call themselves 'Christians'. Indeed, I think they now use my old roundhouse for storage. But I cannot find my way back to Vivian either. We have both done what we must to protect the island, and we have found ourselves on opposite sides of the mists.

I stare past the fire into the darkness of the marsh. My camp is on the northern side of Bol Forla, under the willows where Vivi and I once sat. Before me the old, ruined walkway leads out from the shore to disappear under the dark waters. It is so quiet here. And I am alone. I had sought to be a part of two communities; I can belong to neither. It seems to me that this life is destined to be always a journey, never a home. I look down the old walkway to where it fades in the darkness, and wonder what I might find at its end.

Chapter Nineteen
The Waters

(Vivian)

The light is reflecting off the water. Here and there, where a fish or an otter move below, or a marsh hen scutters by, ripples create patterns, circles and tides, ridges of light and shadow that draw my eye. But upon the broad spread of the lake, there is a bright metallic sheen, a dark silver that makes me want to close my eyes and turn inwards. it looks almost as if the waters are covered with a finely crafted lid.

Yet in some way the power of this reflected light adds to my courage. I get to my feet and, with the warmth of our love filling my soul with such a lightness of joy, such a depth of certainty, I reach out my hand, *Come, my darling.*

But his fingers don't touch mine. I turn to seek him out. He is sitting on the broken walkway where a moment before I had sat beside him. Our eyes meet, yet in his there is a dreadful fear, and it pierces my body like the sharpest lance of yew.

"I can't walk on the water, Vivi," he whispers.

The warmth of the cloth upon my face draws me to wakefulness.

It takes a moment to find comprehension through my eyes, though they are open, and I feel a wish to smile at the gentle face that attends to me.

Morfrenna, I murmur.

"My Lady," she says softly, with a smile that lifts her soul to shine in her eyes.

A child stands beside her, his skin distorted, crusted and
charred from the kind of forced heat that builds when a
roundhouse is set on fire, and he too smiles at me. Then I see
the flames of our own hearth fire flickering through him, and
I realize he is another of the dead.

Is she caring for you too? I ask him.

She wants you to get better, he chirps, like a glas chit in the
full flush of spring. *I've already met my grandfathers, but you're
not dead yet.*

Is that so? I say sadly.

He shakes his head. I close my eyes as again Morfrenna
bathes my forehead with the warm cloth, murmuring, "There,
my Lady." And the young boy continues, *You've been sleeping
for a long time and the seers aren't sure that you want to come
back.* He cocks his head on one side, a little glas chit again,
*They say someone gave you life and now he's taken it away. Who's
that then?*

Why are you here, child?

He shrugs, glancing at Morfrenna. *She's my sister.*

Through the doorway, the dusty light of autumn's end dances
in the wind. A blackbird, his feathers a little buffeted, is
digging into an apple in the clearing just outside. Brown and
brittle leaves, lifted upon gusts, grab at every chance they are
given to explore. Inside, Creyr, tending to the fire, gathers a
handful from the floor that have sneaked in upon the wind,
and sets them into the flames. I watch their spirits shimmer,
released into the air with the merest scent of the earth that has
nourished their growth through the summer's light.

I can feel him watching me. Has he been saying something
important?

His prying eyes leave my face and turn to Sianed.

"Can she see me?" he murmurs.

"The Lady sees your spirit more clearly than your flesh,"
she replies softly. She knows I can hear her and knows how the
druid's words show his ignorance, his lack of competence, yet

she shows no obvious disrespect in her manner. Somewhere inside me I smile to watch the subtle confrontation.

"But does she understand what I've said?"

This is too much and I breathe in through the rasp of my dry throat. My voice is like a rusty blade. "You maggot-infested weasel, I am neither stupid nor deaf. Do you expect me to get up and frolic with joy? Perhaps I am glad you are leaving, for I will not have your scat littering my islands."

He is shocked to hear me speak, to see that I can rise from the trance within which my time now passes. Indeed, I myself wonder how long it has been since last I spoke. Days and days. He gathers up the sloppy edges of his soul and bows, "My Lady." Then he sets his face to justify his action once again, "Surely you can understand, all the help we can give the Silures we must give. Only then do we have a chance -"

"You have no chance," I growl, hearing the grief turned to bitterness in my voice.

Sianed shakes her head, holding her dignity and composure. "Caldreg, the people need you here. Every day we are taking boats out into the marshes, finding those who are fleeing, the homeless, wounded, the dead, and their numbers are not lessening. They need your vision, your rites, your courage."

"Priestess, many are being taken in by settlements that have allied with the Romans. You know that."

"Druid, when your thatch has been set alight above your head, your family dragged out and slaughtered, your children screaming, it is not easy to accept help from those who side with the murderers. People of good heart are starving. Will you leave them behind?"

He rubs his leggings with hands not leathered by the touch of hard work, and gets to his feet, shaking his head. "Priestess," he says quietly and, turning to me with a bow, "my Lady, the decision is made. I will leave before the winter comes in any quicker. With me travel two others of the council, our apprentices and a handful of warriors. Tandreg will go straight to Ynys Mon, where we too shall be heading if things don't go well with the Silures. I know you will not ..."

And his voice drones on, like a wood wasp trapped in the roof thatch, and for a moment I watch him, feeling him drift further from me. Sianed answers, her soul shimmering with her courage and determination, unmoved by the complications of his pompous self-justification. His soul is bent over, carrying the burden of doubt. His visions must reveal to him that to run from his home lands will lose him the respect of the people, a loss that will never be regained, yet he clings to the hope that, by running, he will save something. And what a cruel blade is hope, a blade clung to by those who cannot let the river flow upon its natural course.

I can surely smell the sweet acrid stench of his rotting body already. Come here, druid, let me sniff you! His people being slaughtered, he himself runs to hide, only to be found at the turning of another moon by the hunting dogs of Roma's eagle, his scent of fear like a fire in the wind.

Sianed turns to me, questioning. If she hears my thoughts it only confirms to her that I am now deranged with grief, and here further exhausted by the druid's lies. I close my eyes and let my body slip back again into its stupor.

Laughing, I reach out my hand towards him.

"You don't need to walk on the water, my darling. Why would you want to?"

But his fear is so overwhelming and he looks up into my face with a pain born of not understanding. I crouch before him, briefly aware of my body now being as lithe and strong as it was that summer's day when we first met, and I hold the soft tangles of his bearded face in my hands, offering him the depth of my love without words. As he breathes, so do I breathe, his broad chest lifting and falling with the sobbing of his grief. And the whispers of his soul lift into the cool wind and I breathe in every moment that is filled with his living.

"I can't lose you, Vivi," he whispers. "How can I live now without you?"

I turn to the waters of the lake and it is no more than a moment before I see what I need to see. A sleek black cormorant, perched upon an overhanging branch of willow, spies a fish and slips down through the glistening silver surface into the darkness of the water beneath.

"We have no need to stay in the light, my love."

"But I can't breathe under the water, Vivi."

And for a moment I don't know what to do. I want to jump up and run to where the old walkway planks are splintered and rotting, the stilts collapsed, taking the path into the lake, and there to sing with the joy of this exquisite love I feel so deeply.

Yet I haven't the confidence that he will find his strength to rise and walk those few paces towards me. And in my soul I cry out to the goddess of the marshes. And I cry out to Morla.

How long has it been, Gwenlli?

She sits down beside me and smiles with all the gentle tenderness of her soul.

Since when, my Lady?

Since he died. No, you died. He left. Did he die?

You are getting confused, she says softly.

She lifts the water bowl to my lips.

It is Fianna's face that I wake to, my eyes already open finding focus in this shared world. "My Lady," she is whispering. "Drink, my Lady."

It takes me a moment to break the rage that holds back the grief, yet too to hold my soul steady and indeed to breathe. I look into her eyes and she nods, acknowledging my presence. I sip from the bowl and feel a memory returning to me, a sense of cool clear water. It flickers through me like firelight and is gone. The next sip is hard to swallow.

Across the fire my grandmother sits upon the hides. *Come on, Vivi,* she whispers. *There are things to be done now.*

"What's in the water?" I murmur.

"It is pure water from y Ffynnon Goch, my Lady."

Fianna helps me to sit up.

"I tasted something in the water."

She smiles, shaking her head, and I look into the sadness of her eyes.

"Give me your hands," I say, frowning, watching my own shake as I hold them out. And immediately she lays hers into mine the memory returns.

I look down, almost embarrassed.

She bends to look into my face. "My Lady, what did you see?"

How can I tell her that it was life I saw, just life? It was the touch of her living I had tasted through the bowl. So far have I drifted that its shimmer is surprising.

"How long has it been, Fianna? Since ..." The words are hard to find.

"The moon is full tomorrow, my Lady. She left us when this moon's tide began."

"I have little memory," I start to say.

"We have all been grieving, my Lady."

I have never felt such a weight of exhaustion.

"I would like an apple."

A body jumps from the hay and lands at my side. Wide-eyed, with the soft skin of a young face, she smiles. Her closeness surprises me.

"Bronwen," I say softly.

"Yes, my Lady," she bites her lip to control her smile. "Would you really like an apple?"

Barely have I nodded when she is up and through the door, her voice ringing through the clearing, "Fia! Mama! She asked for an apple!" For the first time in a long while, I hear the hens chattering, a voice singing to spirits a little way off, and the clinking of heavy pots around the community fire.

It is Sianed who comes in, an apple in her hand.

I try to move, to pull myself up, but find that I can't. It seems silly to have forgotten how to do it, or that I can't do it, and I laugh, though not aloud. Sianed smiles, sitting beside me. She takes my hand.

"It is good to see you, my Lady."

There is no expectation in her eyes, no demand, no need about to be presented. I am aware of the absence and feel it both as a relief and a source of anxiety. Through the darkness of my mind, I sense how much of my life has been held in place by the continuous flows of obligation, as Lady of Ynys y Niwl, as elder of the community, as teacher, mother, priestess and student. Memories of days unhampered spill into my mind with a cool wash of clarity, dancing with butterflies, stamping in puddles, playing with lambs, with beetles and thunder clouds. Not yet ten summers old.

And that day, when Eos appeared by the water's edge. What freedom I found that day! With those dark brown eyes, he opened a door within me, a door that led to the world beyond the islands, to a world where nobody knew me.

The grief breaks over me again: that door should never have opened, the door to the world beyond.

I close my eyes, bending over, but I am no longer able to weep. Have I run dry of tears or have I moved into a different land? Sianed takes my hand and holds it with gentle strength. When I look into her eyes she expresses only her committed presence. She does not even ask if there is anything I would like.

I am in a boat, set free upon the lake, drifting, on the surface.

There are moments of lucidity. Cold frost underfoot, an icicle melting into my soul, an inbreath, and I am awake. The rain is softly coming down onto the thatch of the roundhouse.

Morfrenna is playing her lyre.

I turn to her and listen, closing my eyes. They are old songs of the marshes, women's songs, love songs. When she stops to put another log on the fire, I open my eyes. She nods and smiles, *My Lady.*

I beckon her close to me and she comes to sit beside me, and I chuckle at her muddy fingers, her boyish soul holding its right to work and to play. I want to ask how she can play so beautifully with fingers so encrusted with mud. She notices my gaze, laughs and sits on her hands.

I look into her eyes. *Can you understand soul words yet, child?*

She frowns. I take a deep breath, knowing I must find my voice.

"Is he alive?" I say slowly.

The warmth and open affection in her face slips to be replaced by a sadness I can feel deep in her soul. She nods, "Yes, my Lady. He is out on Bol Forla. He is all alone, my Lady. I was told not to talk to him, but ..." She looks towards the door, and then down at the ground, knowing what she tells me is more complicated than she can understand. "But I have left him apples whenever I can, and sometimes bread, cheese and nuts. I've watched him from the marshes on the other side of the river. Sometimes he stands on the shore, looking for who it is who's given him the food. He knows it comes from the waterways and, my Lady, sometimes I've heard him call out to thank the goddess." She pauses, then whispers, "He also thanks you."

Tears slide down my cheeks. The child smoothes them away with the hem of her robe.

"Tell him," i whisper, "to meet me ..."

"My Lady, you cannot move."

"... at the end of her walkway," I touch her hand, reaching for breath.

"On Bol Forla?"

I nod, "When the moon shows her first crescent."

Tears are now falling down the young girl's face.

"But, my Lady," she sobs, looking into my eyes.

"Don't tell anyone," I shake my head. "No one."

From where I lie beneath the yew, the sun's light is no softer. It lances my eyes, arrows of the finest white gold, piercing my soul. I turn away, reaching further into the shadow offered by the old yew, then try again to see the bird, feeling the urgency in my heart, in my belly, in my feet. On its wide spread wings, its yelping cry cutting into the wind, it wheels around letting me see clearly the five dark fingers of its wing feathers and the scattered white markings, and then, as it comes around again, this time even lower over the island, the pale golden brown of his body.

I wonder how long this image has been a portent of death amongst my people. Has it only been such since the seers first began to perceive the eagle upon Roma's standard and, not knowing the source of the killing, noted only the bird? Or has such a bird always brought with it death?

Beside me, upon the mud and grass, the raven dips its head to listen to my thoughts, and I hold out a hand that it nuzzle my fingers with its beak. An eater of carrion, of the dead, she is a companion upon the road, a comfort to any soul who makes the journey, embraced within the darkness of her wings. But she does not bring death.

Again the eagle cries out, and as I shuffle my body to the edge, I can see out through the yew branches, and there I watch the bird land, upon the arm of a man, held up to be its perch. He stands in a clearing that breaks out to the island's shore, and though the blazing sun shines upon him, he seems to thrive in its merciless heat. Smiling, triumphant, he guides the eagle who flies to the hilt of great long sword thrust into the mud. As the bird lands, it turns to gold. There is a cheer, as if a multitude hidden by the veils of time in that moment rises up in celebration. And another part of me dies.

Who are you? I whisper, and across the water the man turns to me. It is Llygethin, the Christian whose name is Trophimus. And I have a strange sense of Eos having sailed down the waters, having sailed away. I seek out a glimpse of him, though the sun reflecting off the water blinds me.

The cracking of wood close beside me breaks my gaze and suddenly I am struggling to open my eyes. Fia is beside me, her hand upon my arm. She whispers, "Settle, my Lady, it is yet night."

The darkness of the roundhouse is muted by a wash of grey upon my seeing. I look up at Fianna, but though she is close she seems a long way from me. Her voice drifts in the air.

I can feel her thoughts, exploring my soul, seeking out how much I know, wondering at my level of clarity. I rise up through the trance of my tiredness, breathing deeply as I find the surface. When I can fix my attention, I gaze into her soul.

You have it. I saw it in a vision, priestess.

And she sighs, conceding.

Yes, I have it.

So tell me.

"My Lady, we are now surrounded by Romans. They know we have nothing of value but the power of the island, and it is said that they do not intend to take that from us, preferring in time to negotiate an agreement for our blessing and visions. When it comes to religion, they are patient, it seems." The door hides are up and for a moment she gazes out into the cold clear air, bringing a fresh openness to the roundhouse and the moments that pass between us.

And the Christians? I ask her.

"They have no interest in us."

They will.

She sighs, "When they have more power they will become a threat to us. As yet, their prayers are an irritation and we protect ourselves from them. Their energy is poisonous to the land and their beliefs too peculiar for the marsh folk to understand, but all our visions confirm that they will not go away."

I cough, seeking my voice, finding only a croak. "Still he gave it to you ..."

"He believed it safer here than taking it north, my Lady." Then she adds, "He needed only to have a surety that you had broken connections with Eosaidh."

I nod.

She touches my arm, gently, then gets to her feet, leaving me for the few moments it takes her to retrieve the blade, time within which I linger upon her last words.

It lies beside me on the deer hides. Crafted by metalsmiths working with the fferyllt of the Deceangli, its depth shimmers in the fire light. I wonder how long it has been in his druid line. By the look of its smooth straight blade and the decoration on its hilt, it can be no more than a few generations old.

According to Sianed, Caldreg believed it would improve our chances, increasing the power of the island, and we had both laughed, or would have done if we had had the strength. She had placed it on the hides with relief simply because in doing so she released its spiritual weight from her hands. She barely wanted to touch it.

I let my fingers slide over the metal ornamentation. The boar's tusks are sharp on my skin, and I sink for a while into remembrance of a vision: druids falling into the sacred waters, their blood spilled red and thick beneath the legs of Roman horses, and one man, a Roman chieftain, leaning down to lift from the waters the unbroken sword of my people. Is it this sword? A sword upon which so many thousands of vows of contract have been sealed, deals between tribes, fostering and marriages begun and ended, deeds of land sworn, cattle traded, conflicts ended. The history of my people.

Yet it is a druid blade still, a long blade, a sword of sovereignty asserted, a blade of declaration, of power proclaimed. That such a blade could deepen any bond with the land is a druidic delusion, a belief held only by those who do not see spirit with clarity, people for whom the land is simply mud not the body of a goddess, and for whom history is about power, not a sacred song of ancestors, a song to sing that the soul may learn.

I lift my fingers from the metal and rub them upon the hides.

What will you do with it? I had asked her.

She looked into my soul and for a while we were silent.

Then she had whispered, *I was hoping for your guidance.*

The boat moves silently through the water. It is good to be outside after a whole moontide lain in the roundhouse. Above me there is mist and to either side, a spell sung upon the boat by Sianed and Fianna. Now Morfrenna sings softly into the damp air, her paddle slipping into the lake without a sound, drawing us across open water hidden by the magic of our grandmothers.

The memory of Sianed's face touches my soul. I knew she was ready and in the way that her being shifted, rearranging itself within the web of life, finding its new position, my trust was affirmed. From within that moment of clarity, with my mother beside me, my grandmother behind me and our blood's roots behind her, spirit to spirit, threads stretching back through time, I gave to Sianed the spells and heard the sincerity of her vows. And she saw that I was with her, and her tears and her fingers clasped about mine sung of her courage, and as we slid together into the waters of the cauldron I knew she would walk with honour.

What I saw in the waters was not my future. I was slow to rise from the depths, but she took even longer, knowing that this was the last time we would journey together, aware of each other's spirit moving close, the tips of our wing feathers now and then almost touching, gliding through the darkness, wakeful and watching as the visions moved beneath us, around us and through us.

Yet, when we both had emerged, our eyes met, and she breathed deeply, and I knew that she had seen a world that she could and would walk within, crafting her own path and that of our people. And I knew too that she had seen me released.

When it was done, I had bowed to her, aware of how strange it felt for the burden of my life to have been lifted, for another now to be Lady of Ynys y Niwl. With grief and relief I had whispered, "Let me go home now."

So do I now lie in the soft damp air of the mist, tears slipping down my cheeks, a part of my soul feeling the lightness of freedom, waiting for the boat to touch the mud of my island, Ynys y Cysgodion, beneath the ancient peeling bark of the old yew I know as Ywena. And when it does, Morfrenna stands to tie the little craft, causing it to rock in the cold still water, but suddenly I feel unable to find the desire to walk again on solid ground.

"Leave me for a while," I whisper.

She breathes in sharply, holding back her grief. I smile - strangely I can feel the shape of it in the wrinkles of my face - and see that it gives her courage. She nods, stepping off the boat onto the mud, then turning to settle it in the swell. Moments seem to stretch, as if they have no edges at all, and I watch Gwenlli beside her on the island, watching me. Leaving the paddle on the furs and hides that cover me, Morfrenna looks down.

"Let the path emerge," I whisper to her, praying to my grandmothers that she has the strength to walk away. Then I close my eyes, listening to the song of the old yew in the evening's breeze.

With darkness falling, the mist begins to lift.

At times I am able to direct my course through the currents, the paddle barely held in the grip of my fingers, breaking the surface of the water quietly, or simply acting as a rudder, the craft following the silent songs of the streams that flow through the marshes. It seems to me a long time and no time at all before I am out in the open water of Llyntywyll.

As ever it does, the darkness of the lake fills my soul with wonder. Yet this time, it is more. The *hiraeth,* the deep longing for the release that comes with going home, shimmers within me like a memory of moonlight upon the water. I breathe in the darkness, the quiet of the lake, and am overwhelmed by the sense of being human and alone.

How long I drift through these moments, I do not know. The first curl of the new moon watches me through clouds that are slowly clearing above me, the sky growing darker as night draws on, the stars beginning to wake and listen. An owl calls and I smile to think that the owls will always call across these waters.

It is with the strength born of that loneliness that I lift myself in the boat, pushing off the furs with arms now thin as twigs in autumn. Feeling the rocking of the boat, out here in the lake, I lift the heavy sword that is Caldreg's blade, and whisper my prayers to the goddess of the water ... *take this, my Lady, I ask you in the name of my ancestors, for all that is sacred, this blade that holds the sovereignty of my land* ... And my words land like snow flakes upon the dark surface, melting, sinking, accepted into her beautiful soul. It is not that I let the blade go, for it too melts, slipping from my fingers into the water's silent song.

I look up. Silhouetted against the indigo sky a raven sits on a high branch of an oak on the lake shore. *Tell him,* I whisper.

Utterly depleted, I close my eyes. And I breathe out, until there is nothing left in my body. In that darkness and quiet, I make my prayers, opening my soul ... *my Lady, my goddess, sacred black water* ...

And I too slip over the side, into the waters of the lake.

Chapter Twenty
The Old Walkway

(Eosaidh)

t was at the full moon of nos Calan Gaeaf the solid mists finally came down over Glyn y Ffynhonnau and stayed. I could see them from the soft round top of Bol Forla, above my camp. It was then I knew the true horror of my mistake that had cut me off from Vivian. My meeting with Vespasian had perhaps bought time, but at the expense of bringing the Eagle of Rome too close in my own person for the safety of the priestesses. Vivi did what she had to do. The mists had to be closed. Only then did I hear with cold clarity the cry of her voice as I crossed the Polden walkway that evening: *Eosaidh, No!*

Often after I heard her call to me, asking me to come to her through the waters. But I could not walk on water, and I feared the darkness of their depths that was always home to her. Nor could I find my way through the mists. Another full moon has come and gone, and it is the dark of the moon tonight. Tomorrow evening, when the sky turns purple, the first silver curve of a new crescent will hang in the western sky. Here in the darkness Morfrenna's words rest in my heart like a hearth-light at day's end.

It is Morfrenna who has been leaving food. Apples, mostly, and some bread and cheese. Sometimes I can see her across the channel that separates Bol Forla from the meadow at this time of year. I call out my thanks, and ask for news of Vivi. But the priestess always disappears into the trees without an answer.

Until a few nights ago. Then, when the moon was just past full, she stood on the bank where I could see her plainly across the water; water I will never cross again. She did not answer me with speech, but I heard her words in my heart: *At the end of Morla's walkway, Eosaidh. There she will meet you, when next the moon shows her first crescent.*

The bright stars of the Hunter are high overhead. This night brings with it a cold, clear sky to call forth the turning of the year during the next moon cycle. But no druids will come to climb the tor for their sunrise ritual, and the people of the marshes will not come to Dolgwyl Waun. Ynys y Niwl must be fully ringed now with Roman forces, making travel next to impossible. From over the ridge, through the mists, comes to my heart a sense of the community of the priestesses. But it comes with heaviness, and I cannot feel Vivi. God help me, I cannot any longer feel Vivi, or hear her voice in my soul. I have not slept all this long night. The pain in my chest is worse.

There is a rustling outside the lean-to. Not loud enough for a Roman patrol; an animal of some size, though. I get up and pull aside the hides over the opening, sensing something nearby. There, I see him in the starlight, not far off, at the start of the old walkway. He is standing still, quietly watching me, Gwyn Hydd, the white hart that came to my hut so many months ago, when the lad had come to me in a vision and we had talked of the Cup of Enaid Las. When I step out into the night he dips his antlered head twice and paws at the hard ground, looking at me with piercing eyes. He snorts, and his breath rings his head with a white mist in the cold air. I can feel the heat of his body, sense the powerful energy of his musk. The hard virility of his presence fills the campsite with the power of life. He tosses his head, once, twice, then holds my eyes in the intensity of his gaze.

For a fleeting moment I think he speaks in my mind.

Uncle, have courage. Your final journey is near at hand.

But then he turns and fades into the darkness between the trees. I want to follow, but am wrapped in sleeping furs and have no boots on. I turn back to the darkness of the shelter, and the coughing begins again, ever worse.

I sit on my cot in the utter darkness, wrapped in all the hides and clothing I can find, and still the cold seeps into my lungs and chills my body to its core. I am holding the old acacia box, empty now, that once contained the Enaid Las. Its shimmering blue shards rest at the bottom of Y Ffynnon Goch, somewhere in the mists. *Release him, Eos,* she had said to me, *Let him go.* But once you have released everything, what is left? The lad is gone. Vivi is gone. Soon I will be gone, but no one will be left to notice. My family in Cornualle must think I have long since perished in the marshes. For what purpose? For the flow of the currents, I think, and reach out to touch the smooth wood of the staff I cut on Wirrheal nearly a year's turning ago. Cerrynt I named it, for Vivi has taught me well about the currents of life.

I will not sleep at all this night. I rise and, pulling aside the hides, find a few sticks for the small fire, to make some tea. The water bag is empty and it is too far to the spring in the dark. Marsh water will do. This time of year I suppose it will be cold and clear, if a little brackish. I have no herbs left, only a bag of whitethorn shavings. Not much taste, but it is good for the heart. A smile comes to my face as I remember little Elwyn stamping her feet on the other side of Wirrheal, perturbed that I had not given her the chance to display her own medicinal knowledge. Somewhere on the other side of the island she sleeps now, while I boil my tea. What is it about old men and the dark of night that makes us constant companions? Vivi had done her best to help me welcome the beauty of darkness, but I never understood the quiet dark heart of my own soul until these long solitary nights under the willows of Bol Forla.

At first I would sit under the willows in the autumn sunshine, letting my mind wander along the south slope of Wirrheal, into Glyn y Ffynhonnau, and up into the mists. There I would stumble about, sometimes recognizing the way, sometimes not. But always, in the mists, I could feel the community of the priestesses: Fia with her young charges, Seren's stern dedication. And Vivi, always Vivi. I never heard her words, but I could feel her heart, knowing she did what she had to do for the protection of her community, feeling the same anguish and heart-longing that I felt. I could never get through, but I lived in hope that one day she would be able to risk sending for me. As autumn became winter, I would often sit on the rise of Bol Forla, remembering the tender joys of our love. From there I could see the great old hawthorn up on Wirrheal as its leaves turned golden and dropped, leaving the crown of rich red berries that now are winter food for so many birds. Soon it will be as bare as when I first saw it, and life will have made a full cycle one more. I no longer wait to hear from Vivi. I think, dear Mother, I think that she may no longer be in this world. And when I think those words, my spirit drops into the depths of an abyss, and my heart yearns for its own release.

The warmth of the tea brings some relief to my burning lungs, but none to the empty ache in my heart. The eastern sky begins to glow with a soft light, as it always has and ever shall, and another night passes. But I have grown too weary of these nights, with only the cold stars for comfort. When it is light enough to see, I step outside, away from the shelter, to piss. As I finish, my head begins to swim from standing again after the long night. Another coughing fit bends me double, and needles of fire pierce my lungs. What I cough up is all red, bright red and steaming in the morning cold. I have trouble catching my breath.

Sedullus' bell begins its cursed ringing calling the Christian community to prayer. Monachoi, they are calling themselves, from monos, alone. They know even less about being alone than they do about the lad. I walk down to the waters' edge to get as far from them as possible. When their prayer is over, the smell of their roasting meat will drift across marsh and meadow, and play havoc with my stomach. In a bit I suppose I will search my stores and have a piece of barley bread. Not to nourish my body, I have no further need of that, but to honor the lad's presence and his gift of life.

The surprise of afternoon sun draws me to the top of Bol Forla. Strange, the slope is far steeper than I remember. I have to stop often to catch my breath, and I am so tired. There is a well partway up where I stop to drink. But my stomach rebels at the thought of swallowing so I only wet my lips. The scores of birds that were here when Vivi and I climbed this rise together are gone. The grasses are winter brown. The brambles are leafless, all thorn, and brittle. A cold wind blows from the open water across the summit, defeating the sun's attempt at warmth. I drop into a shallow depression next to a large stone, hoping for a windbreak. Nearby is the bed of moss and grasses where Vivi and I lay and shared our love on a warm midsummer afternoon. In place of our cries of joy, there is only the wild, lonely wail of the wind in the treetops, and the silent turning of the world toward night.

Eosaidh. Eosaidh.

In the branches of the whitethorn overhead a raven sits, head cocked to one side, looking at me.

My Lady? The reply is In my heart. I have already spoken the last words in my natural voice in this lifetime.

She comes for you tonight, at Morla's walkway, when the first crescent appears in the sky.

I wish to believe it, but I cannot. The loneliness is too great, the fire in my lungs too painful. The raven drops to a lower branch, and studies my face. Can she see the dull despair of death in my eyes?

You said it yourself, Eosaidh. As the currents flow around us, life always returns on the tide. That knowledge is the lad's gift to you, as it was our gift to him. There is no great price on resurrection. It is the way of the world.

In my mind she begins a raven call of the marshes, and in that call I can nearly feel Vivi's presence, though the wind still blows with a lonely wailing across the top of Bol Forla. Its touch upon my face is no longer cold, but bears the gentle warmth of Vivi's fingertips. The pain deep in my lungs is gone.

Prepare, Eosaidh, says the raven. *It is nearly time.*

The winter sky is clear blue and cloudless as I descend the hill. The sun is low in the west, beyond Bryn Llyffaint, backlighting the hundreds of islands and islets that dot the inland sea of Affalon. My camp, on the northeast side of the hill, is already in evening shadow.

A small lean-to is lashed between two ash trees, covered in thatch, with hides and woven cloth hanging down over the wide opening. The small fire from last night has burned itself out. Hanging in a nearby whitethorn is a woven bag containing the last of my provisions. I survey it all in silence as the raven wheels and dives overhead, crying out, playing in the air. I move the stones that encircle the firepit to different places in the underbrush, scatter the cold ashes around the campsite. Slowly, with old fingers that no longer hurt but yet are stiff, I undo the lashings of the lean-to. The larger branches I carry off into the woods. The smaller branches and thatch I scatter around the site. The makeshift cot, and my few remaining provisions I break down a small as possible, then place them into the depression of the firepit and cover them with loose soil. I cannot avoid the appearance of a small mound, but it is not a bad job.

The raven has ceased her play, and watches me from the high branches of an old yew. The evening sky is still bright, the last rays of a setting sun touch her black feathers with highlights of purple. For a moment her eyes flash, and then the sun drops below the horizon. I survey the campsite again. There is no sign I have ever been here. It is good. Sedullus' bell for evening prayer drifts on the breeze, but I no longer notice. They go about their holy routine with no thought for the drama unfolding behind Bol Forla.

There is a singing out in the marshes, heartbreaking in its beauty. In the old marsh tongue, now open to my understanding, a woman sings of tides and currents, of marsh grass and greylag geese, of otters and peewits, of men and women, and of love. In the darkening sky the thinnest silver curve of the new crescent emerges, hanging below Mam Gwener, Aphrodite the Evening Star. At the end of Morla's walkway, where it disappears into the high waters of the winter marsh, there is a shining light from which the song comes. I step to the beginning of the walkway. The cold chill is gone from the evening air. No longer is there the pain of stiffness in my old body. The song is beautiful beyond belief, the crescent moon growing in brightness moment by moment.

As I walk out onto the ancient boards I can see the form of a woman within the light, and it is Vivi, my Vivi. She holds her arms out to me, singing gently of the wonder of what it means to love. Behind her, in the darkness, where the walkway ends and plunges into the waters, is the swift, dark current of the open channel.

I take another step toward her, aware that Cerrynt is still in my hand, the smoothness of the wood where I hold it a reminder of its constant companionship. For a moment I hold the staff close to my breast. Then, stretching my arm out over the dark water, I let it go. With a quiet splash it falls among the reeds and disappears, no longer necessary in this life.

I draw nearer to Vivian, unaware of the broken boards beneath my feet. As I cross the last distance between us, her singing ceases. She looks at me with deep, dark eyes, as black as the waters. Her long hair blows around her as if strayed by marsh currents rather than wind.

Eos, my dearest love, come.

She holds a hand out to me, and the marsh itself is singing its unending song.

Take my hand, my love. You need not fear the waters.
I am not afraid, Vivi. I am ready.

I take her hand, and together we step off the ruined end of the ancient walkway.

Epilogue
Two Visitors

In the very action of slamming shut the car door, I am aware of the distance I am creating between myself and the world beyond. My bag lies on the passenger seat, wallet, keys, mobile phone, and a thousand people crying out to be heard. I close my eyes, taking a deep breath: for this moment, all I need is the small pouch of herbs in the pocket of my coat.

At the ticket office, the young fellow smiles, "Hello there, good lady."

"Hello Sam, busy today?"

He shakes his head, "Not really."

And I smile, relieved.

Passing through the gate, I see an elderly couple sitting down by the waterfall, hand in hand, in the silence of companionship and contemplation. The sound of the water makes me pause, and I too watch it flowing from one sculpted leaf bowl into the next, a series of vulvas and wombs through which the water washes, like the stories of the ancestors, the genes of our blood, splashing out onto the stone and into the pool. The old man coughs, his lungs thick and wheezing, and she rubs his hand with hers, and I think of birth and death. I think of the woman with whom I have just spent the last two hours, the sound of her tears as they flowed, inconsolable and uncomprehending, her soul struggling to understand how to hold the news of her son's death.

The early spring sun barely casts a shadow, yet beneath the old yews the earth is so inviting, and I follow my feet, whispering a prayer to the trees, feeling myself welcomed, my being softly embraced, their dark evergreen canopy above, their roots stretching out beneath me. For centuries they have stood here, breathing sunshine, wind and mud, and I give thanks for their great age, for it offers me that whisper of natural certainty found in the current of continuity.

Finding, in the stillness, a better awareness of my own roots deep in the dark and nourishing earth, I feel the rich spring water that flows beneath me. A part of me longs to release my soul into the current but, if instead of submission I listen, in its song I hear the whispers that draw me on towards its source.

* * * * *

Therefore, Father, send your Holy Spirit upon William, and make him a priest in your Church.

I took the old, faded calligraphy from the wall and held it for a moment, debating between the packing box and the waste basket. In the end, I saved it. One does not throw away the memories of a life passed simply because the experience of it has come to an end. The bishop cloaked his response to my renunciation in cordiality, but we all knew he was glad to see me go, to be finally rid of a troublesome priest who saw God in too many places, or perhaps saw too many gods.

I have come to Glastonbury seeking answers to questions that have no answers. Sunlight glints off the dancing waters of the Vesica pool as I approach it at the foot of the Chalice Well gardens. An old couple rest near the waterfall quietly holding hands. I sit gently myself by the edge of the pool hoping not to disturb their solitude. In spite of the March chill, I pull off my shoes and slip my tired feet into the cold, clear embrace. The energy of the achingly cold water moves up and into the rest of my body, bringing me back to life after a wearying journey.

Above the pool, a hawthorn spreads its bare branches, leaf and flower buds nearly ready to burst open. Beyond stand a pair of old yews, towering over all, a flurry of ravens croaking and calling from their branches. The whole world is alive in a way I have never felt before. It hums in the earth beneath me, in the waters about my feet, in the air that brushes gently across my face. I close my eyes and let myself feel the hum, let my own body begin to vibrate with it.

* * * * *

The garden is so beautifully kept. Even now, in March, a week or so before the equinox, with the lavender cut back, bare branches glowing with buds, the dry stalks of herbaceous perennials tied neatly into winter clumps, the white snowdrops singing softly in the breeze, yellow and purple crocuses calling their songs a little louder, the rich mud turned and free of weeds, the place feels like a temple to humanity's relationship with nature.

Yet the hoe is harsh and with sadness I feel nature giving in to the will of the gardeners. I remember not so long ago (or was it as much as twenty years?), when this was a far wilder place, overgrown with herbs and shrubs untamed, the untended grass overshadowed by trees. It felt easier to sit here in my truth back then.

Walking up the gentle incline, I stop for a while to watch early bees exploring the creamy sweet haven of hellebores. A wren lands on the stone of the terrace wall behind, looking at me with her head cocked. *What are you thinking, priestess?*

Nothing to disturb you, I whisper, feeling the easy smile she provokes in my soul.

What am I thinking? I crouch at the path side and lift a handful of the soft cool mud, rubbing it between my fingers, feeling its depth beneath my feet, breathing it in. The hoe is harsh. How wrapped about I am with the demands of my role, with the need to guide and care, to support and affirm those who look to me as their priest. Is this the hoe that now cuts back the wild growth of my soul?

I rise and walk on.

A siren breaks the air and I turn, looking down the hill to the town that hums beyond the garden walls, instinctively the prayers rising in my soul, spilling out into the breeze, sending courage and serenity into the swirl of sound and the hearts of those who run with it. Yet for a moment I am filled with a seeping horror; the brutal spread of civilization, of human need and litter, still finds no place to sit in my soul.

I close my eyes, murmuring to my gods as I walk on, calling to the gods of my ancestors, *Sacred currents of life, guide me, allow me to understand ...*

* * * * *

After a while I rise. Something is calling me up the hill. I stuff my hiking shoes into my backpack, wanting to feel the earth through my feet as I walk.

In Arthur's Court, a few people sit silently on the edge of the healing pool, their feet in the water. A young man stands by the waterfall, where the cold spring leaves its orange red stain as it falls across the rocks. His eyes are closed, arms folded across his chest, feeling a presence that brings peace to his face. I suppose that must be so with individual human spirits everywhere, finding connectedness as and where they may, without concern for the dogmas of others who would herd them into religions, honouring the credal statements of dead men rather than the mud and waters of the embracing earth.

Still higher and farther in I walk, through a springtime garden alive with colour and the earliest bees, but as I stop to smell the mingled scents of the blossoms, I realize this brightness and buzz of life is only the outer clothing of what I seek. Somewhere, my heart tells me, there is a cool silent centre.

The words on the pathway arch say, 'Chalice Well', and here it is quieter still.

* * * * *

The song of the old yews that overhang the well ever fills my soul before I am even close and today is no exception. Sitting on the cold stones laid around its shaft, I murmur notes of that song as it drifts through me, longing to cry out into the wind, hollering a wail that is both of wondrous celebration and ancient desolation. Yet at the same time, I am vividly aware that my call would be another clamour of humanity given into the web of life.

I shift my legs, aching with my years of living, until cross-legged I can bend over like a cockle shell closing. And in doing so, my soul slips from me, through the imprisoning iron grate, into the temple of russet clear water in the well before me. I breathe in its cool energy.

The modern overlays dissolve.

And before me lies the ancient pool, fed by the spring that rises into the blood-soft earth beneath the ancient yews, rough stones laid around its edge, yew roots and my roots intertwined in the precious mud. And it is here that I cry out the ancient prayers of my soul, *my Lady, sacred waters, within the sanctity of your womb I touch the essence of life, oh my Lady, accept my soul into your ancient black waters ...*

It is here that I let my soul slip into her song.

* * * * *

Here is the ancient well head of the Red Spring, so deeply moving to so many that no religion has been able to claim it as its own.

There is a woman seated on the stones before the well, her back to me, dressed in black with long black hair flowing over her shoulders. Rather than approach, I find my way to the wooden bench in a small alcove on my left. It is shaded by overgrown shrubs and the old yews that hang above. I can feel the damp coolness of the well on my face, closing my eyes and ears to all, drawing into myself.

In the silence I travel down, ever deeper, ever more silent, ever more still. A voice speaks in my heart, Seek the darkness,

Will, seek the frightening gentle heart of darkness within you.

I know that voice. I have never in my life heard it before, but I know the voice.

My eyes open upon the well head before me, the woman with long black hair is still seated on the rounded stones before the well. She turns her head and looks at me. Her face is expressionless, yet bears a heart rending mixture of sorrow and love. Her eyes, as black and deep as the waters of the old marshes, hold mine in a dark embrace, piercing to my soul. It is only for a moment, yet it is for a thousand years. And then she drops her gaze, and turns her head.

I rise from the wooden bench and take a step, not knowing whether it will bear me back down the hill through the garden wall into the rush of Chilkwell Street, or to the old well head, and the strangely silent woman in black.

Glossary

Affalon	Avalon, the marsh, lakes and islands that are the centre of the tale
Bae Fyrtwydd	Myrtle Bay
Bol Forla	Morla's Belly, Morla's Hill (modern: Bride's Mound)
Bryniau'r Mendydd	The Mendip Hills
Bryniau'r Pennard	The Pennard Hills
Bryniau'r Pwlborfa	The Polden Hills
Bryn Cadoedd	Hill of Armies (modern: Cadbury Castle)
Bryn Llyffaint	Hill of Frogs (modern: Brent Knoll)
Bryn Fyrtwyddon	Hill of Myrtles, Wirrheal Hill, now Wearyall Hill
Bryn yr Afalau	Hill of Apples, now Chalice Hill
Bryn Ddraig	Dragon Hill (The Tor)
Caer Iwdon	Yew Hill Fort (modern: Dundon)
Crib Pwlborfa	Polden Ridge
Croth Ddraig Las	Blue Dragon Womb
Derwydd	Druid
Dolgwyl Waun	Festival Meadow (modern: Beckery)
Glyn y Ffynhonnau	The valley of springs
Y Gors Chwerw	The Bitter Marsh
Fferyllt	Alchemists
Y Ffynnon Goch	The Red Spring (modern: Challice Well)
Y Ffynnon Wen	The White Spring
Llw Ffynnon	The Tribal Wells, The Oath Wells, (modern: Wells)
Llyn Cimwch	Crayfish Lake
Llyn Hydd	Hart Lake

Llyntywyll	Lake of Darkness
Llynwen	White Lake
Maen Wyddraig	Dragon's egg stone
Pentreflyn	Lake Village (modern: Meare)
Yr Wyddfa	The Tomb (modern: Snowdon)
Wyddonwrach Wen	Thorn Witch at the Dragon's Stone
Ynys y Cysgodion	The Isle of Shadow
Ynys Hyddwen	White Hart Island
Ynys Mon	Mother Isle
Ynys y Niwl	The Isle of Mist (modern: Glastonbury)

Other titles form Thoth Publications

INVENTING WITCHCRAFT
A Case Study in the Creation of a New Religion
by Aiden A.Kelly

This extensively revised edition contains new research which was unavailable at the time, as well as detailed textual comparisons of Gerald Gardner's own manuscripts, magical books and rituals that could not be included in the earlier edition. It contains contributions from people who helped Gardner create modern Witchcraft and looks at the sources of his inspiration. Both liberal Wiccans and religious scholars hailed the earlier book as a classic in the new field of Pagan Studies. This revised edition is a must-have for anyone interested in Witchcraft and modern religious history.

Aidan A. Kelly received his Ph.D. in theology from the Graduate Theological Union in 1980, in a joint program in advanced humanities with the University of California, Berkeley. He has taught at the University of San Francisco and other colleges, and served for five years on the steering committee of the prestigious Group on New Religious Movements of the American Academy of Religion. He is well-known in academic circles for his argument that all religions begin as new religions. He is also a founder of the New Reformed Orthodox Order of the Golden Dawn, an eclectic Wiccan tradition and of the Covenant of the Goddess, a national church for American Witches.

ISBN 978-1-870450-58-4

THE DRUID WAY
by Philip Carr-Gomm

In The Druid Way, Philip Carr-Gomm takes us on a journey through the sacred landscape of Southern Britain, and as he does so, we learn about Druidry as a living tradition of the land and its people, a tradition that is as relevant today as it was for our ancestors.

As we walk the ancient tracks across the South Downs we encounter dragons and giants, ancestral voices and ancient places that speak to us of the beauty of a spiritual way that still exists and can still be followed. We learn how Druidry can help us to sense again our kinship with Nature, and how following the Druid Way can lead us towards a profound sense of oneness with all life.

This new edition has been extensively revised and includes the complete ceremonies of three Rites of Passage, a guide to the sacred sites of Sussex and a Foreword by Cairisthea Worthington.

This whole book is a delight. It is the diary of a sacred journey, through sacred space, and through the heart and mind - a book to use, to keep and to remember.

Wood & Water

This book provides inspiration, soul-food and encouragement to those who long to be part of the richer life of this beautiful planet.

Caitlin Matthews

ISBN 978-1-870450-62-1

THE GRAIL SEEKER'S COMPANION
by John Matthews & Marian Green

There have been many books about the Grail, written from many differing standpoints. Some have been practical, some purely historical, others literary, but this is the first Grail book which sets out to help the esoterically inclined seeker through the maze of symbolism, character and myth which surrounds the central point of the Grail.

In today's frantic world when many people have their material needs met some still seek spiritual fulfilment. They are drawn to explore the old philosophies and traditions, particularly that of our Western Celtic Heritage. It is here they encounter the quest for the Holy Grail, that mysterious object which will bring hope and healing to all. Some have come to recognise that they dwell in a spiritual wasteland and now search that symbol of the Grail which may be the only remedy. Here is the guide book for the modern seeker, explaining the history and pointing clearly towards the Aquarian Grail of the future. John Matthews and Marian Green have each been involved in the study of the mysteries of Britain and the Grail myth for over thirty-five years.

In *The Grail Seeker's Companion* they have provided a guidebook not just to places, but to people, stories and theories surrounding the Grail. A reference book of Grail-ology, including history, ritual, meditation, advice and instruction. In short, everything you are likely to need before you set out on the most important adventure of your life.

"This is the only book that points the way to the Holy Grail in the 21st century." *Quest*

ISBN 978-1-870450-49-2

THE FOOL'S COAT
by Vi Marriott

The story of Father Bérenger Saunière, the poor parish priest of Rennes-le-Château, a remote village in Southern France, who at the turn of the 19th century spent mysterious millions on creating a fantastic estate and lavishly entertaining the rich and famous, is now as well known as "Cinderella" or "Eastenders". He would never divulge where the money came from, and popular belief is that in 1891 he discovered a priceless treasure; yet Saunière died penniless, and his legacy is a secret that has continued to puzzle and intrigue succeeding generations.

Since *The Holy Blood and the Holy Grail* hit literary headlines in the nineteen eighties, hundreds of solutions have been suggested. Did he find documents that proved Jesus married Mary Magdalene? Was he a member of The Priory of Sion, a sinister secret society that knew the Da Vinci Code? Did he own the equivalent of Harry Potter's Philosopher's Stone?

A literary mosaic of history, mystery, gossip and myth, THE FOOL'S COAT investigates Father Saunière's extraordinary life against the background of his times, and suggests that the simplest solution of his rise from penury to riches is probably the correct one.

Vi Marriott is a theatre administrator, writer and researcher. Her play *Ten Days A-Maze*, based on Count Jan Pococki's *Tales of the Saragossa Manuscript*, had seasons in London and Edinburgh; and she contributes regularly to three "house" magazines concerned with the mystery of Rennes-le-Château and other esoteric matters.

ISBN 978-1-870450-99-7

NATURAL DRUIDRY
by Kristoffer Hughes

Natural Druidry is a deeply personal account of one man's journey through the dappled groves of culture and tradition. Exploring the inspiration of Druidry through the eyes of a man in love with heritage and the land, Kris takes you on a journey into the mysteries of the Druid tradition, into the shadows of the past and the magic of Druidry.

Written with simplistic clarity, humour and tears, Kris invites you to share his journey through tradition, descending into the mysteries of Druidry and of its practise in the twenty-first century. Exploring the fundamental principles of Druidry from ritual, connection, mythology, shamanism and finally to a personal ride through the Druid year.

Share in a world of wondrous beings, of sheer potentiality beyond comprehension and the awe and childlike surrender one feels when confronted with the enchantment of Druidry.

Inspiration lies at the heart of this book, where the joyous experience of the flowing spirit of Druidry known as Awen sings through dry ink. Journey with Kris into the magic of the past and the present, deep into the vast cauldron of spiritual enlightenment that sings from the land, that whispers to us upon the breeze as the breath of our ancestors.

ISBN 978-1-870450-67-6

TEUTONIC MAGIC
by Kveldulf Gundarsson

Tales of Teutonic magic have thrilled the world for centuries. Now bringing together the dark stuff of sagas, Kveldulf Gundarsson reveals the personal magical path behind the legends and explains the practical techniques of the Northern Tradition. Gundarsson is a well known expert on the esoteric lore of the Teutonic people. This, his first book Teutonic Magic brings a lifetime's worth of expertise to the subject. Blending historical lore with practical experience of esoteric skills, Gundarsson presents the reader with a spiritual path walked by the ancient and dark age Germans.

He explains the magical writings of the Teutonics, including the uses of each of the runestaves, the laws of magic in the Northern tradition. He provides the key to unleash the awesome might of the Northern magical tradition.

This is not a dry academic book. Gundarsson's writing flows like the sagas themselves, covering subjects such as Norse deities and rituals. It describes the structure of the spiritual realms in which the Norse Magician would walk. It is no wonder that this book is considered the classic text book of anyone who would study Runes or the Northern Tradition.

ISBN 978-1-870450-22-5